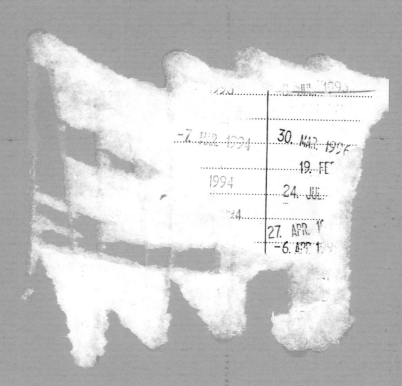

Colette

Colette

A LIFE

by
Herbert Lottman

SECKER & WARBURG
LONDON

920 · COLE

First published in Great Britain 1991
by Martin Secker & Warburg Limited
Michelin House, 81 Fulham Road, London SW3 6RB

Copyright © 1991 by Herbert Lottman

A CIP catalogue record for this book
is available from the British Library
ISBN 0 436 25746 7

625396

Book design by Robert G. Lowe

Printed in England by Clays Ltd, St Ives plc

Contents

Colette

Prologue

CLAUDINE: in the early years of our century it would have been hard to escape her, unless one kept one's distance from the gossip columns, never went out to the theater or to a cabaret, and took no notice of what young women wore. In France, certainly, Claudine was everybody's brash school-age kid, though one prayed that one's own children would not behave the way she did in *Claudine at School*. When the book opens, she is living in a village on the northern edge of Burgundy, a village on the way to nowhere else. It sits on a slope, its houses tumbling down, as Claudine puts it, "from the top of the hill to the bottom of the valley." The woods are virtually at her back door.

Her story begins when she has just turned fifteen. On that birthday she wears a long skirt, for her legs are starting to draw glances. Having lost her mother early, she has been brought up by an absentminded professor of a father. He lives only for his research (on snails and such things), and his indifference to the ripening Claudine borders on idiocy. Her classmates are the daughters of shopkeepers and farmers, for the more well-to-do pack off their delicate daughters to boarding school in the district capital. Claudine is the exception to this practice, thanks to her father's insouciance. Among her friends at school is big Anaïs, who is "cool, corrupt, and so impossible to disconcert that she never blushes, the happy creature!"

That school year is to be eventful. The decrepit main building, with its filth and smells, is being replaced. A new headmistress, Miss Sergent, arrives. She is "a well-built redhead, with a plump figure and hips, but terribly ugly." Miss Sergent soon has an assistant, the pretty Aimée Lanthenay, who pleases Claudine as much as her superior *dis*pleases her. Claudine is impertinent toward the older woman, though privately she concedes that she is not a bad teacher.

Soon enough Claudine has become infatuated with blond little Aimée, to the point of arousing Miss Sergent's jealousy. To have more time with Aimée, Claudine arranges to take private English lessons from her.

Then there is Dutertre, a local councilman and the official medical inspector for the school. He is a frequent visitor, spending most of his time with the older girls. Dutertre, says Claudine, "reads our homework, brushes his mustache against our ears, caresses our necks." He is also believed to be Miss Sergent's lover. When the devious doctor notes that Claudine is first in her class in composition, Miss Sergent protests, "But it's not her doing, she's just clever and doesn't work hard." Once, in order to read Claudine's notebook, Dutertre places his hand on her shoulder; another time he draws her out into the corridor for a medical checkup, murmuring, "Oh, little Claudine, I like you with your warm brown eyes and your crazy curls. You are like an adorable little statue, I'm sure." He kisses her before she can tear herself away. (We know, because Claudine has told us, that "if my face makes me look younger than I am, my figure is eighteen years old.")

Meanwhile, Miss Sergent has her way with the lovely Aimée. One day Claudine surprises the teachers in a long embrace. On another occasion she creeps quietly up the stairs and, through a door that is not quite shut, sees more.

Then Aimée's younger sister Luce, who is Claudine's age, shows up at school. She falls for Claudine as Claudine fell for Aimée. We follow Claudine to the district capital for her final exams (once again

French composition saves her), then back to her village for a school
ceremony. The mother of Miss Sergent, deus ex machina, surprises
Dr. Dutertre in a compromising encounter with her daughter. She
chases him with a broom, and the whole village is there to witness
the event.[1]

We next meet Claudine in Paris. Her father has written his book on
snails and has moved there to be closer to his publisher. During a
visit to an aunt, Claudine meets Marcel, who is at least as interested
in other young men as she once was in Aimée; they exchange titil-
lating stories. She also meets Marcel's father, Renaud. He's a young
father, she thinks.

Soon she is in love with the handsome Renaud, and one night, as
a carriage takes them home from the theater, she tells him as much.
To preserve Marcel's rights as heir, she decides that she must be
Renaud's mistress and not his wife, but he insists that they marry.[2]

So we find Claudine married, after a brief engagement during which,
she confesses, she goes around with "the drawn features of a cat in
heat." The newlyweds travel, yet Claudine remains at heart a country
girl: Renaud smiles when he finds her "more enraptured by a landscape than by a painting." Although she continues to be passionate
with Renaud, she learns that for him "pleasure consists of desire,
perversity, frivolous curiosity, licentious play." On the way home
from a summer Wagner festival, she persuades him to stop for a day
in her childhood village. Miss Sergent, the headmistress, asks him,
"Is she still as young and devilish as she was?" but she invites her
visitors to spend the night at the school. They sleep in Aimée's room,
for the younger teacher has gone home for the holidays. Claudine is
disappointed; she was hoping that Renaud would see these amorous
women together.

Her husband enjoys himself all the same, though, thanks to the
girls who have no families to go home to. Spending the evening with
these Claudines who are too young even for him makes him a memorable bedmate for the original Claudine that night. The next day

Renaud kisses his favorite among the schoolgirls. In turn, one of the girls kisses Claudine, who confesses, "For a year and a half, I have felt the progress of a slow and agreeable corruption which I owe to Renaud."

In Paris their life is intensely social. At one of their receptions Claudine is drawn to a woman called Rézi, whose husband is a retired British officer — Rézi whose eyes are amber-gray, whose black dress is tight across her rounded, mobile hips. . . . For her part, Rézi is soon running her fingers down Claudine's neck. She can't be proper, thinks Claudine, she's much too pretty! That night Renaud receives the benefit of Claudine's aroused sensuality.

Soon the two women are inseparable. Claudine calls on her new friend each morning before she gets dressed. "I'm mad about three things," Rézi tells her. "Travel, Paris, and you." Renaud surprises them in their first kiss and encourages the flirtation. When Claudine asks how he can condemn his son's homosexuality while accepting hers, he protests that "it's not the same thing! You women can do anything. It's charming, and without significance."

Rézi therefore asks Renaud to help them find a hideaway for their trysts. He rents a flat for them but holds on to the key so that the women must appeal to him each time they desire each other. Claudine becomes ill and spends three weeks in bed; when she can go out again, she finds Renaud and Rézi together in the rented flat. Her response is to return to the village of her childhood.

She grieves, but she cannot be entirely lost there, with her favorite cat, her "vague papa," and their enchanted garden. Renaud writes to apologize, claiming that curiosity alone motivated his betrayal. Claudine is distressed, realizing that she does not love Rézi but does love Renaud.[3]

Claudine and Renaud appear again in *Claudine and Annie,* the fourth of the Claudine books, but this time only as supporting players. The heroine is now Claudine's friend Annie, who is in the process of freeing herself from a domineering husband. Claudine advises her to divorce him, warning, "You'll carry the mark of the chain for a long time."[4] Then, in *Retreat from Love,* Claudine and Renaud move back to center stage, or rather Claudine does. For her husband is desperately ill, in a Swiss hospital; she is waiting for him at Annie's country house. Now divorced, Annie is so passive that it sometimes appears that the house belongs to Claudine and not to her. What Annie needs, it seems, is physical love. Then Marcel, Renaud's homosexual son, invites himself to stay, disturbing Claudine's tranquillity and arousing Annie. "Don't give him a baby!" Claudine tells her good-humoredly. Annie ignores the warning and assaults Marcel — to no avail. Since he is penniless, Claudine offers him cash to sleep with Annie, but even this does not work.

When at last Renaud arrives, Claudine finds herself face-to-face with an old man. (In fact he is fifty, she twenty-eight.) When he dies, she will return to her native village, surrounding herself with beloved household pets. She does not think she will yield to temptations of the flesh — not with Renaud watching over her.[5]

Those are the Claudine books. Writing in the frivolous weekly *La Vie Parisienne* in 1908, a year after the last of Claudine's adventures was published, Sidonie Gabrielle Colette, who called herself Colette, confessed that she often ran into Claudine. She had seen her that very day and been greeted with, "Hello, my Double!" So Colette had to warn her, "I am not your Double. Aren't you fed up with this misunderstanding that makes us one and the same . . . ? You're Claudine and I'm Colette. Our look-alike faces have played hide-and-seek long enough." People thought that Colette had a woman friend named Rézi, or that her husband, Willy, was Renaud. Claudine might have found her "retreat from love," but Colette decidedly had not. She demanded to be allowed her own identity, a private life of her own.

Many things distinguished Claudine the character from Colette the author, declared Colette. "You cannot imagine what a queen of the earth I was at the age of twelve! Solidly built, a rough voice, two

ONE

The Real Village

AT FIRST APPROACH Saint-Sauveur-en-Puisaye is not a congenial place. But it was there that Sidonie Gabrielle Colette was born and grew up, and there that she attended the school that Claudine was to put on the map. The real Claudine left Saint-Sauveur in sadness and shame, when she was an impressionable adolescent. As an author obliged to sign her books "Willy" and then "Colette Willy" before she could call herself simply "Colette," she was to return to Saint-Sauveur again and again in stories, though rarely in reality.

At first approach, too, Saint-Sauveur is unlikely to impress. A county seat in the Yonne district, some 120 miles south of Paris, it lies an inconvenient cross-country drive away from the district capital at Auxerre. Its streets are graceless, its facades undistinguished. The house on Rue de l'Hospice (now Rue Colette) in which Sidonie Gabrielle was born — and about which she wrote with convincing nostalgia — even that house disappoints. One can feign admiration for one of the town's "attractions," a renovated castle going back (in parts) three centuries, but only the ruin of a round tower — the "Saracen tower" that Claudine mentions — is apt to rouse the imagination. If the castle is unremarkable, however, it nonetheless allows "a delicious view" of rolling, fertile fields and meadows, with a "vast and somber forest" enveloping the site. So says a guidebook even older than Colette.[1]

But of course we return to one particular street to place ourselves before the featureless facade (which has one feature all the same: a double staircase with more steps on the uphill than on the downhill side) of the house in which Sidonie Gabrielle Colette was born.

This may be Burgundy, but it is not prosperous Burgundy. It is nearly as far from the cradle of that rich and secret wine culture as it is from Paris. And in this humble region of indifferent natural and man-made features, of hapless village and farm folk, how fared the Colettes? Sidonie Gabrielle was about twelve, the age at which she remembered herself as being a "queen of the earth," when a neighbor reported, "The poor Colettes are miserable. They owe money everywhere and pay nowhere."[2] Even in one of her sentimental journeys back to that time, Colette recalled her mother's anxiety about the likely fate of her "children without fortune," in this household with a mother in poor health and a father who was crippled and ineffectual.[3]

Begin with the mother: we know a good deal about "Sido." Her name at birth was Adèle Sidonie Landoy. The Landoy family was from the Champagne region, east of Paris, but Sido's grandfather settled with his wife in the French Ardennes. Colette was to claim that her mother's father had some measure of black blood, and Sido spoke of him as "The Gorilla." Colette guessed that he was a quadroon.[4] No one has been able to say more.

Adèle Sidonie's parents were in Paris when she was born, on August 12, 1835. Her mother died less than eight weeks after giving birth to her, so a nurse was found for the infant in the hospitable Puisaye countryside.[5] Later she was raised by her older brothers, journalists both, in French-speaking Belgium, where she learned "to understand and love rare and beautiful things."[6] Colette remembered that she herself was so permeated with Sido's recollection of her rich and heady growing-up that when other six-year-olds would sigh "Paris," she would think, "Brussels."[7]

All the same, Sido never forgot the land that had nourished her infancy. And when the time came for her to take a husband, at twenty-one, Puisaye took *her,* in the person of Jules Robineau-Duclos, a landowner of Saint-Sauveur who was exactly twice her age.

History is sometimes kind to us. Documents of seemingly limited interest are conserved and suddenly answer riddles. Thus we know something about the situation of Jules Robineau at the time he married Sido, in 1857. He had inherited considerable property and had even added to it. Yet there were things that Sido and her protective brothers could not have known about him. This husband whom the matchmakers had found for her was a drunkard and a brute; his fellow townsmen called him The Ape.[8] Two months after his marriage to Sido, drunk, he tried to beat her up. She reacted by throwing everything within reach at him, including a lamp stand with sharp edges, which he received full-face; he bore the scar until he died.[9]

More: two years before Jules Robineau married Sido, his sister and her husband went to court to have him declared incompetent. He admitted to a court investigator that he drank too much brandy, but he denied the specific charges against him, including the allegation that he had threatened to kill his servants and use them as bait for crayfish; nor could he recall taking shots at them, another act of which he was accused. The examiner noted that Robineau had difficulty answering questions; he seemed precociously senile.[10]

It was also true that the sister and her husband had much to gain from a declaration of incompetence, and everything to gain if Robineau died a bachelor. So other family members counterattacked, deciding to marry him off so that the sister would be kept away from the succession. A prospective bride appeared in the person of Adèle Sidonie Landoy, down from Belgium on a visit to the Puisaye family that had nursed her.[11]

We can guess what Sido's first marriage was like. Robineau remained the town's best-known drunk; meanwhile, they had two

children, Juliette and Achille. When Robineau died, after eight years
of marriage, he left debts as well as property. One of the debts was
a commitment to a young woman who had borne his third child,
this one out of wedlock.[12]

Sido found a new husband in no time at all. Jules Colette was not
far away; in fact, if anything, he seems to have been too close. For
another curious document has been dug up: the report of a local
justice of the peace concerning the selection of guardians for the
minor children of Sido's first marriage. The judge made no attempt
to veil the notorious behavior of the deceased Robineau, but he could
say nothing nice about Sido, either. He was certain that she had been
having an affair with Jules Colette. Indeed, he wrote, "there is no
one in Saint-Sauveur who is not convinced that the second child of
Madame Robineau [Achille] is the work of Monsieur Colette."

Robineau had died alone in his room, during an attack of apo-
plexy. The inquisitive man of the law was astonished that no one
had suggested that Sido and her lover, Jules Colette, might have
contributed to her husband's death. At the very least, the two of
them had allowed him to "kill himself in peace."

After the funeral it did seem as though Jules Colette was in charge.
The usurper took care of little Juliette and Achille while Sido visited
her brothers in Belgium, and he helped to set up the board of guardians that was to protect their interests. For over half of the estate left
by Robineau consisted of woodland, whose value could be reduced
significantly by an inexpert or unscrupulous manager. Further, as
the judge observed, Sido was "a woman without order, without a
sense of money"; she had more servants than she could afford, even
if Jules Colette paid his share. (He was the local tax collector and
also had a military pension.) But above all, the examiner feared that
Jules Colette himself was reckless with money. He was believed to
have ruined his parents, and in his adopted Puisaye he had incurred
a financial obligation in the shape of a girl whom he had impregnated while courting Robineau's wife. The town, which, according
to the report, "is accustomed to being a witness to immoral acts,"
was scandalized by this situation.[13]

Scandal or no, Sido married Jules Colette on December 20, 1865. The couple elected the community of property rule, which gave them equal rights to any property acquired by either of them after the marriage. Jules Colette had only his personal effects to declare, plus the bond he had deposited when he obtained the tax job; Sido, of course, brought to her second marriage all her rights over properties deriving from her first.[14]

Although he was imprudent, even reckless, Jules Colette seems to have been a good soul. He was born in Toulon on September 26, 1829, the son of a naval officer. He himself chose dry ground. He was admitted to the Saint-Cyr military academy and came out a second lieutenant assigned to the legendary Zouaves (Frenchmen clothed as Arabs). When war broke out in the Crimea, pitting the French and British against the Russians, he was wounded and promoted. At twenty-six he was a captain, posted to Algeria for the colonial conquest. Then Napoleon III went to war in Italy, in support of the Piedmontese against Austrian domination. One of the fiercest battles of that war took place at Melegnano, in June 1859. Captain Colette lost a leg there, when he was not yet quite thirty.

All her life long, Captain Colette's daughter, Colette, held on to an envelope on which she had written "My father's military record." She also kept a photograph of him in full uniform, wearing his medals. In a brief narrative called "A Zouave" she lets us see him being carried off the battlefield, joking all the while. Napoleon III visited his hospital; when questioned about his wound, Captain Colette reportedly replied that it was "nothing, Sire . . . a scratch." When the emperor asked what he could do for him, he protested that he had enough medals as it was. "Can I give you something else?" Napoleon inquired. "Well, yes . . . a crutch, Sire," came the answer.

"Ah!" Colette's mother would sigh, telling her daughter about her husband. "If you had known your father then! If you had seen him as I did for the first time, with his waistline of a young maiden, his light complexion. . . . If you had seen how the girls followed him, and how jealous they were when he chose me!"[15]

He was a man with ambition who would go nowhere. With tenderness his daughter returned again and again to those aspirations of his, usually to mock him gently. He tried politics, for instance. His campaign for election to the district council of the Yonne in 1880 is important to our story, for among his rivals was a young doctor named Pierre Merlou. Merlou won[16] and became the Colette family bugbear; Captain Colette's daughter (who accompanied her father on his speechmaking tour) would never forget him. Later, when she had an opportunity to write about her childhood, she would invent "Dr. Dutertre," the libidinous inspector of young girls' notebooks and bodies, the villain of *Claudine at School*.

Captain Colette saw himself as a writer, but he wrote nothing other than a couple of poems. His writing daughter remembered listening as he recited one and telling him that he used too many adjectives. She also recalled a shelf that held a row of cartons, each bearing a title in Gothic lettering: "My Military Campaigns," "Lessons of the 1870 War," "Marshal Mac-Mahon Seen by One of His Military Comrades," and even the touching "From the Village to Parliament," a dozen subjects in all. Each carton contained 150 to 300 sheets of paper, all of them blank. They were the "mirage" of his career as an author.[17] Colette was fascinated, too, by her father's meticulous preparations for writing, the care he took to keep the right equipment at hand. She would remember that and imitate him when the time came.[18]

TWO

Growing Up

CINEMA BUFFS can sometimes catch a 1930s movie called *Claudine at School,* though they may be sorry if they do. The movie version of Claudine dwells in a mansion, for the French invent their own Hollywoodian distortions. The true house in Saint-Sauveur is hardly that grand. Colette later remembered her parents' bedroom, the room in which she was born, as having "little warmth or comfort."[1] The room that the Colettes later ceded to their growing daughter was a low-ceilinged bridge over the carriage gate. To find any real space one had to go out back to the garden, which figures so significantly in Colette's writing. Later she would say that she could recall each species of flower that blossomed there, and each tree, exotic or common.[2] Note also (for Colette fails to mention it) that in order to reach the toilet it was necessary to leave the house and cross the lovely garden.

Adèle Sidonie and Jules Colette had been married ten months when their first child was born. That was Léopold, who would never be called anything but Léo — hapless Léo, a dreamer destined to be a musician and trained as a pharmacist, who in the end became nothing at all. He was forever being protected, even in maturity.[3] In a memoir written after his death, Colette lets us see Léo as a child in the back garden, designing tombs for their dolls.[4]

The couple would wait another five years after Léo's birth for Sidonie Gabrielle, born on January 28, 1873. Meanwhile, Sido's children from her unhappy first marriage were growing up. Juliette was nearly thirteen when her sister was born, Achille just ten; Colette's earliest memories of them would be as young adults. She remembered Juliette, without affection, as an enigmatic, somewhat solitary woman, but that may have been because of what happened later. Colette spoke of her "black Mongol eyes" and "her curious head, which had an appealing ugliness, with high cheekbones and a sarcastic mouth."[5]

Achille, on the other hand, was not odd. Later Colette confessed that although he was only her half-brother, she had preferred him; they had been "attuned."[6] He was predestined to be a doctor, and he became one.[7] He earned his degree at the Ecole de Médecine in Paris, but his real training came out in the countryside, far from hospitals and nurses. His very first patient was a well-digger whose leg had been blown off by dynamite. The teenage Colette did not witness that operation, but she did see others, for she would accompany him on his rounds. At the age of fifteen or sixteen she could sew up a cut lip. She even thought that she herself might become a doctor.[8]

It should be clear that the Colette household was not typical of rural France. The father could have been a writer; the mother was definitely a reader. Colette said that her mother taught her to read before she was three (and she would do the same for her own daughter).[9] When young Colette read, she read Eugène Labiche, Alphonse Daudet, Prosper Mérimée, Victor Hugo.[10] Colette thought that she was seven when she began her lifelong infatuation with Honoré de Balzac, counting herself lucky that no one ever told her that she was too young to plough through the twenty volumes of the family's black leather set; she simply skipped the difficult or boring parts.[11] One scholar found references to no fewer than fifty-five characters from Balzac in Colette's works, some of them mentioned more than once.[12]

No nonsense about prayers in that house; even a Christmas celebration was too much for this rational family.[13] Although Sido was a conscientious atheist, she had her daughter baptized, allowed her to attend catechism lessons at the age of eleven, and, scowling all the while, let her go on to first communion and confirmation. And confession? Sido felt that it would be better to punish oneself. She was nevertheless on good terms with the town priest and went to Mass with everybody else, though to the priest's exasperation she always brought her little dog along.[14]

Colette's mother practiced her own kind of morality. She raged against the practice of corseting unmarried women to hide their pregnancy: how could a pretty if unrepentant girl with a full belly be bad? When her daughter, along with the rest of the catechism class, placed flowers on the altar of the Virgin and then brought a "blessed bouquet" home, Sido laughed her "irreverent laugh" and asked, "Don't you think it was *already* blessed?"[15]

Colette at school: how much nicer she was than the impertinent Claudine. At the close of her life Sido remembered her daughter as her "sunshine"; when the child entered a room, she lit it up. Perhaps the proper word for her was *angelic*.[16] School, the only one she ever knew, was right there in Saint-Sauveur, minutes from home. It was a humble, tumble-down village school; the new building whose inauguration is described in *Claudine at School* would be ready almost too late for her. She entered at the beginning of the 1878–79 term, shortly before her sixth birthday. It was quite a winter, she remembered; she walked to school between walls of snow taller than she was.

In class the children read from a New Testament; their elderly teacher had not quite seized the lay spirit of the times. Another recollection involved the use of individual charcoal footwarmers, which came in handy for heating up chestnuts or potatoes and for bashing other girls during recreation period. The fumes from the warmers made everyone drowsy.

In 1885, at the age of twelve and a half, Colette passed the examination leading to her first diploma. That wondrous French practice of saving every scrap of paper with writing on it gives us the text of a dictation concerning Victor Hugo's love of birds; Colette got a 9½ (out of 10). Yet she and her classmates all failed an assigned essay. The subject may be mentioned here, for it would come up again during the Nazi occupation of France (and cause Colette to stumble again). The pupils were asked to discuss German claims that Burgundy was part of the German empire.

Colette got her diploma all the same. Yet while both her brothers and her sister had gone on from elementary school to boarding school, Colette stayed home, stayed in the very same classroom, despite the fact that her teacher had little competence beyond the primary grades. She began to receive proper schooling only when the town created a secondary program and a headmistress, Olympe Terrain, appeared.[17] "We were twelve or thirteen, the age of precocious chignons, of leather belts buckled tightly, of shoes that hurt," Colette remembered. "We were slim, tanned, mannered, and brutal, as awkward as boys, impudent, blushing at the very sound of our voices, bitter, full of charm, incorrigible. . . ."[18]

Mademoiselle Terrain, the model for the terrifying Miss Sergent in *Claudine at School,* was only twenty-four when she reported for duty in Saint-Sauveur. She found herself in charge of a school with five lower grades and the new secondary class. She had been recommended by Dr. Merlou, who was by then the mayor of Saint-Sauveur (and still the political enemy of Jules Colette); it would be whispered that he and she were lovers.[19] As Merlou's protégée, the headmistress had to deal with the hostility of the Colette family, and later she would also remember weeping with outrage at the lack of classroom discipline. Sidonie Gabrielle Colette, it seems, was the ringleader; the girls played marbles in the courtyard and climbed trees. (Proper young ladies, of course, did neither.) She also recalled that Sidonie introduced the practice of using only last names, so Mademoiselle Colette became Colette.

Headmistress Terrain was nonetheless to say some positive things about her turbulent pupil, and this long after Colette had invented the headmistress who slept with her assistant, the comely Aimée, in *Claudine at School*. As a student Colette was both intelligent and agreeable, gifted in French and in music, if hopeless in science. The teacher actually enjoyed her cheekiness.[20] Whatever the assignment, Colette in her written work showed "a rare precision, the right word, the colorful expression, the unexpected that creates an agreeable surprise," as Mademoiselle Terrain was to tell one of her pupil's first biographers.[21]

The headmistress recalled that Colette once took part in an agricultural contest and spoke poetically about animals. And then at last Mademoiselle Terrain led Colette and her classmates to Auxerre for their final exams, in July 1889. Her recollection of the saucy Colette at this moment was not very different from the portrait Claudine painted of herself at the same time and place. When asked to explain the composition of ink, Colette replied haughtily, "I buy mine at the grocery store." Mademoiselle Terrain whispered to the shocked examiner that this student had been raised in a barracks-room atmosphere.[22]

A scholar who traced the steps of the girls that week tells us that Mademoiselle Colette was one of four pupils who faced the examining board. Another of the young women being tested, described in *Claudine at School* as resembling "a little black ant" (she would go on to become headmistress of a school in her own right), remembered the participation of Colette in that event as being unsettling. She strutted about, changed dresses three times in two days, and succeeded in arousing some of the old professors — though she did not manage to impress the one responsible for the physical and natural sciences. After replying to one question with too much nonchalance, Sidonie Colette seemed to realize the fate that was in store for her, so she addressed the examiner in a tone "half insolent, half whining," asking, "You're not going to fail me for that, sir?" She was not failed for that.

In the end she did well enough on the written tests; with a mark of 17 out of 20 in French composition, she went to the head of her group. She did less well on the orals, with 10 out of 20 in explication of text, 15 in arithmetic, 10 (the average) in history and geography, 10 (the maximum) in music, and 6 in the physical and natural sciences. In all, 133 points. The "black ant" got 136½.[23]

THREE

The Village Lost

PERHAPS SOME of the schoolgirl shenanigans, the provocations, even Colette's displays of peacock pride, were invented to distract attention from the family drama. While the model for Claudine was preening in Saint-Sauveur, the Colettes were finding it more and more difficult to meet their obligations. Much later, the woman who as a girl was observed to change dresses three times in two days would remember wearing "a little jacket cut from the non-moth-eaten part of one of my father's old dress coats."[1]

For the brave Captain Colette, who could have been so many things — author, public speaker, leader of men — was a mediocre manager. Colette's mother would tell him, "Everything you touch shrinks."[2] At this remove it is difficult to determine how much of the problem was preexisting, consisting of debts left by Sido's first husband in his downward slide. It is at least possible that the first property sales by Jules Colette and Sido were designed to pay off these obligations. Early in their marriage they sold a vineyard, woods, and meadows, and settled a debt that Robineau had owed to his sister. Among the other properties they disposed of was the house in

Toulon where Jules Colette had been born.[3] The captain did what
he could to make the farms prosper, but he was simply not up to
the task. The tenant farmers got the best of him, demanding expensive repairs. To pay for these, he borrowed money from the farmers
themselves, who thus eventually became owners of the Colette properties.[4]

The records reveal a cascade of property liquidations beginning in
1885. One of the heirs of the deceased Robineau was his daughter,
Juliette, who was now married to a Dr. Charles Roché, also of Saint-
Sauveur. In order to pay out her share of the legacy, the Colettes
had to sell property for cash. So Juliette, now and forever, became
the villain of the story. But perhaps the story is not true, after all;
Sido, Juliette's mother, later said that within weeks of her marriage
Juliette swallowed poison rather than sign papers that would have
spelled the ruin of her mother and her family. She did not die; the
property *was* liquidated. The Robineau estate was divided among
Sido and Achille and Juliette, the children of her first marriage.
Achille's share included the house in Saint-Sauveur, then still occupied by the Colettes.[5]

Sido saw Juliette's marriage as a mismatch. Her daughter had
given herself, she thought, to "the first dog with a hat on."[6] Soon
the Rochés and the Colettes were not even on speaking terms. Then
began the war of the property lawyers, with accusations that Jules
Colette had disposed of family possessions in an "improvident" and
"inexcusable" manner. On their side, the Colettes were obliged to
borrow at "usurious rates" to meet the demands of Juliette's new
husband.[7] The feud was the talk of the village, and later, when she
came to write about it, Colette knew how to dramatize that. In a
vignette in *My Mother's House,* Juliette, estranged from her family,
is shown at the moment of giving birth. Colette stands looking out
her window in an effort to see or guess what is happening in that
shuttered house so nearby and yet so far away. Suddenly she notices
a familiar form in a housedress: her mother, who crosses their street
to be a little closer to the Roché house. There is a scream — Juliette
in labor. Colette watches as her mother kneads her own hips, ob-

viously wishing to ease the birth pangs of her ungrateful daughter, unreachable and suffering.[8]

The day came when the Colettes could no longer hold on to Saint-Sauveur. It was time for Sido's older son to help. After finishing medical school he had settled not in Saint-Sauveur but in Châtillon-sur-Loing (now called Châtillon-Coligny), a county seat only slightly larger than Saint-Sauveur, some twenty-five miles to the north and west. Here Achille was able to provide temporary quarters for the refugees.

The forsaking of her village was a wrenching experience for Colette, and she was to return to it again and again, making a myth of Saint-Sauveur. What actually happened remains confusing. A seemingly authoritative biography tells us that the house in Saint-Sauveur, the house of Colette's birth and growing-up, was sold at auction. In fact, it was not sold at all. Nor was the furniture put up for sale by court order, as Colette herself said it was. An advertisement in the local newspaper has been found, so we now know that there was a "Voluntary Sale of Furniture" (on June 15, 1890) because the owners were going away. Beds and armoires and mirrors and candlesticks, oil paintings and other art objects, leather-bound books, including the works of Voltaire, Goethe, Schiller, and Musset, though not those of Balzac — all went to the highest bidder.[9]

So on their arrival in Châtillon the Colettes moved in with Achille. Soon they had a house of their own just across the road. The living quarters seemed constricted after Saint-Sauveur, but they did have a garden. And school was over for Sidonie Gabrielle.

It is hard to imagine what this overripe, overworldly village girl would have done had she not . . . but she had. Found a man, that is, and a Parisian into the bargain — one of the most Parisian men one could hope to meet, not a product of the boulevard but a creator of its wit, its fin de siècle studied insouciance. He was a journalist, best known as Willy, born Henry (actually Henri) Gauthier-Villars, born so long before Colette (on August 10, 1859) that he was already well established in his career, already somewhat notorious.

It might indeed be helpful to stop the clock here so that we can appraise Henry Gauthier-Villars as the Colettes might have, just at the moment when his flirtation with their daughter began to look as if it would turn into something more permanent. When Henry was still an infant his father had acquired the printshop and bookstore that were to be the nucleus of the scientific publishing house owned and operated by the Gauthier-Villars family almost to our day. Henry himself, however, was destined for a less commercial track. While in law school he was already writing theater reviews under such pseudonyms as Henry Maugis. He also liked the name Jim Smiley, taken from Mark Twain's story "The Celebrated Jumping Frog of Calaveras County" (Henry later wrote and lectured on Twain). In no time at all he was mixing with leading writers of his day, including the Symbolists (then the avant-garde). Late in life he remembered being published in the same magazines as Verlaine and attending receptions at the modernist *Mercure de France* alongside Guillaume Apollinaire. At the time of his engagement to the girl from Saint-Sauveur he was writing music criticism under still another pen name, The Usherette, displaying the erudition and dexterity for which he was becoming known.[10]

Let Willy describe himself at this time. (Willy, his most famous pen name, seems to have been nothing more than a diminutive of Villars; Colette and presumably everybody else pronounced it "Vili.")[11] "Thinning blond hair, baby-faced, a bit conceited; the heavy lips of a sensualist, myopic eyes, still young-looking": this is the Usherette writing about Willy. It is not a flattering portrait, but to judge from both photographs and character witnesses, it seems to be an accurate one. "Has considerable success with women, and lets it be known. In music, possesses deliciously vague notions," the description continues. He sums himself up as a patent fraud. In a collection of the Usherette's reviews there are no fewer than sixteen mentions of Willy. One of these reports the presence of Willy and "Willa" at a concert, for one must be accompanied by a missus, though not necessarily one's real wife.[12]

"Mr. Willy was not enormous," remembered Colette, "but bulging." This was much later, when she was saying mean things about her former husband. "A powerful skull, popping eyes, a stub nose without bone, jowls — everything rounded." She gave him a dainty, agreeable mouth but spoiled the compliment by saying that he was right to hide his weak chin behind a short beard. He was said to resemble Edward VII; Colette felt that the truth, less flattering, was that he looked more like the king's mother, Queen Victoria.[13]

There have been brave attempts to explain how this man-about-town won the heart of a rural grade-school graduate. She herself stated that he was the son of a classmate of her father's in military school; Willy later claimed that he had known her since she was ten years old.[14] When he managed to escape Saint-Sauveur, Captain Colette enjoyed being able to drop in at the Gauthier-Villars store in Paris to exchange reminiscences with the owner. Colette remembered that her father once shipped a giant pike to his "Crimea comrade Gauthier-Villars."[15]

In September 1889 Willy had a child with a woman who was married to someone else. She divorced the other man and Willy recognized the child, but then this woman whom he adored died suddenly, leaving him with the two-year-old Jacques.[16] Desperate, he called on his country connections for help, according to the same tradition that had sent Colette's mother to the Puisaye to be nursed and nurtured.

So they had indeed known each other — the old-young man who called himself Willy and Sidonie Gabrielle the saucy schoolgirl — for a long time. Colette remembered writing love letters to Willy when she was sixteen or seventeen, three or four years before their marriage. "My very dear darling, I didn't close an eye all night," she wrote. "You were at once too close and too far away."[17] To hear her tell it (at least when she was telling it unkindly), the Parisian bachelor was casual about the engagement, coming down to see her only occasionally. He would bring gifts and then disappear again. For her the memorable thing was the exchange of letters.[18]

Still, it was not a very plausible match, even if Colette was more like the Claudine of her stories than she was willing to admit.

Perhaps it was to justify the strange union of country girl and dandy that Colette later offered an excuse: "Let's just say that if so many young girls place their hands in a hairy paw, offer their lips to a greedy mouth, look with serenity at the enormous masculine shadow of a stranger, it's only because sensual curiosity whispers irresistible counsels." This in *My Apprenticeships,* her harshest settling of old scores, whose subtitle is "What Claudine Didn't Say." She goes on, "In a very short time a man without scruples turns an ignorant girl into a prodigy of dissolution, whom nothing can disgust." Disgust comes later, she adds, like honesty.

One thing that Claudine *did* say was that the young girl could take the initiative. During a visit to Paris, where she was staying at the home of another military-school comrade of her father's, Colette went out with Willy. Two glasses of sparkling wine went to her head, and in the carriage on the way home the nineteen-year-old girl told the thirty-three-year-old man, "I'll die if I'm not your mistress!"[19] Willy made sure that the episode was woven into *Claudine in Paris.*

To the rest of the world the union may have seemed shocking. Later, when *he* was angry, Willy suggested that Colette was the one who had had to be married off because of her scandalous behavior. In one of his novels he has the man-about-town marry "Vivette Wailly" — this at a time when his former wife was known as Colette Willy. Here she appears as an intelligent and sly country girl, poor as a churchmouse, who cannot marry in her own village because of a fugue with a music teacher.[20] In this context — Willy having indicated that Vivette prefers women to men — the music teacher is also a woman. Colette later confessed to having had a crush on a chestnut-haired woman piano teacher, but that was a couple of years *after* her marriage, and in Paris.[21]

As the bride later remembered it, she had no pressing need to marry, and her parents actively opposed the match.[22] She confided to a friend that were it not for the pressure exerted on Willy by the Gauthier-Villars family, he would not have gone through with the marriage, despite their three-year engagement. Her mother, said Colette, detested Willy. But what could a girl do? It was marry Willy or become an old maid, or a teacher. So she made him a gift of her twenty years and her five-foot length of hair, and for a time he was amused by her.[23]

"I'm marrying the daughter of Captain Colette," Henry Gauthier-Villars wrote to his brother Albert, "happy to offer this token of gratitude to a family that was so wonderfully good to Jacques [his infant son]. She happens not to have a dowry, which does not lead our parents to rejoice." Willy did not think that it was going to be a "marriage of love." When one had a chance for love, he added with obvious bitterness, one buried it (as he had buried Jacques's mother).[24]

He was to recall how friends teased him when he took his fiancée out in Paris in the evening: "Be careful, Willy, the law doesn't fool around."[25] There was also some teasing in the press, as when, less than a fortnight before the marriage, a Parisian daily reported:

> There is much talk in Châtillon of the intense flirtation going on between one of the best of the Paris wits and an exquisite blonde known throughout the region for her extraordinary head of hair.
> Nothing is said about marriage.
> So we advise the pretty owner of the two incredible golden plaits to give her kisses . . . only with a ring on her finger.[26]

At that time dueling was the expected response to a newspaper gibe; Wilky challenged the editor and wounded him.[27] He could be tender. To a friend he described himself as being "quite stunned by the fluttering grace of my pretty little Colette." Soon they would be married, "and I won't have a cent. All right!" (The last phrase was written in English.)[28]

They went before the mayor of Châtillon on May 15, 1893. The groom submitted a statement from his parents, who were absent from the ceremony but consented to the marriage.[29]

One of the most revealing photographs ever taken of Colette presents us with a stuffy upper-middle-class family at teatime. The
Gauthier-Villarses are formal but friendly; their son is pensive. In
the foreground there is a young woman with an hourglass figure and
bangs. She looks bored, or even languid, but she is the only one with
enough curiosity to look at the man behind the camera.[30]

FOUR

The Literary Life

*I*N THE YEAR he married Colette, the man who called himself Willy was, among other things, on the brink of a prodigious career in literature. An editor and critic, and an original writer when he cared to be, he was nonetheless more often an impresario for other writers, whose work he would pass off as his own. Books by Willy were likely to have been written by anyone but Willy himself. Yet in 1893 he seemed at the peak of his powers, an authority on whatever subject he chose. He was a man of salons social and literary, of the theaters and cafés of boulevard Paris.

Their married life began modestly enough, however. Willy then had a bachelor's apartment at the top of a house on the Seine that served both as the offices of the family publishing house and as the residence of family members. Their rooms were "furnished with shameful file cartons," the bride observed with distaste; under a "tired bed" the dust was thick as snow (gray snow). "Piles of yellowing newspapers occupied all the chairs; German picture postcards floated about, glorifying women's underclothing with ribbons and buttocks."

But within a matter of weeks they had moved some streets behind the quay, to a three-flight walk-up on Rue Jacob. In the first apartment Colette had been bothered by traffic noise; now she was trapped in a building surrounded by other buildings. Later she would admit that she had been too young to appreciate Rue Jacob's eighteenth-century facades; for this twenty-year-old they were merely depressing. Her only activity then, she remembered, was waiting for Willy to come home.[1]

We have a portrait of Colette at the dawn of her new existence, by the actress Marguerite Moreno, who was to be her lifelong friend: "Your interminable tresses enlaced you like a snake. . . . I see your eyes, your little pointed chin, . . . I hear the way you rolled your r's. . . ."[2] The artist Jacques-Emile Blanche was invited to lunch and arrived full of curiosity to meet "the nth victim of that gobbler of female flesh and souls." The visitor scrutinized Colette, with "her burgundy dress, the high collar of a boarding-school girl on holiday, her triangular face resembling a cat's. . . ." She was engaged in crumbling a piece of bread on the tablecloth, embarrassed by the presence of an unfamiliar visitor. "Willy scolds her; furious, but obedient, she turns her head away. . . ."[3]

Most portraits — both verbal and visual — of Colette at the outset of her life with Willy concur in depicting a young lady with head bowed; not everyone discerned the fury. Some of the recollections, recorded later and benefiting from hindsight, attribute a degree of cunning to this bride who was more childlike in appearance than in actual years. She remembered herself as being anything but pampered. Her mother came up from Châtillon and discovered that in the middle of winter Colette had no coat. She found it natural to live without money, just as she had before marriage: life meant reading and munching on candy. She was being punished, she would say later, for having wanted to be the plaything of a mature man. It helped that she was unsocial by nature: "I drifted into daydreams, half-light, vagueness, the habit of keeping my mouth shut. . . ."[4]

In a fictionalized version of her years with Willy, she has her husband strike her. He is unfaithful and does little to conceal his infidelities; she is jealous to the point of contemplating suicide. He is brilliant, and their friends feel that without him she would scarcely exist.[5]

A vignette: a young music critic remembered a visit to Rue Jacob. While talking to Willy he heard sounds of splashing in the next room. "It's Colette," Willy told him. "She's taking a bath. Do you want to see her?" The young man smiled vaguely, as one does after a bad joke, and later wondered what would have happened had he nodded yes.[6] As for Colette, she was to remember how women would repeatedly write to her husband to offer themselves to him,[7] a circumstance that, if true, would seem to belie the portrait she paints of a physically repellent Willy in *The Vagabond*. Was she totally innocent? In the photographs she posed for, she looks as if she wants the world to see what a hard time she could give anyone — even the ringmaster that Willy made himself out to be.

He was a very public man by now. His books were beginning to be talked about, at the very least by friends and writers who were beholden to him. There were collections of his music and drama reviews, prefaces, works written with others. His collaborations soon assumed a form peculiar to him: he would invent a plot for a novel and recruit a writer to fill in the details; he himself would then add the spice, lacing the narrative with puns, kindly allusions to friends, and slurs on enemies. The books would come out with Willy listed as the sole author. This literary factory of his produced some fifty books before the machinery finally broke down. Willy novels played up Willy's wit and his attraction to ladies; he generally turned up in them as Henry Maugis or Jim Smiley or even Silly. He varied the pace by publishing intermittent works of erudition, which were not necessarily written by him either.[8]

To hear his estranged wife later tell it, there was something perverse about his frenzied activity. He seemed to want to appear desperate and to relish the idea of being pursued for nonpayment of debt. His favorite expression became "Hurry, little friend, we don't have a penny in the house!" And off his secretaries would fly, rushing to the post office with piles of dispatches for his ghostwriters, demanding more novels, more articles. But in spite of the bitterness of their separation, Colette conceded that this man who did not write possessed more talent than those who wrote his books for him. He could talk about the article he had in mind better than any of his young assistants could execute it.

He devised complicated means of covering musical events. Assistants passed notes to other assistants; there were passwords, discreet rendezvous. It would have been simpler for this born musician to write the reviews himself. All the same, his helpers included some of the most admired talents of his day, among them the composers Vincent d'Indy and Claude Debussy![9]

Much of his own talent went into advertising. His helpers competed with each other to see who could concoct the most eulogistic biography of the master. "Willy! Those two syllables, enigmatic and haunting, which one sees constantly and everywhere, in the slightest of literary sheets as well as in the most luxurious of magazines, excite and intrigue us" — and that from a writer who was not even on his payroll.[10]

On a visit to Châtillon, it was all Colette could do to maintain the fiction that she was happy in her marriage (or so she remembered). It took some time for her to learn how to laugh again. She told stories about the famous people she had met, but then she would break down.

The worst was yet to come. Colette put the event at just a year after her marriage. Alerted by an unsigned letter, she hopped into a carriage for a ride up the Montmartre slope to a tiny mezzanine flat, the hideaway of a wild young woman named Charlotte Kinceler. She found Willy with Charlotte; they were not in bed but going over a ledger together. The young woman grabbed a pair of scissors, ready to defend herself. Willy wiped off some sweat. "You've come for me?" he asked. Colette was surprised to find herself so cool, and so was he. The bitterness would come later. And still later she would become friends with Charlotte Kinceler, as she got into the habit of doing with the mistresses of her husbands. This particular one was "a little brunette . . . not pretty, but passionate and graceful."

Perhaps Colette's discovery of Willy with an apparently domesticated mistress was responsible for the long illness that followed, for it is not otherwise explained. "There is always a moment, in the life of young people, when dying seems as normal and tempting as living, and I hesitated," she would later write. She was rescued by friends of Willy's who were also her friends (but not her lovers). Older even than Willy, by ten years, Paul Masson was to be immortalized in Colette's novels as the selfless confidant. Marcel Schwob, writer and critic, lover and then husband of Marguerite Moreno, was perhaps the most brilliant of this circle. Colette lets us see him at her bedside, reading from (and translating) Mark Twain, Jerome K. Jerome, Charles Dickens, and Daniel Defoe.[11]

In Paris Schwob lived in a suite of low-ceilinged rooms on Rue de l'Université, steps away from Rue Jacob, making his living by writing literary criticism. In 1890, at the age of twenty-three, he had begun to write for the influential *L'Echo de Paris,* which also became Willy's chief source of revenue. Eventually Schwob took over the literary section of the paper, along with one of the best-known critics of the time, Catulle Mendès.[12]

Colette's convalescence was spent on Belle-Ile-en-Mer, the largest island off Brittany, known then for its isolation as well as its spectacular scenery. The Willys were accompanied to the island by Colette's other bedside companion, Paul Masson. He must have been good company for Willy, too. Masson had given up a legal career to play literary games, loving puns as much as erudition. Colette remembered "a gray face, unobtrusive and unforgettable, a little beard of dried hay, the look of an evil priest, a slight, grating laugh." At Belle-Ile, Masson always wore a dark suit. But he kept up with the twenty-one-year-old Colette in her enthusiastic embrace of sun, sand, and salt-sea air (the latter new to her). Willy spent his days writing — letters, mostly, perhaps to commission more books that he would sign as his own, perhaps also to keep up with women friends.

"But I was already learning to look the other way," Colette confessed (afterward).

She saw Masson as her first friend in maturity. He helped her to become a woman, giving her confidence in herself, finding qualities in her that no one else had found. For on the surface she was an enigma with two long braids, a wild creature fed like a monkey, on nuts and bananas. Masson seemed to know what was going on *inside*.

The bachelor Masson would be assailed by fisherwomen in high lace caps venturing, "You don't need anybody?"

"To do what?" he asked.

"To sleep with you," came the reply.[13] It was a good story, and in her novel *Retreat from Love* Colette would repeat it, though in that context the fisherwoman offers to sleep with Claudine and her husband both.

In the same fiction Colette also tells another Belle-Ile story. She is dressed in a sailor suit; when she and her husband make love on the beach, local people assume that her husband has seduced a cabin boy. From then on he is known as "the disgusting Parisian."

Colette wrote her first almost-grown-up letters to Marcel Schwob — almost-grown-up because she was in her twenties but sounded fifteen. The first of these that has been found goes back to the previous December (1893), when a young woman who lived with Schwob died unexpectedly. No one told Colette anything about it, so that when Schwob called at Rue Jacob she was her usual carefree self. "Willy scolds and pushes me and shouts," she wrote to Schwob. "He would have done better to explain things and not to surround himself with useless mysteries as he always does."

Schwob wrote a book called *Le Livre de Monelle,* a somewhat disconnected tale in the Symbolist manner. The final pages, evoking the death of his mistress, brought Colette to tears as she read them in their Belle-Ile hotel, "and Willy had to calm me down in bed and put me to sleep in his arms, and he cursed you for upsetting me so." She was still the child bride.

The Willys were in Belle-Ile from late June until the end of August, going from there to Châtillon. Her mother bickered with Willy all day long, Colette reported to Schwob, and "that keeps me merry."

She was delighted by a line from Defoe's *Moll Flanders,* published in Schwob's translation; it ends with Moll's confession, "I own I was much wickeder than he."[14]

FIVE

Inventing Claudine

IF COLETTE STILL needed to grow up, Paris was the place for her to do it. Willy's world was for quick-witted pupils. She accompanied her husband to the boulevard cafés, where he would recruit his young writers. (They were almost of her generation, she thought, and yet a kind of barrier — "a man worse than mature" — separated them from her.) She watched as Pierre Louÿs's mistress ran her fingers through his hair, musing that *she* had never touched a man's hair lovingly (Willy was bald). She dreamed of "a passionate adventure, secret, normal," with one of these young men. She later said that she had created the homosexual Marcel in *Claudine in Paris* so as to be able to describe a good-looking younger man.[1] This character was modeled on X. M. (for Marcel) Boulestin, Willy's secretary, who kept Colette company on those long afternoons when her husband was off on mysterious errands.[2]

And so on into society. Léontine Arman de Caillavet, who had been kind to Colette during her illness, was the hostess of one of the most brilliant salons of turn-of-the-century Paris, a gathering of men of state, poets and playwrights, and women who were more than just beautiful. A permanent fixture of this salon was the writer Anatole France, whom Madame Arman de Caillavet hoped to make "the Voltaire of his era."[3]

Marcel Proust was still in the army, fulfilling his draft obligation, when he began attending the Caillavet afternoons. The hostess got Anatole France to write the preface for Proust's first published work, as well as for the book of another young hopeful, Charles Maurras — this before the cataclysmic Dreyfus case drove a wedge between arch-nationalists such as Maurras (and Willy, too, for that matter) and the Arman de Caillavets, Frances, and Prousts. Later, when she could confess such things, Colette would recall that she had not been impressed by the young Proust, with his excessive deference and his formal dress.[4] A curious document has survived in the form of a thank-you note that Colette sent to Proust to acknowledge compliments he had paid Willy. Colette could only come up with more compliments for her man: "My Willy is so original (even if he hides that fact carefully)." She hoped to see Proust again at Madame Arman de Caillavet's salon, she said, "for it seems to me that we have many tastes in common — a taste for Willy, among other things."[5] And she accused *him* of being excessively deferential!

There was also a musical milieu, consisting of music makers and music lovers, that was of capital importance in the life of Gauthier-Villars the music critic. On a typical evening a composer who is now part of musical history would sit at the piano, with a male singer standing nearby and a woman singing from her chair. Occasionally two composers (their names might be Gabriel Fauré and André Messager) would join in a four-handed exercise. A Claude Debussy would applaud.[6]

Until the Dreyfus affair the Willys were familiars of the Natansons, Thadée and Misia. Thadée, the descendant of wealthy Polish Jews, founded the influential literary magazine *La Revue Blanche* with his brothers, and his young wife was the child of minor Polish nobility. Misia remembered the Colette of that time, "with her triangular face and her wasp's waist, which gave her a schoolgirl's silhouette." Willy was Colette's teacher, thought Misia, who deplored the crude stories he told.[7]

Colette had first met Marguerite Moreno when the actress was the companion of Catulle Mendès, Marcel Schwob's mentor at *L'Echo de Paris*. After the sudden death of Schwob's young mistress, Marguerite moved in with him, and Colette was able to get closer to this winsome and intelligent woman, with her "long silhouette." Everything about the regal Marguerite "humiliated and enchanted the displaced country girl that I still was," Colette wrote.[8] His biographer tells us that Schwob was still in full possession of his powers when he fell in love with the actress, but illness soon troubled their life together.[9] We now know that he was suffering from bubonic plague, as improbable as that may sound, and that he was being treated principally with morphine to relieve the pain.

Maurice-Edmond Sailland, who began his literary career as a ghost for Willy and who wrote under the odd pen name Curnonsky, remembered of Marguerite Moreno, "For an intellectual, an artist, a poet, she was the ideal pale and bewitching muse, whom one should have wished to take up the lute for, bestow a kiss upon, and do the rest."[10] Born in Paris in 1871, she was Colette's senior by two years. She was only nineteen when the Comédie Française gave her a starring role.[11]

An aspect of Colette's relationship with Willy is revealed by a note she sent to Marcel Schwob. He was to accompany her to a party at Léontine Arman de Caillavet's (Schwob's mother had been Léontine's teacher). "Willy," she wrote, "asks only that you get out of the carriage a few yards before her door, so that people don't go around saying that we are 'flaunting our liaison.' "[12]

It was easier, as Colette remarked, to dream about a fair but inaccessible creature such as Marcel Boulestin. Others describe him as small, round, and faintly comic in his dandyism. He spent his time arranging receptions and outings for Willy and decorating the house "artistically" with flowers. He would later go on to open a splendid French restaurant in London.[13]

There was Charlotte (or "Lotte") Kinceler, who had apparently admired Colette's cool reaction when she surprised Willy in her Montmartre flat. For her part, Colette now said she felt grateful to Lotte, who had taught her to be on her guard against Willy. The incident in Montmartre had spelled the end of Colette's youth; from Lotte she learned "tolerance and dissimulation, and how to compromise with an enemy."[14]

Willy loved his bohemian existence; Colette often found it distressing. At times it meant waiting part of the night in a newspaper office for proofs of a theater review, "legs hanging over a bench, punch-drunk with sleep, . . . tired of not having eaten, tired of eating. . . ." Only when some eminent wit joined them — it might be the playwright Georges Courteline — would she brighten up. Then it would be finished. Was she terribly thirsty? Willy asked. Thirsty for sleep above all. But they would wind up in a café.[15]

In 1895 Colette's name was affixed to some musical reviews in *La Cocarde,* a short-lived daily published by Maurice Barrès, an ideologist of the anti-Dreyfus crusade. One can guess that Willy was only making use of his wife because he was publishing reviews under his own name in other newspapers. The voice in these reviews is that of a seasoned critic; one begins, "Monsieur Colonne has undertaken to let us hear all of the works of Berlioz, good or bad. We've admired the good ones. Yesterday he gave us *Lélio.*" She put her name to six such reviews, and then a seventh appeared in the same paper under Willy's byline.

His biographer tells us that it was also in 1895 that Willy opened his novel-writing factory.[16] And Willy's wife was invited to join the work force. As she remembered it, the day came when Willy said, "You should jot down your recollections of primary school. Don't be afraid of spicy details; I might be able to do something with them . . . money is tight."

But it always was. She recalled that although she was still somewhat indolent after her illness and convalescence, she managed to procure a stack of school composition notebooks with lined paper and red marginal bars — hers was a classroom assignment, after all.

She wrote at one corner of a desk, "with application and indifference," and when she was done she handed the closely written pages
to Willy. He read them and then told her, "I was wrong; I can't do
anything with this." Into a drawer went the notebooks.[17] As Willy
remembered it, he actually took the material to his regular publishers, who turned down this first draft of *Claudine at School*. One of
them commented that it would not sell a hundred copies.[18] Willy
may not be entirely reliable on this point, however; his "regular
publishers" would not become regular publishers for another two or
three years, if Colette produced her schoolgirl story in 1895.

But this is a detail. It is likely that Willy provided his ghostwriter-
wife with guidelines, perhaps even a scenario. The classroom antics
had to be naughty, the dialogue racy. The novel as we know it is a
well-constructed fiction, with fully developed scenes. We can be sure
that there was more than one version of *Claudine*.

Note, too, that the Willy couple made a pilgrimage to Saint-
Sauveur in July 1895. Willy even remembered that they went there
so that Colette could show him the scene of her childhood romps;
the idea for the book supposedly came out of that visit. As the episode was related by Colette's teacher Olympe Terrain, the visitors
joined the headmistress and her staff for lunch, and since the other
teachers had been classmates of Colette's, the day was devoted to
reminiscing.[19] Willy added that he and Colette were invited to spend
the night at the school, an event imaginatively reproduced in *Claudine Married*.[20]

For a true vacation Willy took his wife to the Jura Mountains.
His parents had a house in Lons-le-Saunier, and they stayed there
for a time. Colette remembered a large and Catholic family, a
mother-in-law, sisters-in-law, aunts, and cousins, all discoursing on
pious matters.[21]

Willy was a Wagnerian, and his presence at the annual Bayreuth
music festival was indispensable. Colette accompanied him there in
the summer of 1896 to follow Wagner's Tetralogy.[22] There Willy
acted the part of "the odious tyrant, the kind master, the chubby cat

crying like a calf at *Die Götterdämmerung,*" as Colette described it to a friend.[23]

She was to publish her first piece of writing now — the first, that is, that was not only signed but also probably written by her — and although it does not appear in the bibliographies, it is worth mentioning. On December 5, 1896, a sober weekly called *La Critique* printed her four-paragraph review of a play called *Omphale* by a Monsieur de Saussine, a name that seems not to have survived the nineteenth century. The plot is simple: a rich American woman seeks to secure the fame of the sculptor she marries, and then she discovers that she really cares about him. No sleight of hand in this review, no racy allusions, no puns; the author expresses some reservations about the acting and wishes that the actress playing the American heiress were prettier.[24]

SIX

Ascension of the Willys

ONE OF THE THINGS this climbing couple could do
now was move from the dark Rue Jacob to the newly developed Rue
de Courcelles, almost as far right as one could go on the Right Bank.
A first impression of this artist's studio six flights above street level
was likely to be favorable; only later would Colette discover that
skylights and high windows signified excessive heat in summer and
relentless cold in winter. It was already fashionable to take over a
studio like this one and to furnish it casually with a garden bench
here, a refectory table there. Bohemian when they moved in, the flat
would become much more so before they left it.[1]

To hear his son, Jacques, tell it, Willy did his writing there, as
visitors came and went, exchanging gossip. He would add his own
comments and make his phone calls while messengers carried off his
pieces to various newspapers.[2] Colette, on the other hand, remembered that she had to whisper to her visitors so as not to disturb
Willy, who sat on the other side of a glass door, in a white-walled
room that looked like a pastry shop transformed.[3]

To escape bohemia, there were outings. Even the portly Willy
would mount a rented bicycle, his wife beside him on a racing bike
that lacked brakes and a mud-guard (he had won it in a lottery).

They canoed on the Marne and the Seine with others of their circle. For the men this sporting life would conclude with a winy lunch followed by a snooze. Colette missed the real country.[4]

In 1898 Willy signed his name to a novel titled *Un Vilain Monsieur!* (A Naughty Gentleman), in which he appears as Henry Maugis, as Jim Smiley, and, in yet another disguise, as Robert Parville. Among the other recognizable characters are Léontine Arman de Caillavet and Anatole France. She is depicted as a hunchback, a hook-nosed screech owl.[5] In *Claudine in Paris,* written in 1901, she is Mrs. Barmann, again a screech owl, with the same hooked nose; in *Claudine Married* (1902) she is "that stoutish screech owl," while Anatole France is "the noisy camp follower who shares her destiny." In the manuscript for the same novel Colette identifies one of Mrs. Barmann's regular guests as "a young kike writer"; the reference is to Marcel Proust, but this time Willy was a prudent editor and changed it to "a young and handsome writer."[6]

The Willys had been welcomed into Madame Arman de Caillavet's drawing room often enough, and she had befriended them, comforting Colette in her dark days.

But two things had happened since then, and one could argue about which mattered more to Willy. In 1894 Captain Alfred Dreyfus was convicted (on faked evidence, it would be revealed) of passing secrets to Germany, the hereditary enemy. The "affair" divided France, with nostalgics for the Old Regime and a dominant Church on one side, and resolute democrats on the other. For traditionalists, for anti-Semites, surely, Dreyfus had to be guilty. Willy himself was a congenital anti-Semite,[7] and he and his closest associates, along with their newspapers and magazines, were firmly in the anti-Dreyfus camp. When the Natansons' *Revue Blanche* launched a campaign to support the army's prisoner, Willy refused to join the signatories. "It's the first time that he hasn't wanted to sign something he didn't write," quipped Pierre Veber, a onetime ghostwriter for Willy. (Jules Renard, who recorded this in his diary, had his own comments on Willy's literary career: "His glass isn't tall, but he drinks from other people's"; "Willy *have* a lot of talent.")[8]

Willy did sign one manifesto, an appeal for funds for the widow of Colonel Hubert Henry, who had helped to fake the case against Dreyfus. The money was to be used to sue a supporter of Dreyfus.[9]

The Dreyfus case was heard for a second time in 1899, but still not to the advantage of the luckless officer. He was pardoned all the same, and later (in 1906) rehabilitated. The schism would endure.

For Colette, the rural suspicion of urbanized Jews was hard to shake off. A letter survives from her mother, for example, expressing concern that she was doing business with Jews.[10] As she grew in years and experience, and grew away from Willy, Colette was to throw off some of her prejudices; some of her best friends . . .

But there was another reason for the Willys' hostility toward their benefactor Madame Arman de Caillavet. Apparently Willy had taken advantage of his easy access to her home to attempt the seduction of her attractive daughter-in-law. Madame Arman let Colette know what was happening and was so upset by it — or so Willy told another salon guest, Marcel Proust — that she nearly lost her eyesight.[11]

We do not have to use much imagination to picture the Willy couple as the century turned. Photographers, and more than one portraitist, have done it for us. At work they sit at the same desk (a large Directoire-style table) at the Rue de Courcelles studio. (Willy scribbled on this photograph: "Perfect union, shared labor, household peace — Nuts!")[12] Formal studio portraits show Willy in top hat and gloves, Colette looking resigned. When Jacques-Emile Blanche painted them, he thought them a "sad couple," she still a girl with lowered eyelids, her lord and master treating her like a child. Blanche says that he destroyed the revelatory product of their sitting.[13] Colette remembered that he had painted the portrait over an existing oil of a young woman; after a while the original reappeared, effacing the Gauthier-Villarses.[14]

Never mind the vanished portrait. Another one, by Eugène Pascau, survives, and Colette herself interpreted it: "On my features one can see, as in most photographs of me from the same period, an expression at once dutiful, impassive, half sweet, half doomed, of which I'm rather ashamed" — a shame she still felt nearly forty years later.[15]

The former child-wife spoke mockingly of the sheer volume of portraits that Willy commissioned of himself (she called it "a photographic madness"), not to mention the statuettes, the cardboard and rubber effigies, the silhouettes in carved wood, the inkstands in the form of top hats. She found "significant" the marble cross on which Willy's features appeared in bas relief. He had this frightful object reproduced on postcards, one of a series of cards that he ordered by the thousands to use for his daily correspondence.[16] In a word, he had discovered that his personality was his most marketable commodity, and he became an expert at marketing it.

The publishing history of *Claudine at School* seems uncomplicated to the point of suspicion. In cleaning out his desk, Colette maintained, Willy came upon the notebooks in which she had scribbled her memories of Saint-Sauveur. "Well, well," she quoted Willy as saying, "I thought I had thrown them out." He opened one of the notebooks and leafed through it, then murmured, "That's nice." He opened another, then another, and finally exclaimed, "My God! I'm an idiot!" So he rushed off to see a publisher, not forgetting his inevitable top hat. But first he suggested that she liven up the story by sprinkling it with local dialect, improvising a few classroom pranks, and *also* adding a lesbian angle.[17]

A colleague of Willy's remembered being asked — by Willy — to look over the manuscript. He was impressed with what he read, but when he inquired as to when the book would be published, Willy remarked, "I do have to work on it a little." [18] Later Willy would insist (unconvincingly) that far from contributing spice, he had instead fought to keep the book decent — fought Colette, that is. As an example, he said that she had written, in reference to candy sold in her village, "It smells like a belched apple." [19]

We will never know who wrote what in the original manuscript of *Claudine,* for it has not been found. What we do know is that Willy alone put his name on the book. In the preface he explained that the manuscript had been sent to him "wrapped in a pink ribbon." Colette later claimed to have taken it all as a joke. She read the preface only after the book was printed, and was amused by the jacket illustration of a country girl in wooden shoes scribbling in a notebook.[20] The novel was published in March 1900. Willy had his claque in the popular press, where this book's readers ought to be found, but he also had friends among the more sophisticated critics. He himself was to say that Charles Maurras made *Claudine.*[21] That talented man — a classicist by day, a militant *antidreyfusard* by night — assured his readers that *Claudine at School* deserved their attention. For Claudine was a serious person, and Willy had *treated* her with great seriousness.[22]

Willy had another friend in Alfred Vallette, founder of the literary journal *Mercure de France,* the organ of the Symbolists and promoter of everything that seemed new. Vallette's wife, Rachilde, wrote fiction that was bold for its time as well as influential book reviews for *Mercure de France.* Her appraisal of *Claudine* appeared in the May 1900 issue, and it was ecstatic. "Whether by a tour de force of his wit (and he has plenty) Willy, the man-about-town, the gossip columnist, the brilliant author and delicate virtuoso, actually created the character of Claudine, or whether he plucked these pages from a woman's beloved hands, as one picks flowers to arrange them artfully in a precious vase, I don't really care," she wrote. "This is an astonishing creation, and that's saying enough." If Willy had written it, it was a masterpiece; if "Claudine" had, it was the most extraordinary thing a beginner could do.[23]

Willy confided to Rachilde that he and Colette had written the book "together." He had used her notes and, above all, her conversations, for she had been talking to him since she was ten. The docile Colette sent Rachilde a thank-you: "You know, I had this pile of notes for years, but I'd never have dared to think that they were readable." It was thanks to Willy, who had "removed and attenuated the raw language that was too Claudine-ish," that *Claudine* had become publishable.[24] True or false, the myth had a life of its own now.

To hear Colette tell it later, there was something sadistic in Willy's insistence on his authorship of the novel, after he had sworn her to silence. He would invite her in to hear others praise *Claudine* and would pat her on the head and say, "But you know, this child was precious to me."[25]

Closer to our own time, regional historians have traced the characters in the Claudine books to real-life models. Some 200 such persons were utilized by Colette, and more than 150 of these have been identified as living in Saint-Sauveur during her growing-up years. Often she employed real or only slightly disguised names,[26] and her invented village itself is faithful to Saint-Sauveur down to the trees and flowers and fruit.[27] We don't of course know whether Colette realized what this would do to her old friends and neighbors, or to what extent the stress on their quirks and their vices was Willy's doing. Later he would go on record with a portrait of Saint-Sauveur as a veritable Sodom, claiming that Luce, for instance, Claudine's classmate, was based on a true "perverted peasant girl."[28] But he also remembered that the model for the doctor-politician Dutertre, who is shown coddling the girls and sleeping with their teacher, was hurt by the publication of *Claudine at School*.[29] In fact, the real Dutertre went on to become a minister of finance and a diplomat; there is even a street named after him in his hometown.[30]

The certain victim of all of this was the headmistress, Olympe Terrain, portrayed at once as girl-prone and the doctor's mistress. She denied committing the unnatural and even the natural acts attributed to her, and there is little evidence but hearsay to contradict her. "An evil genius led her astray," was her own explanation for her former pupil's treason.[31] She let it be known that because of *Claudine,* the real-life model for Aimée had missed out on marrying a teaching colleague, and the model for Luce had been wed only after a vigorous investigation.[32] Big Anaïs, who married a man who was to become a member of parliament, herself became a distinguished lady of the district and never forgave Sidonie Gabrielle.[33]

It was Claudine this, Claudine that. No vaudeville show could be without its schoolgirl sketch. And Willy had a new theme for his picture postcards: on one of them Colette, in a schoolgirl uniform, kneels before a large sheet of paper, making a sketch of Willy in top hat and goatee.[34]

Even worse — or even better, if you were Willy — budding Claudines threw themselves at the novel's supposed author. Colette found portraits of schoolgirls in his pockets, and some of these Claudines went so far as to show up at their door.[35] According to Willy, they came in couples — lesbian couples — and he received them in a bachelor's flat.[36]

SEVEN

The Claudine Factory

SUCCESS CALLED OUT for a sequel. The second *Claudine*, called *Claudine in Pais*, would allow Willy to introduce a bit of the wit and the vice of his Paris. In the new novel Claudine would come up against sophisticated salon life and encounter some of the personae (including Willy himself) that Willy and his ghosts had created for other novels published under his signature.

But in *Claudine in Paris* the country girl also meets Renaud, a more digestible Willy, a Willy that a girl could embrace with more enthusiasm. There is room, too, for another Willy alter ego, Henry Maugis. Later Colette would see Maugis as the only confession Willy ever made about himself. For it was he, not she, who invented this character who is a musicologist, a Hellenist, a literary man, a "swashbuckler, sensitive, unscrupulous," a lover of foreign brandies and puns, an amorist who prefers half-dressed women to naked ones, and girls' socks to silk stockings. . . .[1]

He locked her up so that she would write: this is the cliché that has come down to us of the bride-martyr and the satyr-impresario. Colette herself was responsible for this image; she lets us hear the key turning in the lock. She would be released from her writer's jail when she could show pages of finished manuscript. Not a flattering memory, she admitted. Thanks to her jailor she learned not how to write but how to deal with an enemy — and how to blackmail. "Perhaps I'd work faster in the country," she suggested. And so they got a country house.[2]

It was near Besançon, in southeast France, not far from the mountain retreat of the Gauthier-Villars family. Colette adored the place and could see herself and her books and her pets settling there forever. The house, called Monts-Boucons, had a Directoire-style facade, but its surroundings were purely pastoral. Colette felt like a shepherdess on her hilltop, eating the fruit of her orchards. Her pets were given names that would become familiar to her readers: Toby the dog, Kiki-la-Doucette the "subtle angora cat" (though she called her husband that, too). As for Willy, he came and went, and each departure was wrenching. But his absences taught her how to live alone, how to survive.[3]

A first-time visitor to Rue de Courcelles remembered Colette as being "muscular and slim," with little dark-blue bulbs for eyes, set "in the triangle of her face, under short-cropped hair."[4] Colette's own recollection of exactly when she was shorn of her floor-length tresses is unreliable, contradicted by photographs. The heroine of *Claudine in Paris* has cut hers, and we can guess that by the time that book appeared, in March 1901, Colette herself had yielded to practicality and the new fashion. Certainly she was new-style in behavior. The first-time visitor soon became a regular guest, but on one occasion, when she entered Colette's drawing room, she appeared hesitant. Colette noticed this and called out in front of everybody, "Do you want to pee?"[5]

When Natalie Clifford Barney first saw her, Colette was no longer the slender adolescent with long braids but a filled-out young woman with solid legs and a well-rounded backside; she was bold in language and manner, yet given to catlike silences. Barney also spoke of her "triangular face"; with that face, and her elongated eyelids, Colette could look seductive without really trying.[6] And Natalie Barney had an eye for seductive women; her drawing room would collect the most emancipated of them.[7] Late in life she showed a biographer a list of her female conquests, both liaisons and demi-liaisons, and for whatever it is worth, Colette was in the latter category (apparently because Willy's jealousy kept her out of the former). Barney's lifelong servant did remember the two women having a fling, which seems to be confirmed by a letter in which Colette says that Willy kissed Natalie's hands, and Colette everything else.[8]

Yet Natalie Barney seems to have excluded Colette from her circle of literary women in love with one another. In a memoir of what she referred to as her Academy of Women, she noted that "Colette loves seascapes and open horizons, little dogs, being backstage, and having one man at a time to keep her in slavery."[9]

Natalie was the daughter of Albert Barney, the heir to a railroad fortune back in the States, and Alice Pike Barney, a painter and writer whose father, of Dutch Jewish origin, was described in an obituary as one of "the most prominent merchant princes of the land." Born in Dayton, Ohio, in 1877, Natalie Barney went to school both in the United States and in France, following her mother in her travels. Later she took her own trips with the gorgeous Renée Vivien (born Pauline Tarn), going as far as ancient Lesbos (now Mytilene) in the hope of reestablishing a colony of women poets there.[10] In Liane de Pougy's 1901 novel, *Idylle saphique,* Natalie becomes Florence Temple-Bradfford, also called Flossie. Her female lover tells her, "Your perversity frightens me. . . ."[11] Both the name Flossie and the reputation for perversity stuck. In Radclyffe Hall's *The Well of Loneliness,* Natalie appears as Valérie Seymour; she becomes Evangeline Musset in *The Ladies Almanack,* attributed to Djuna Barnes.[12]

At this time Natalie was living in Neuilly, in a house with a garden large enough for memorable parties. She remembered calling on Colette in order to invite her to one of her afternoons, one that promised to be sensational, for the exotic Mata Hari was to perform Javanese dances in the nude (for an exclusively female audience). Willy was angry that he could not come along, and he insisted that Colette meet what Natalie Barney considered to be indecent conditions before he would consent to her going. Natalie does not tell us what these conditions were, but she has Colette admit to her, "I'm embarrassed that you've had a chance to see the chain I wear."[13]

Let this serve as background to Colette's third novel, *Claudine Married*. For Claudine and Renaud are indeed married, though with his complicity she begins a torrid affair with another young married woman. Renaud is now less a silver-screen idol than a jaded debauchee, the impresario of Claudine's lesbian liaison, a voyeur and then a full partner.

By this point in the Willys' marriage, anything was possible. In her memoirs Colette confessed to cowardice in allowing her husband to play around in Paris while she spent summers at their house at Monts-Boucons.[14] And in a novel written after their separation, Willy describes Vivette Wailly (read Colette Willy) as selfish and incapable of loving a man, even going so far as to tolerate her husband's mistresses so as not to be disfigured by pregnancy.[15]

In *Claudine Married* the young women, Claudine and Rézi, meet at a reception. Later Willy was to say that Colette was introduced to Georgie Raoul-Duval, an American married into a French family, at the literary salon of Jeanne and Lucien Muhlfeld. Colette proceeded to pursue her in an "ardent, brutal, tenacious" way that scandalized their friends. On her side, Georgie was dangerously seductive, "and perfidious, enjoying unnecessary danger." As Willy told the tale, this seductress known as Georgie would arrange a rendezvous with Colette and another with him, in the same bedroom but an hour apart. Once he recognized Colette's perfume on Georgie and warned her that if Colette found out what she was up to, she would shoot her. Georgie was indignant at the suggestion that Colette might try to kill her and not Willy.[16]

In *Retreat from Love*, the last of the Claudine novels, the Claudine-Renaud couple takes the American Suzie to the Bayreuth Wagner festival (for Renaud's sake). In fact they did all go to the music festival in 1901; a directory that documents the French presence there mentions both the Gauthier-Villarses and a Madame Duval of Paris.[17] "There is good music, mediocre food, and some frankly nasty things," Colette wrote to Jeanne Muhlfeld, "but we're of good cheer, and Georgie is merry."[18] Colette did not really like Bayreuth, and even the company of Georgie was not enough to sweeten the pill. What she craved and soon got was the sentimental retreat of Monts-Boucons. If she did have an affair with Georgie, it was now over, except in the pages of the new Claudine novel.

Claudine Married — or *Claudine in Love,* as it was to have been called — is the first of Colette's books written with or for Willy for which the original manuscript survives. It is definitely in her hand, with many changes — either suggested or ordered — in his. In it one can see how Colette followed Willy's suggestions on the same or subsequent pages, and a scholar who published a facsimile of the manuscript observed that there is no page of the handwritten text without some contribution or other from Willy, whether concerning form, vocabulary, grammar, dialogue, or transitions.[19]

What is lacking, of course, is a camera sequence of Willy standing over her, Willy urging her to insert this, to stress that, Willy carrying out his vendetta against Georgie, to the consternation of Colette, for this is the way she explained the situation to Jeanne Muhlfeld: "This vindictive fellow, having had a serious falling-out with G. R.-D. (I told you it would happen!) is now transforming, with brutal re-touches, Claudine's Rézi into Georgie. She is — she'll be — fright-fully recognizable. She mustn't be." Colette was worried about Willy first and foremost. "I have reasons for being less interested in . . . Claudine's friend." She wanted the Muhlfelds to turn Willy away from this madness; they would be doing him a favor.[20] When the publisher received the manuscript, he too found it hard to take. So it was Colette's turn to defend the book: there was not a single contestable word in it, she insisted.[21] (No doubt Willy got her to say that.)

But someone who read the manuscript recognized Georgie as the model for the lascivious Rézi and warned her. The publisher had already printed *Claudine in Love,* but Georgie blocked its publication, forcing him to either scrap his stock or sell it to her. We know this because copies have been found, and one can be consulted in the rare-book room of France's National Library.

The intrepid Willy now offered the book to another publisher, his friend Alfred Vallette at Mercure de France, a sister company to the journal of the same name. It appeared in May 1902 under a new title, *Claudine Married*. Of course the monthly *Mercure de France* had only good things to say about it. "It is impossible for a young woman to be more ingenuous than this in her sensuality," the reviewer announced, thereby guaranteeing good sales.[22]

It is true that hardly anyone was ever negative about anything in Willy's time. All the same, however, there was a note of dissent in a magazine called *La Renaissance Latine,* whose critic observed that the novel began with "repeated caresses," continued with further caresses, and ended with Claudine's desire for more. He did not wish to appear prudish; we are all voyeurs, he allowed, since we do read *Claudine.* He found talent in the novel, especially in Rézi's seduction of Claudine. But if only Willy would provide red meat instead of candy, French literature would be the better for it.[23]

At the beginning of 1902, before the latest *Claudine* had reached the bookshops, Claudine went on stage. Knowing the audience at the Bouffes Parisiens, a small theater specializing in popular musical comedies, Willy and his coauthors adapted not the first but the second Claudine novel, *Claudine in Paris;* later they added a one-act prologue dealing with Claudine's school days in the fictional version of Saint-Sauveur. The play opened at the height of the Claudine craze, when the streets were filled with Claudines. It had a winning actress in the cabaret entertainer Polaire, who was even more of a gamine, even smaller and slimmer, than Colette herself.

In her memoirs Polaire identified herself as Emilie-Marie Bouchard, born of a French mother and an Algerian father; the latter had given her her almond-shaped eyes. She claimed to have been eighteen when *Claudine in Paris* took her away from singing in cabarets, but she looked even younger because of her incredibly slender waist and her cropped hair. She seems actually to have been twenty-one at the time.

She remembered going to Rue de Courcelles to meet the Willys. Colette pushed a bench in her direction, rolling her *r*'s as she invited her to put her behind on it. Soon all of Paris was talking about this threesome, for at Willy's insistence Colette and Polaire began to dress alike, strolling the boulevards with the top-hatted Willy between them. It was even said that Willy himself sometimes mistook one for the other.[24] One could fill a book with all the photographs of Colette dressed as Claudine, Polaire dressed as Claudine, and Colette and Polaire together, with or without their master. In her memoir of those delirious years Colette says that it was at this point that Willy asked her to cut her braids, to enhance her resemblance to Polaire. She obeyed with relief, she wrote, for her floor-length hair had become a burden.[25]

To hear Colette tell it later, Willy's persistent requests of his lookalikes embarrassed her. She did not enjoy providing the spectacle of a threesome, even a false one. Colette told a friend that in any case Polaire would have refused to make love to her, for she detested what Colette liked to call "unisexuality."[26] For her part, Polaire confided to Marcel — Willy's secretary and Colette's friend — that she "hadn't even been" Willy's mistress.[27]

There may or may not really have been a dinner party, hosted by the playboy artist José Maria Sert and held in a private room of a Paris restaurant, at which dessert consisted of a giant cake that was carried in by four servants in livery. Two naked women were said to have emerged from a mountain of whipped cream — Colette and Polaire, Colette laughing as she splashed the dinner guests. True or false, the story has come down to our time.[28]

A sadder story: Colette remembered that one night Polaire summoned the Willys to her flat, saying that her lover was beating her. Colette found herself confronted with something entirely new for her: "love in its youth and brutality," a young man's bare chest, a young man's muscles. She realized that she was jealous.[29]

EIGHT

Squirrel in a Cage

THANKS TO CLAUDINE, if not to Colette, Henry
Gauthier-Villars had moved beyond the relatively small circle of boulevard wits in which he may have seemed first among equals. A
smart fortnightly, *Revue Illustrée,* featured a formal portrait photograph of Willy and Colette on its cover (predictably, the picture was
labeled "Willy"). The accompanying eulogistic article was illustrated
with portraits of Willy at ages seven, fifteen, twenty, and twenty-
seven, in each of which he is wearing the appropriate suit or uniform.[1] Soon after that a popular weekly published a story about
Willy written by none other than Henry Gauthier-Villars, adorned
with a portrait in the familiar top hat, twirled mustache, and goatee.
He would have liked to be tall, dark, and slender, he explained, but
Nature had decreed otherwise, "decorating my fat face with pale blue
eyes that reassure — too much — timid souls who might be frightened off by a belligerent curled mustache." His neck measured seventeen inches, exactly the same as Polaire's waistline.[2]

Fame brought a certain prosperity, and prosperity meant that they
were able to move, though not too far away (from 93 they transferred
to 177 bis, also on Rue de Courcelles). It was a town house, somewhat
more appropriate to the ascension of the Willys, even if they occupied

only one floor. Colette found the two-flight walk-up gloomy and
again did what she could to liven it up with applied eccentricity,
which she said was the response of the shy to the challenge of their
surroundings. One example of her method was a solid wood balus-
trade painted white and planted dead-center in their salon to divide
it in two.[3]

This time Willy acknowledged Colette's role in the family part-
nership by making sure that she got her own desk and a good lamp.
Her refuge was up a narrow staircase, in a painter's studio equipped
not with easels but with gymnastic equipment, including a trapeze.
She made use of the gear, feeling like a prisoner doing the required
daily exercise. The studio also served as her private drawing room.
Marcel brought his young men to see her; she remembered this as
her introduction to the male homosexual universe.[4]

Later Willy's son would seek to temper the grim picture Colette
painted of the house. She slept late, he pointed out, making up for
her long evenings out. Willy, on the other hand, would usually be
at his desk, in his bathrobe, as early as nine, having left it at one or
two in the morning after finishing a review of a play. There were
afternoon outings — Willy and Colette together in their own horse-
drawn carriage. Or Willy would go out to see publishers, and Colette
to shop; they would meet at some fashionable tearoom.[5]

Still, Colette's misery eventually found tangible expression, first in
defiance and revolt, then matching treason with treason. Yet escape
did not even occur to her: open the door to the cage of a captive
squirrel or bird or even a wild beast, and its first reaction is not to
leap out but to retreat to the back of the cage. Certainly, for the
village girl she was, the prospect of deserting the marital domicile
was not without its terrors. It was safer to retreat to the studio and
its trapeze.

The camera caught her there, in a blouse and long skirt, with
Toby the bullterrier at her feet as she leans against the parallel bars.
Her expression is downcast, sly.

Willy, meanwhile, was busy with new Colettes, new Claudines.
Colette remembered one whose picture was prominently featured in

Willy's book *En bombe;* he would even send her upstairs to be photographed in the studio. This young woman used to go out in the carriage with them, until the day she complained that she always got the jump seat.

Colette found out about the new Claudines indirectly. "Monsieur Willy's daughter bought the same hat you did," Colette's milliner informed her one day.

Later on — and remember that this is Colette's version, told decades later, after Willy's death, but with no apparent lessening of bitterness — later on she could not decide whether she had still been in love with Willy then. How can you tell, she wondered, when it's your first love, that it's over?[6]

Summer was a consolation. After visiting her parents she would go on to Monts-Boucons. "It's raining on me, it's sunning on me, I get up at six and go to bed at nine," she exclaimed to Jeanne Muhlfeld in July 1902. "I'm the color of a pigskin suitcase." Willy was sharing her holiday at the time, and was even being nice to her.[7]

She never mentions her writing in the letters that have come down to us. At the moment, Willy "were" working on the fourth of the Claudine stories, *Claudine and Annie.* This manuscript provoked their bitterest arguments, Willy remembered (when he too was bitter), since she wished to "drag into the mud" all the women with whom she had made love, along with all of those whom she suspected Willy of having been involved with — wrongly, he was quick to add.[8] In truth, this novel has been read as a settling of scores by Willy, who did not even bother with a plot, making this the least satisfactory book of the series. Claudine is not even the main character; instead, Annie Samzun (who is in a sense another incarnation of Colette) holds center stage. There are also Marthe Payet and her cuckolded husband (Henry Maugis is the seducer), and there is Bayreuth.

Colette later declared that she detested all of the Claudine books, had not liked them when they were written and did not like them thirty or more years later. She placed *Claudine in Paris* and *Claudine and Annie* at the bottom of the pile. She had written what she was asked to write, written to hurt.[9]

Willy published another book under his pseudonym that year —
with a ghostwriter, of course (and Colette may have helped him as
well). *La Maîtresse du Prince Jean* (Prince John's Mistress) exploited
the success of the Claudine series as fully as it could. The front and
back jackets portrayed Willy in the act of caressing either his heroines or their effigies. One is a naked Claudine in a tub. When the
novel appeared in installments in a magazine, Willy was brought to
court on a charge of obscenity (specifically because of a scene of
"prolonged voluptuousness"). When the book came out, it contained
the plea of Willy's lawyer, who argued that the indictment was only
an excuse to get at the author of the Claudine books, which everyone
had read. He introduced testimonials to the honorability of Henry
Gauthier-Villars. One of these was from Jules Renard, who said that
his fourteen-year-old son had already read *Madame Bovary* and
would probably soon be trying *Claudine* but would never, he hoped,
succumb to "any handbook of moral foolishness."[10]

Then at last Colette appeared as the author of a book of her own
(signing herself "Colette Willy"). The year was 1904, and these were
the first *Dialogues de bêtes* (Animal Dialogues), a collection of playlets
in which household pets — Toby the bullterrier, Kiki-la-Doucette
the chartreuse cat — talk over their quotidian preoccupations, and in
so doing pierce the veil of the human behavior that they cannot help
witnessing under the same roof. A sober monthly called *La Vie Heureuse* published one of these sketches, illustrated with photographs of
Colette at her desk, Colette with her cat and dog. As he sat with her
in a living room resembling a Dutch tavern, an interviewer for the
magazine noted Colette's appearance, her "short hair, curly, over sly
eyes that occasionally sadden, a pointed face, a schoolgirl's short
skirt." He was reminded of the squirrel in a cage mentioned in the
inscription of a book by Francis Jammes, which he had noticed on
a nearby table. Colette told him of the recent death of a cat of theirs;
it was to console Willy for that that she had written the *Dialogues*.
She revealed a desire to leave Paris and "this absurd round of openings and first nights," to live in the country — as soon as Willy was

ready. The interviewer found her introspective, speaking of her lost province with nostalgia.[11] He was remarkably perceptive.

As for Francis Jammes, Colette liked what she had read of his. He wrote about nature, rural life, and animals, though his basic beliefs were light years removed from hers and his work was to become increasingly impregnated with Catholic dogma. He corresponded with Colette from his retreat in the Pyrenees; the two were never to meet. She had taken pains to autograph a copy of the original edition of *Dialogues de bêtes* and send it to him. He in turn had sent her one of his novels about country life, inscribed "To Madame Colette Willy, with the admiration one offers a squirrel in a cage." (This was the book that the interviewer saw in the drawing room.) And she had a reply ready: "Willy is a fine squirrel master. The cage is charming, and the door open. He has given me lovely squirrel toys: a trapeze and parallel bars. . . ."[12]

Soon she would make a curious request of her pen friend. Mercure de France was planning to publish an expanded edition of her dialogues; would Jammes write a short preface for it? He said yes! His preface took the form of a letter: from his southwestern province he had to tell Paris that Colette was "a true poet" as well as a woman "who dared to be natural and is much more a village bride than a depraved woman of letters."[13] In her response she told him, "This Rehabilitation of Colette Willy will be the beginning and the end of my literary pride."[14] Her letter was written in October 1904; in November, the naughty weekly *La Vie Parisienne* published another of her dog-cat dialogues, abundantly illustrated with their portraits.[15]

So it was Colette's year. Yet shortly after the appearance of the first volume of *Dialogues de bêtes,* another novel, *Minne,* was signed by Willy alone. Colette had wanted to put her own name on it; Willy said no, even though her role was less of a secret by now — and no secret at all to the literary community. In this brief story, half fairy tale, half thriller, a young girl imagines violent lovers but grows up to marry a very conventional man, the cousin to whom she has been promised. In a sequel, *Les Egarements de Minne* (Minne's Transgressions), her cousin proves to be a disappointing bedmate. She seeks satisfaction with others, in vain, only to reach ecstasy at last in the arms of her lawful husband. Later, when Colette had become master of her own fate, she would combine the two novels into one volume, *The Innocent Libertine*.

Around this time, the popular daily *Gil Blas* published a drawing of a top-hatted and bemustached Willy by the versatile Sacha Guitry. "He looks like a famous man," noted the celebrated wit. "And I can't imagine anyone besides God, and also Alfred Dreyfus, to some extent, who is as famous." As far as Guitry was concerned, Willy's chief claim to fame was Claudine, "depraved, and charming, and universal." He concluded, "Ah! if only that man would allow himself to be publicized! . . . But he is unbending!"[16]

It almost comes as a relief to discover a dissenter in the person of the critic Jean Ernest-Charles, who in an article entitled "The Willy Case," published in the influential *Revue Bleue* in the autumn of 1905, examined not only those books signed by Willy but also the hagiographic writings about this singular man. For Ernest-Charles, Willy was little more than a publicity hound; his books were products, not literature. Even immorality was utilized in the service of publicity. As for Madame Willy, he found her *Dialogues de bêtes* "unbearably pretentious," though he discerned in them some of the qualities found in the Claudine books, including the "precisely observed detail, a delicate and occasionally poetic sensuality, a feeling for nature. . . ."[17]

NINE

Claudine Walks Out

NOTHING WAS EVER NORMAL in the life of the Willys. On the first of May 1905 both parties to the marriage agreed to an amicable separation of property. Family legend attributes this decision to the elder Gauthier-Villarses, for their son Henry was to receive a substantial legacy, and why should Colette share it? In fact — the actual facts are hard to nail down, but the outline is clear — much was happening in the Colette-Willy household. For one thing, the couple was spending more than it was earning, and after the separation of property Willy was obliged to sell off assets (which contradicts the story that he was comfortably endowed). The Willys had also embarked on a dangerous slide in their private life, having given each other license — license that was liberally used.[1] It is difficult to guess which of the two, in that pivotal year, committed the irrevocable act, or rather, perhaps, which of them committed it first. Willy found a new Claudine in a young woman named Meg; Colette discovered the comforts of a protector in a mature woman named Missy.

The book that was to record Colette's independence, *Les Vrilles de la vigne* (The Tendrils of the Vine), got a first airing in May 1905, when the fortnightly *Le Mercure Musical* was launched. Colette introduced that issue with a brief monologue concerning a nightingale. In earlier times, she wrote, the bird did not sing at night; it slept, often on a vine. One night, when one such bird was sleeping, the "spurs of the vine, these tendrils brittle and tenacious," grew out so quickly that they ensnared the creature. Eventually it tore itself loose, but it swore never again to sleep while the tendrils of the vine were growing. Instead it would sing, thus becoming "the desperate singer" we know.

The writer herself, she said, had once been ensnared by the tendrils of a bitter vine, had slept on in confidence. But now she had broken those twisted threads, and she sang to stay awake, and free.

They had begun the year as a couple. A postcard survives from a journey to Monte Carlo, dated February 14; they were to return to Paris later that week so Willy could cover a Sunday concert.[2] Before the end of that montth, their friend Marcel Schwob, long martyrized by his incurable disease, died at thirty-seven; there was a funeral for them to attend. They were also seen together at the Arts and Fashion Circle, a restaurant and gambling club on Avenue Victor Hugo that drew men of letters, ladies who lived for men (such as Liane de Pougy and the courtesan known as the Belle Otero), and women who lived with women (such as Missy). That year the Circle had begun to publish an elegant magazine called *Le Damier* (The Checkerboard), whose second issue contained a tribute to Colette, with formal photographic portraits, the reproduction of a page of manuscript in her hand, and a piece of Claudiniana.

This last was a letter from Claudine to her dear Renaud, which could have been (but was not) appended to *Claudine Married*. In it she speaks of jealousy — both her own, which is banality itself (for when he looks at other women, she wants to *kill*), and his, when she was in love with Rézi. For she *did* love Rézi once, "if to love is to desire to the point of burning, to wish — momentarily — the death of a creature for everyone else, to dream — only in passing, of course! — of running away with her, of a love-kidnapping. . . ." She no longer loves her, however. Nonetheless, her husband, Renaud, is keeping her far from Paris, and that sets her mind to wandering. Living without Renaud is such an abnormal situation that all her acts became forbidden ones. It is as if, from Monts-Boucons, Colette was warning Willy that wanderlust could be dangerous both for the seducer and for the woman he has left behind.[3]

If she was indeed straying, if Willy's indifference or betrayal or complacence encouraged her to stray, it seems to have been in the world of what she called unisexuality. That very year, in *Maugis amoureux* (Maugis in Love), a novel published under Willy's name, there were references to the secret vice that had made a best-seller of *Claudine Married*. Claudine does not like men, we read, even if they like her. If she loves her husband, it is only because he is more girlish than all the Rézis of the world put together.[4]

It seems likely that Colette met Missy at the Circle. Missy was Mathilde de Morny, who since her marriage (a brief one) had been the Marquise (or Marchioness) de Belbeuf. Her great-grandmother was Empress Josephine, her grandmother Queen Hortense, her uncle Napoleon III, her father Duke of Morny; on her mother's side she was descended from the Romanovs of Russia. She was no longer young and seems never to have been very attractive. She made herself even less so, at least to the uninitiated, by her masculine clothing and deliberately virile behavior.[5]

But she was generous, and warm, in her gruff way; she could be protective toward a child bride, or toward a thirty-two-year-old woman trained to behave like one. She herself was ten years older than that when she met Colette, sufficiently senior to be a credible protector.

Then, in the other corner, we have Willy and Meg Villars. Meg was also a friend of Colette's, and for a time the Willys and Meg may have been a threesome. Or perhaps Meg's affection for Colette was only a feint, a Willy-inspired ploy to make the action more interesting and to conceal his own urgent interest in Meg. Perhaps he encouraged Colette's liaison with Missy for the same reason.

In her own skin Meg was Marguerite Maniez. She was not, as her pen name and pen biography would have it, English; although she was born in London, her parents were both French. The story goes that when she called on Willy to have a copy of *Claudine at School* autographed, she was the same age as the fictional Claudine — that is, a dozen years younger than the real Colette. Willy liked what he saw.[6]

Meg was a dancer — "an English dancer," so they said. But Colette could dance, too. Apparently her first public performance was for a very special audience, at a party in Natalie Barney's garden in Neuilly in June 1905. In a pantomime created by Willy she was a shepherd, playing opposite a nymph danced by a ravishing American actress named Eva Palmer.

Otherwise, the summer went badly. Captain Colette was dying. Sido kept her daughter informed of his rapid decline. Although suffering from emphysema, he could still walk to Achille's house for lunch, after which the doctor would drive him home. He died on September 17, a week short of his seventy-sixth birthday. Willy and Colette drove to Châtillon in a rented car, encountering every possible nuisance, including three flat tires, and finally getting there to find the funeral procession already at the cemetery. The finest of funerals in a village burial ground, with the captain in a military uniform still showing shrapnel tears — so Colette dramatized the scene. Her small, hard mother stands at the edge of the grave, murmuring words of love that only he is meant to hear.

Sido detested mourning clothes, so Colette tells us, and expressed the wish that Colette not wear them when *she* died.[7] Another detail: Sido's older daughter, Juliette — she whose marriage had compromised the family's financial stability — was not informed of the captain's death until after the funeral, and even then Sido made sure not to let Achille know that she had written to his sister.[8]

When they got back to Paris, Colette wrote to her dear Flossie — Natalie Barney — about the loss of her father, "so young at seventy-six, so much in love with my mother, so loved by his children." And she told Natalie what she had brought back as her share of the paternal legacy: a ribbon for the Crimea campaign, a medal for Italy, the rosette of the Legion of Honor, and a photograph.[9] This legacy was always close at hand, and was found intact at Colette's own death.

So at the captain's funeral the Willys were still a couple, or at least they were pretending to be; they seemed even to be making plans for the future. "You're not giving up the idea of having a car," Sido said to her daughter, "in spite of the horrible breakdowns you had?" Colette even asked Sido to lend Willy whatever capital she still had — at a high rate of interest, of course.[10] And when the couple went to Monts-Boucons in early autumn and Colette stayed on after Willy's return to Paris, he wrote to a friend, "Colette is finally coming home tomorrow. I wasn't made to be a widower."[11]

She returned with a resolution: she was going to earn her own money, if not from the writing of best-sellers — Willy's monopoly — then through her newly discovered taste for the stage. "So you're going to earn a thousand francs an evening!" exclaimed Sido. "Jesus-Marie, what a lot of money!" But she was worried all the same, fearing that Colette's earnings would only serve to pay off debts. When would her daughter be able to build a nest egg of her own?[12] Later, Colette would contend that her stage career had been Willy's idea. She would be on the road a lot, he said, so they could give up their apartment, change their routine. She got the message. He was trying to get rid of her, at the very moment when she herself was seeking a way out. When Willy said, "There's no hurry," she understood: "It's all over."[13]

If she was going to perform in pantomime, she could not have found a better teacher than Georges Wague. A year her junior, he had begun dancing in school and was a real trouper who knew how to travel.[14] Colette's first appearance in a proper theater was in a pantomime called *Love, Desire, and the Chimera,* on February 6, 1906. She played a faun. Evidently she was good enough to be encouraged, and on the best stages, not only in Paris but in Brussels, Nice, and Monte Carlo — and this before audiences were drawn to her performances because she was a subject of scandal, a famous writer.

In *Retreat from Love* she would laugh at herself, in her portrait of the frenzied mime Willette Collie. In *The Vagabond* (a very autobiographical novel) she confides that she is said to have a gift for dancing in addition to "an impeccable physique." There is abundant evidence, in the form of photographs, that she was not afraid to show her legs and a bit more, at a time when such things were not done in-respectable theaters.

An honest critic, looking back over her years of miming, later summed up her career as a "sad exhibition." He explained, "If Colette already had her spiritual wings, she did not succeed in attaching them to her body on the stage."[15] But such enthusiasm! A partisan of Willy's, who therefore was to become a lifelong foe of Colette's, found her vulgar. She was the "solid, healthy, exuberant, ungraceful peasant," he said, "good for a roll in the hay." Her gestures, too, lacked grace. And yet her performance was captivating; her liveliness was all. Her legs were too heavy, their muscles too apparent, her belly was too prominent, her breasts were too heavy; her knees were ungainly, her feet ugly. "But at the slightest movement, all her body went into action in a prodigious spurt of energy, a lyrical offering of herself, so that only the movement counted."[16]

And still there was Willy. At the end of winter (in March 1906) she traveled with him to the South of France to visit Natalie Barney's splendid and unpredictable lover Renée Vivien at her villa in Nice. They stayed through the Mardi Gras carnival and gaped at gamblers at the Monte Carlo casino. A piece that she wrote about the trip centers on the idle rich, ancient and active courtesans, lesbian couples. It is also her first halting homage to a landscape and a climate different from those of her France.[17]

Back home in Paris, she performed in a play coauthored by Willy, billed as a Parisian love story ("As Parisian as my Burgundy accent," she would remember later, when she came across a stage photograph of herself in male attire; she found it ugly and destroyed it).[18] A reviewer lets us see her dressed as a very young man, in short pants and with her hair in curls; she was "brazen, with a determined air." She took over the stage with her enthusiasm, all the while remaining in control of her gestures. It was this exuberance that struck the audience. "She burned the boards," noted the reviewer, "rolled her *r*'s, laughed, swaggered, enjoyed herself, and amused her comrades, who were delighted to play alongside this astonishing woman."[19]

But the enthusiasm was still not universal. There were boos both for Colette and for Marcel Boulestin (Willy's secretary and her "unisexual" confidant). Willy dismissed the negative response as the desire of this proper audience to punish Colette for having abandoned society for the stage.[20] For her part, Colette informed Francis Jammes that she would not be writing to him anymore because she had become an actress and that must diminish her in his eyes. He replied at once that it was precisely because he did love God that he could not think of her as humiliated.[21] This was the Belle Epoque, the pre–World War I decade that represented not so much a fulfillment as a promise.

For Colette it was also a transition. She was at work on the last of the Claudine books, *Retreat from Love,* writing it at Monts-Boucons, which was so much hers that it could have been her birthplace. By the time the novel was ready to be published, she and Willy were no longer a couple, and she signed it "Colette Willy." The reader was warned: "For reasons that have nothing to do with literature, I have ceased to collaborate with Willy."

In fact they *had* collaborated, that one last time. As usual, his contribution was the ribaldry, a few scandalous situations. Scholarship has nonetheless determined that pages and pages of *Retreat* are devoid of any trace of Willy. There are numerous instances of suggestions made by Willy that Colette, manifesting independence at last, simply ignored.[22] Toward the end of the book, Claudine, whose beloved Renaud has died, assures a confidante, "I have not lost my love." Willy scrawled in the margin of the manuscript, "Nor I."[23]

Years later, a publisher who wished to do an illustrated edition of *Retreat from Love* prompted Colette to pick up the old novel with a fountain pen in hand. She removed what she considered to be unseemly language. Among the more substantial cuts she made was the episode in which Claudine offers money to the homosexual Marcel to make love to her friend Annie (who so much craves a man).[24] For better or worse, these excisions were not carried forward into later editions; we read the book today with the naughty parts left in.

Colette spent part of the summer of 1906 rehearsing for an engagement at the prestigious Olympia music hall. She was to appear in another pantomime, this one called *La Romanichelle* (The Gypsy). Willy ended the summer in the country, not alone. Writing to his friend and helper Curnonsky (he was asking him to give Colette's performance a favorable review), Willy confided that he was vacationing with Meg Villars — "my daughter," he called her. "Meg is Miss Gauthier-Villars here, convinced that she really is, as sweet as an angel, and insisting on being spanked when she takes too long to do her hair or has spent too much on chocolate. . . . The spanking is done with a brush, in an interesting way: I spank, we laugh, then we're ready for the rest. Rule Britannia!"[25]

Curnonsky, as requested, reviewed Colette's performance (in a vaudeville weekly): "The debut of Colette Willy will certainly lure all of Paris to the Olympia," he astutely began. "The famous name, the literary and social reputation, the talent and beauty of the young debutant make her one of the most important stars discovered by a music-hall director in a long time." He realized, he said, that some spectators would not be prepared to see a good writer transformed into a savage little gypsy, only just clothed in rags that revealed her bare skin. Indeed, he continued slyly, it was something of a shock when she appeared without tights, but "the audience will just have to get used to this." Artistic truth required nudity; "the abolition of tights has become a necessity in dance, and two lively and pretty legs showing muscles under the skin seem more chaste than overclothed and boring limbs. . . ." Curnonsky pointed out that Colette was not the first to abandon tights; Isadora Duncan had slipped hers off first.

Having aroused his readers' basest instincts, the clever Curnonsky went on to say that Colette danced well, with "all the vigorous originality of her talent as a writer."[26]

Willy returned to Paris, but not to Colette. In a fictional account of her life up to that time, Colette dated the end of their marriage to the day when her husband showed her to the door of her own home so that he could receive a mistress.[27] On the other hand, a friend who accompanied Willy to Rue de Courcelles one day remembered that Willy rang twice before going in — a friendly warning. They found a woman on the trapeze; she did a complete turn so the visitor could admire her backside.[28] In his own vengeance-by-fiction, Willy has "Vivette Wailly" drive him to ruin and then go off to lead a life of dissipation with the "Baroness de Louviers," an old morphine addict who dresses in men's clothing[29] — a reference to the Marchioness de Belbeuf, or Missy, who of course never showed her backside on a trapeze.

But at the time all of this was happening, there was less bitterness, more complicity. Willy and Meg and Colette and Missy seemed to be together more than they were apart in the early months of their new couplings. Then, too, there is the letter, signed only "The English Girl," in which Willy's "daughter" confessed to Colette, "Never was a night as long as the one I have just spent — I still felt the taps you gave me yesterday. If I say that I am very much in love with you, that would only be a way of speaking . . . but I'm so entranced that it comes to the same thing." Was the "English girl" playing on Colette's penchants or on penchants that *Willy* wished to encourage? Colette's correspondent went on to invite her to lunch in the Bois de Boulogne, so as to be able to gaze at her. Willy could join them if he desired, said Meg, but wouldn't that bore him?[30] Later there would be photographs — Colette and Meg together, recalling Colette and Polaire.[31]

Colette moved to a small flat on Rue de Villejust, but she could more often be found at Missy's, just around the corner on Rue Georges Ville. "Your theories about marital relations are quite different from mine," Sido declared in an understatement, "even though I always felt that to sleep with my husband was neither healthy nor proper. But to put streets and walls between one's husband and oneself is going rather far. . . ." That was on November 6. On November 12 she wrote, "Now you're amused by the charms of your husband's mistress! Strange, strange!"[32]

But independence did not consist solely of the freedom to select one's sexual partner. Colette also had to be able to succeed in a career without Willy. Thus Sido to Colette: had she read the review that said exactly the same thing Sido had been trying to tell her, that it was a pity that someone who could write the way she did was wasting her time on the stage?[33]

Yet early in November Colette appealed to Georges Wague, her mentor in dance: could he give lessons to the marchioness, who wished to perform in *La Romanichelle,* taking the role of the leading man?[34] Another scandal loomed. On the front page of an otherwise sober daily newspaper, *Le Journal,* a headline announced:

THE FORMER MARCHIONESS DE BELBEUF
PLAYS PANTOMIME

The accompanying photograph showed Missy in a dinner jacket, with Colette, in décolletage, leaning on her shoulder, the caption making it clear that the marchioness was in costume for a rehearsal. The reporter wrote that when he called at the noblewoman's home, Colette had informed him that Missy would be performing in a private club, and that it was no business of the press's. Still, he had been allowed to watch a rehearsal in a drawing room filled with antique furniture and precious hangings, as well as a marble bust of Napoleon Bonaparte. He recorded the presence not only of Wague but of Willy, and noted, rather maliciously, how easily the marchioness seemed to wear male dress.[35]

The columnists could hardly ignore this plum of a story. One weekly let it be known that Colette had been offered a considerable stipend by the Moulin Rouge cabaret to perform with the marchioness, who had refused on the grounds that she did not know how to sing. "I've a frog in my throat," she was ambiguously and perniciously quoted as saying.[36] Soon after that the theater page of the same weekly reported Colette's appearance at an opening night, seated up front. When asked where Willy was, she replied that he was farther back, with his "little friend." The columnist observed that Willy's new friend was the opposite of Colette, "a well-built, pretty blonde." Just then the little friend, Meg, came up to where Colette was seated to greet her, accompanied by Willy, and they all sat together eating fruit.[37]

This item brought a protest from Colette. She enjoyed the paper's gossip column, she said, for it had been spoiling her with generous mentions. But she regretted the inclusion of this last story. She pleaded, "Don't tie together so . . . intimately, in the minds of your many readers, two couples who have arranged their lives in the most normal way possible, which means for their own pleasure."[38]

TEN

Missy

COLETTE'S NEXT stage appearance should not have given rise to scandal. In another pantomime, *Pan,* which opened at the end of November 1906 at the Marigny theater, her teacher Georges Wague was the costar. The sensationalistic press, however, reported that Missy had been slated to take the masculine role but had gotten stage fright. It also made a good story to say that some spectators assumed that Wague *was* Missy.[1]

Today, when we look at the old photographs, Colette's roles and costumes seem interchangeable, her expressions uniformly overdrawn. But surely that was the best way to hold the audience in that curious medium, melodrama for the variety stage. In a review of *Pan,* a critic calling himself Snob described the action: "After a rather pretty musical overture, Colette appeared as Paniska — in a kind of gypsy costume, with a short and tattered skirt showing her leg and thigh naked to the hip. Accompanied by string instruments, she struck some ceremonial poses, during which her skirt rose still higher, and the Mytilene elite became delirious." The reference, of course, was to the lesbian colony, though why men should not also have been titillated by Colette's thighs the reviewer did not explain.

Colette was playing to other women, he concluded, with "the famous marchioness" as leader of the claque.[2]

Henceforth Missy was a public figure in her own right. Before the end of the year an entertainment magazine would devote two full pages to her. One of the photographic illustrations for the spread has Colette gazing up, with love in her eyes, at the cropped-haired Missy, who wears riding breeches and a man's jacket and tie. The writer compared the Missy of twenty-five years earlier, when she had resembled a Diana, the virgin goddess of hunting, to "the shadow of herself" that she now was. Today she seemed "a creature without sex, with a puffy, pasty face, and the fixed stare of an ether addict."[3] Missy sued for libel and won, but she received less compensation than she had hoped for because, said the court, Colette's letter to the editor following the "little friend" episode had proclaimed their affair and thus proved that Missy behaved as the magazine said she did.[4]

Sido came to Paris just then and of course saw how her daughter had arranged her life. She did not express shock. "You're all too nice to me," she wrote to her daughter after her return to Châtillon, "Missy included. Surely it's because you think I'm going to die soon."[5]

Colette's flat on Rue de Villejust was on the ground floor. From the courtyard a gate led to another courtyard garden, this one serving a house on another street. Renée Vivien, Natalie Barney's ardent friend, lived there, and sometimes Colette would call on her, though only rarely, because she had little patience for the odors of incense, flowers, and overripe apples that surrounded Renée. On one occasion these "funereal perfumes" actually made her nauseous; she tried to open a window but discovered that it was nailed shut. Clearly Colette moved on a slower track. She found Renée Vivien puerile and watched from a distance her rapid decline — the result, apparently, not only of too much alcohol but of too much sex.[6] Barney and her circle were persistent in their quest for new sensations, but that was not Colette's way. Whether it was Missy's is another question.

She lived around the corner, in a house that may have shown some evidence of her "sensual" bachelor's life, though Missy herself (to hear Colette tell it), in her sober masculine attire, was anything but reckless. Pale "in the manner of certain ancient Roman masters," she had a soft voice, a man's nonchalance, and elegant manners. Writing long after those years, at a time when she was again living with a man, Colette could speak frankly of the attractions of women who loved women. Dependability was one of them. Men came and went, but "two women absorbed with each other don't fear or even imagine separation any more than they would tolerate it." A woman withdrew from her man to rest, to bathe, and when she was ill, but this was not necessary with "twin bodies who suffer together." It was a matter not only of sensuousness but of identity. "A woman enjoys the certainty in caressing a body whose secrets she knows and whose preferences are suggested by her own."[7]

Did Missy see herself with equal lucidity? The innumerable portraits of her in male attire, bearing the serious expression of a child wearing Indian feathers, do not help us with an answer. Perhaps she enjoyed or even encouraged the caricaturists. The photographs she posed for often seem satirical, as when she is shown wearing an officer's cap and surrounded by women admirers, Colette among them. A source whose reliability is in doubt said that Colette told him that Missy sought to tame her by using a whip on her ample buttocks.[8]

There *was* an element of self-destructiveness in the determination of Missy and Colette to show themselves to an audience. And at the Moulin Rouge, no less! Missy played the masculine role opposite Colette in *La Romanichelle* on December 20, 1906. "A new artist is born," proclaimed the satirical magazine *Le Rire:* "Yssim [Missy's stage name], a name which the ladies pronounce on their knees. We lick our chops over the program, if we may say so. . . ." In the original French, the allusions to lesbian sexual acts are even cruder. The reviewer reported that members of the "corrupt nobility" had protested noisily during Missy's performance, convinced that she was dishonoring her lineage.[9]

But the two women were not to be stopped. Colette and "Yssim" immediately began rehearsing another pantomime that seemed to have been written just for them (as indeed it was). The announcement poster bore the arms of the house of Morny:

?   YSSIM   ?

and

COLETTE WILLY

in

EGYPTIAN DREAM

A pantomime by
Madame the Marchioness de Morny

Ten performances were to be given at the Moulin Rouge at the beginning of January 1907.

There were no empty seats on opening night, and the audience was seen to be wearing evening clothes appropriate to a premiere. When the master of ceremonies announced that the sketch that was about to be presented had been written "by a marchioness whom everyone will recognize under her pseudonym Yssim," there were boos.

The curtain rose on a gentleman consulting an ancient tome; in the background could be seen a mummy in its sarcophagus. When the gentleman was seen to be the marchioness, there were further audible protests. But let a reporter for *Le Figaro* tell the rest of the story: "During the quarter of an hour that the pantomime lasted, the tumult didn't cease for a minute, and the actors confronting the storm continued the performance with a perseverance worthy of a better cause." When Colette rose from the sarcophagus "to mime a love scene with her partner, Madame de Belbeuf," the shouts grew even louder. There were cries of "Get out!" as well as invective that the reporter said the newspaper could not print. Women in the front rows threw cushions and other projectiles.

Then Willy was spotted, seated in a box with a lady friend, and the crowd directed its fury at him. He was escorted to safety, but the protestors — estimated at two to three hundred persons — managed to get close enough for blows to fly, and the police had to intervene to handle the mob.[10] The next morning the director of the cabaret was summoned to police headquarters and warned that if *Egyptian Dream* remained on the program, the place would be closed down. That night, January 3, "a noisy packed hall waited impatiently for the curtain to rise on the pantomime," according to another press report. At length an announcement was made over the clamor, to the effect that *Egyptian Dream* had been banned and was being replaced by another pantomime, entitled *Oriental Reverie*, with Georges Wague substituting for Yssim as the male lead. There was another storm of protest, with spectators chanting in unison, "*La Marquise!*" The whistling, shouting, and laughing went on for the entire fifteen-minute duration of the sketch.[11] Some members of the audience, in an ironic reminder of the stories in the press about *Pan*, believed that Wague was really Missy after all.

The management had had enough, but it was the police commissioner who finally settled the matter with a total ban on the sketch, title change or no, Missy or no.[12]

One immediate consequence of all of this was that Willy lost his good job at *L'Echo de Paris*, which, as the leading conservative daily, did not take such things lightly.[13] He was presented as the innocent party by at least one defender, his friend Sylvain Bonmariage. He could have prevented Colette from appearing in public but decided not to; the job he lost was worth 150,000 francs a year, an enormous sum for a journalist. It was now, said Bonmariage, that Willy decided to make a definitive break with Colette, but he would not fight her or Missy or anyone else, and he did not try to prevent Bonmariage (said Bonmariage) from seeing her. "In a word," Willy was quoted as having exclaimed, "everyone is angry with Colette except me!" It is interesting to note that Bonmariage's book was published only after Colette's death, though he said he had been prepared to publish it earlier.

Bonmariage, who met Colette a year or two before the Moulin Rouge affair, found her spiteful, but he also remembered her as "a voluptuous beast," smelling of "men in rut"; she was "a cat in heat for whom life is a succession of rooftops." She spoke meanly of people and had a false sincerity. Her language was crude and she farted in public, then joked about it. He claimed to have heard Apollinaire say of her that she reminded him of a chambermaid who thought she could do as she liked because she was sleeping with the master of the house.[14]

Whether or not Willy was the offended party, he did seem to have the most to lose as life was lived during the Belle Epoque. A man could very well be seen about town with a "daughter" like Meg Villars, but his wife was not to dally. It was Willy who sued for divorce, on grounds of desertion; a legal separation was granted in February 1907. After reading about it in *Le Temps,* which was the most austere of Parisian dailies but which nonetheless had room to report on Willy and Colette, Sido wrote to her daughter, "This doesn't tell me anything I didn't know and I'm not particularly sorry, but I'm worried about your finances." She was sure that Willy had led Colette to do what she had done because it would give him an opportunity to throw her out. Her mother had a piece of advice for her: she had one true gift, as a writer; now was the time for her to make use of it. Everything else was uncertain — even Missy, because of the hostility of her powerful family.[15] Sido's was an acute observation, but Colette herself felt that she had not one true gift, but two. The theater was in her blood now.

An entertainment weekly quoted a woman named "Folette" concerning her divorce. Folette explained that her husband, eighteen years older than she, had introduced her to the world, but then the world had discovered that it was *she* who had the talent. That made him jealous, and then, because of their age difference, he began to worry that she would cheat on him. So he looked for a way out, setting her up with girlfriends until she went too far. He feared ridicule, for he had been cuckolded all the same; divorce now seemed to be the only solution. Folette supposedly told the interviewer that Willy had not really been cuckolded, for she had never had another man, and few of his friends could have said as much![16]

If this was not an authentic interview, it was close enough to the truth.

In any case, she did not ignore her mother's advice. She was still working on *Retreat from Love,* though Willy managed to get to their regular publisher first and obtain an advance payment.[17] She countered by approaching another publisher (the house that had done her animal dialogues) and explaining that she had a novel in hand and wished to publish it quickly as a way to compensate for the bad press she had gotten over the Moulin Rouge affair.[18] Then she let Willy's publisher know that she was claiming as her own property her "share" of the new novel, and was giving it to a different publisher. She was sure, she said, that Willy would produce a book of his own to honor his obligation. "Mine is ready," said this plucky woman, "and I'm taking it. It's a race in which I got there first, and that's it." Willy pleaded with her: one ought not to treat such matters so lightly . . . he was prepared to accept a compromise. . . .[19]

She won, easily. Her contract with Mercure de France was carefully worded: she was Madame Colette, authorized by a legal separation of property to sign her new book "Colette Willy."[20] Her mother scrutinized the novel, looking for a key to the couple's rupture, but she found nothing. In *Retreat from Love* Claudine's beloved husband dies, and she is miserable; Sido felt that the book proved that her daughter had suffered considerably, without confiding in her. As for the plot of the novel, Sido guessed that Willy could not have appreciated being depicted as a sick old man.[21]

The curious thing is that both Willy and Colette showed signs of regretting their break. A letter exists in which Willy tells a friend, "At bottom, I miss her a lot, more than I want to admit to myself." He speaks of her as his "widow" and calls himself "the late Willy."[22] Another of his friends was certain that Willy still loved Colette, despite his flirting around. Following the Moulin Rouge explosion, Willy had written to him, "It's all going to end with a pistol shot," which he had interpreted to mean that Willy was contemplating suicide.[23]

What was more, Willy's apologist Bonmariage remembered "piles of letters" in which Colette begged Willy to come back to her. "I owe you everything. . . . Without you I'm nothing," she would write, or, "What will you do for me if I leave Missy?"[24] Some such letters survive. In one (written in mid-February 1907) Colette assures Willy that she would have preferred to stay with him; Missy would have understood their threesome. Other people would have been indulgent, and all would have been for the best in this best of demimondes. Colette and Willy, says Colette, were made for each other. If he came back they could pursue separate careers, and Missy would not object.[25]

Missy herself even joined the discussion. "I don't always understand your two characters," she wrote to Willy, "and at the beginning I often regretted your need to publicize our situation (a situation certainly desired by you), which could have remained the way it was but with more discretion." When Willy pushed Colette into her arms, Missy said, she had known what would happen. "I therefore don't deserve to be blamed by Colette, who is a confused child without much moral sense, though that is certainly not her fault. I can understand that she is bored by my old and melancholy person, and I'm sorry about that, but a human being can't transform itself."[26]

For her part, Sido was puzzled. "You love Willy," she asked her daughter, "you say you love him a lot, and he leaves you for a young and pretty girl?" She blamed Willy, but if she was wrong about that, it was surely because Colette had not told her everything.[27]

Now more than ever a career was necessary for Colette. And it was with Wague and not the marchioness that she traveled to the Riviera in March to perform the no longer incendiary *Egyptian Dream*. The theaters were filled; the audiences liked what they saw.[28] "You will have had a lovely journey all the same, and gotten ideas for your future books," her practical mother summed it up. Sido wished that she could see Colette dance, for she never would have thought that her daughter would be good at that.[29]

The experience could indeed be written about. *La Vie Parisienne*, which had earlier published some of Colette's animal dialogues, published a new one, "Toby the Dog Speaks," on April 27. In it the bullterrier tells the chartreuse cat what he has overheard their mistress say. "I want to do what I want," she has declared. "I want to play pantomime, even act in comedies. I want to dance naked, if tights bother me and spoil my appearance. . . . I want to write books that are sad and chaste. . . . I want to cherish the person who loves me and give that person everything I own: my body that refuses to be shared, my soft heart, and my freedom!" Toby the dog hears his mistress talk about "him," and how he is surrounded by girls who beg him to marry them if and when she dies. He does marry them, she adds — one after the other. "He could choose. He prefers to collect." Oddly, in the book in which it was collected, this piece is dedicated to "Miss Meg V. . . ."[30]

ELEVEN

Making It Alone

SHE WAS CERTAINLY going to do what Toby the dog
had heard her promise she would: go on the stage (and with a
dog, too — this one named Poucette). She even acquired an automobile (with Missy's help) and learned how to drive it. By June
1907 she and Missy were wandering along the Channel coast looking for a vacation house. They found it between Dieppe and Le
Touquet, in a fishing village called Le Crotoy. The beach was
adequate but not elegant; the best thing that could be said for Le
Crotoy as a summer resort was that it was one of the closest ones to
Paris.

They arranged to have interesting neighbors: Willy and Meg. The
two couples seemed not to be able to get away from each other. Sido,
for one, found Colette's relations with Miss Meg "unbelievable" and
warned her to be cautious: "I'm more suspicious than you, especially
about anything that is abnormal and illogical." [1]

Her daughter *should* have been suspicious of Willy. Without telling Colette, he accepted a lump-sum payment from the original publishers of the first four Claudine books in exchange for all present

and future rights, thus ruling out any future income from these novels for himself or his former wife.[2]

This autumn she was to go on the stage again, this time in a pantomime called *La Chair* (The Flesh), written by Georges Wague; he
was the bandit, she his mistress. At the climactic moment, when he
is struggling with her, he rips her dress, exposing a breast.

La Chair opened in Paris on the first of November 1907, and of
course the bodice-ripping was a sensation. "I worry that you'll be
asked to perform in far-off countries," Sido wrote.[3] One of those far-
off countries was the United States, and indeed *La Chair* did make
it to New York, though without Colette.

Writing to Count Robert de Montesquiou, whose life-style had
made him a model for Proust's Charlus, Colette confessed that she
was thought to live in an unusual way; she knew that some blamed
her for that, especially since she offered no explanation for her break
with convention. "But I assure you that I'm not a horrible person,
and that there is no evil intention in my behavior!" She believed that
a woman could live alone and earn her own livelihood; was that a
crime?[4]

"Dear friend," Colette began a letter to an author who was known
to be adapting a book for the theater. "Is the pantomime written *for*
someone? . . . If not, let me remind you, with charming modesty,
that I play pantomime quite well, especially Oriental parts." Had the
man seen her in *La Romanichelle* or in *La Chair*? "Excuse me," she
pursued, "but I am guided by the mad ambition to earn my own
living, both on the stage and in literature, and I assure you that it
takes obstinacy!"[5]

Then Willy struck again. This time — we are at the beginning of
1908 now — he liquidated what was supposed to have been her private domain, Monts-Boucons in southeastern France. Looking back,
she would say that it was because Willy had taken it away from her
that the house remained so precious a memory.[6] But by now she
thought she knew how to use the press to her own advantage. On

the front page of an art and entertainment daily, *Comoedia,* she explained why she had missed a theater engagement. "To my deep regret," she said, she had been obliged to travel to Besançon for the sale, "by order of justice and other stupidities," of the estate that she loved so much. She pretended not to be able to comprehend why it had been necessary to dispose of the house just because of her separation from Willy. The *Comoedia* editor who published her letter suggested that *it* ought to have been read out loud on the stage, instead of the love letter Colette was to have recited that evening — for it was, after all, a letter from a woman, and a curious one. (Whether it was the letter or the woman that was being described as curious is not clear.)[7]

Once again Sido found it hard to understand her daughter. She was convinced that Willy had been *Comoedia*'s anonymous editor; obviously he was holding her up to ridicule.[8]

Even as she played the ingenue in public, Colette was writing some of her most incisive essays, confessional but mature, soon to be collected as *Les Vrilles de la vigne* (The Tendrils of the Vine). Here childhood reminiscences and descriptions of nature are utilized both to conceal and to reveal present feelings. Paradoxically, before they were given form as a small book they were published one by one in that frivolous magazine *La Vie Parisienne.*[9] As Sido put it, "The drawings in *La Vie P.* are rather pornographic, but that's surely the latest fashion."[10]

Mixing high seriousness with frivolity never bothered Colette. Then and later she had no qualms about lending herself to advertising. One such advertisement included her photograph along with a poem in which she made a final rhyme out of "Negri toothpicks."[11] "What a success!" was Sido's reaction when she came across the ad in a newspaper.[12]

In February 1908 Colette was back on the Riviera, once again playing opposite Georges Wague in *La Chair.* To a friend she wired, "Much success, though Maritime Alps Prefect made me cover left breast."[13] We can imagine what her road shows were like thanks to a sketch she wrote called "Music-Hall," which portrays her arrival in a "large Mediterranean city," where she sees posters advertising her pantomime as a "terrifying melodrama." The first performance takes place in an undecorated theater (even the paint is scarcely dry); during the love scene, spectators exchange opinions, taking the side of the lovers against the husband (whom they call a scoundrel and a cuckold).[14] From now on Colette would write some of the most authentic accounts of backstage life in literature — always before the paint was dry.

In March she lectured for the first time; that would be another way for her to make a living.[15] Then *La Chair* was scheduled to run in Paris for the whole month of April, and it was clear that audiences could not get enough of that left breast. "You're exhausting yourself," worried her mother. "Fortunately Missy is with you."

Sido read in *Le Temps* that the Paris police were planning to arrest women who danced naked in vaudeville shows, and Colette's theater, the Apollo, was mentioned. Was Colette to be interrogated? she asked. Colette was not. She told her mother about a scarab bracelet and an opal necklace that Missy had given her recently. "How she spoils you!" Sido commented. Then she read an article praising Colette as a writer and expressing regret (as Sido herself did, once again) that she was wasting her time in pantomime.[16]

But the books Colette was writing now could not earn her a great deal of money, and stage work paid quickly. Now, at the age of thirty-five, she had an opportunity to play in *Claudine in Paris,* taking the part that Polaire had made famous: the schoolgirl Claudine. A difficult role, Sido warned, "but since you were able to create it in literature, perhaps you can interpret it." [17]

In an interview published in *Comoedia* and signed (in English) "Nobody" — and we can guess that it was Henry Gauthier-Villars who was hiding behind that pseudonym — Colette spoke about Claudine during rehearsals for the play. She admitted that Polaire would be a hard act to follow, for she had made the heroine *younger* than she was; in Colette's interpretation she would be "mature." [18]

Summing up her daughter's theatrical success, even Sido had to concede, "I never imagined that you were up to it, for you were always so unbending, and for the stage you need a flexibility, both physical and moral, which I didn't see in you. You've adjusted in both senses, that's a fact."[19]

That summer Colette and Missy had a proper house in Le Crotoy, though what was proper for that time and place looks like ugly brick-villa resort housing to us. "We're on the edge of this water desert, which is a sand desert when the tide is low," Colette told her mother (on a postcard picturing it). "And not a soul in sight. . . . One is not-immediately struck by the charm of this flat beach with its dunes covered in pink morning glory . . . but you become attached to it after a while, I promise you."[20] Before that summer was over, duty had summoned her to other resorts: she played Claudine in Aix-les-Bains and took the leading role in someone else's play in Geneva. (Here she shared in the box-office receipts; it was the most she had ever earned — 973 francs for two performances, she announced in triumph to Georges Wague. She did not tell Wague that she was traveling with an "English nurse," in Willy's expression — none other than Meg Villars.)[21]

In Bordeaux that autumn she played opposite Wague again in *La Chair*. Missy stayed home, so Colette kept her informed. She reported that the theater manager had asked her to meet an admirer who came to the theater every single night to see her; she had agreed, but only for lunch. Colette added that Missy was going to find her old and ugly; she was sleeping badly and ruining her eyes with reading. And she had just finished a piece for *La Vie Parisienne* (probably the dramatic account of a storm at sea, witnessed from their Le Crotoy villa). "I love you," she assured Missy. "I can't wait to be finished here. I kiss you, my sweetheart, my true Reason-for-Living."[22]

Back in Paris, home was now a ground-floor flat on Rue Torricelli, just below the Boulevard Pereire in the northwest corner of Paris. When Colette asked her mother to ship her the furniture and bed linens that were being kept for her in Châtillon, Sido wondered what she would do with all of it. Surely some part of it was intended for

the "Willy-Meg household"? "Silly you!" was Sido's indulgent comment.[23]

This time Sido had news of her own. Colette's half-sister had died
suddenly, at forty-eight, and that had caused a stir back home. The
announced cause of death was heart failure, but Sido was convinced
that Juliette had been taking a sedative for her heart and that she
had died of an overdose. Her doctor husband denied that she had
been under medication; Sido remained skeptical, though she stopped
short of accusing Dr. Roché of having murdered his wife. Juliette
had suffered above all from a lack of love, and that had hastened
her end.

No one, in any case, accepted the official explanation of her death,
and Sido thought it possible that her husband would be forced to
abandon the little Yonne village where he practiced.[24]

For the moment Colette did not have to choose between being a
writer and being a performer. In *Comoedia* it was a man of the
theater who praised her writings, proclaiming, "Among living
women writers, Colette Willy is the most mysteriously gifted." [25]
When she received a copy of *Les Vrilles de la vigne,* however, in
November 1908, Sido observed that it was merely a collection of
pieces written for a magazine — *La Vie Parisienne,* of course. "You
really don't have enough time to devote yourself to a full-scale work,
and that is a real pity, but I don't despair, provided that you don't
let yourself be taken over by the theater," she told her daughter.[26]

Collection or no, *Les Vrilles* was a good book, and it confirmed
Colette as a writer as well as a free soul. This distinction was recognized at once by another free soul, the poet-critic Guillaume Apollinaire, who utilized a female pseudonym to review "sister" writers
in a Symbolist monthly. "Certainly all who read this book will admire its overriding delicacy, which will lift Colette Willy straight to
Paradise when the time comes," his review asserted. The male/female
critic, "Louise Lalanne," concluded that the freedom manifested in
the book was a good sign for the future of literature.[27]

It comes as something of a surprise, then, to find Colette contemplating a return to the Willy factory — for there is evidence that she was prepared to work on another Claudine novel. So Willy informed his ghostwriter Curnonsky, at least; he had spoken to Colette, he said, and she was bored. "With an outline," she supposedly told Willy, "I'll knock it off in two months." She did not want anyone to know about it, however. In the end, nothing came of the project, but Willy's letters make it clear that he was following every turn of his estranged wife's career.[28] They were definitely on speaking terms, in any event, and some of the sketches in *Les Vrilles* were even dedicated to Willy and Meg. The dedications vanished in later editions, after Colette learned that her ex had given away all future rights to the Claudine books and kept the cash for himself.[29]

TWELVE

The Vagabond

COLETTE AND *CLAUDINE* were in Lyon in December 1908. "What a business!" she sighed, loud enough for her mother to hear. It gave Sido another opportunity to express her regret that Colette was acting instead of writing. She was concerned about her daughter's overworking (which Colette admitted caused headaches) and her traveling alone at night.[1] Colette confessed (to others) that she lived in a daze, in a permanent state of hunger and exhaustion. She had signed up with a traveling theatrical troupe; there were daylong rehearsals now. "It's a good school, but a rough one," was her summing-up of it.[2] "A wild success here," she reported from Lyon to Charles Saglio of *La Vie Parisienne,* "but I'm not paid enough."[3]

The Lyon tour could not possibly have flopped, she explained to Missy; she had encountered "a public determined to find the slightest grimace of your unbearable false-child charming, even though I played it all wrong." But that was what her admirers had been expecting; what counted for her, she assured Missy, was back on Rue Torricelli, and she had "ash-blond hair and dark brown eyes that appear black. . . ."[4]

Perhaps her heart *was* in Paris, but she would have to keep moving nonetheless. She had found a way to combine her two careers, the stage and writing; indeed, she could even write for the stage. At the beginning of 1909 she finished a featherweight play called *En Camarades* (As Comrades). It may not have been the new literature that Apollinaire had discovered in *Les Vrilles de la vigne,* but it was the kind of play she could use as a vehicle for her own theater career. In act 1 Max and Fanchette, though married, live as good friends, each in theory free to do as he or she wishes and then to confess. Max flirts with another woman, so Fanchette decides to try a young man whom they call The Kid. In act 2 she goes to see this young man; she tries to relax but finds that she cannot. Then her husband — jealous in spite of their arrangement — bursts in on them. Max and Fanchette agree that in future they will do everything together, even though this seems as ridiculous as their supposed freedom.

Léon Blum, a respected literary critic, thought he could see beyond the boulevard comedy. In *Comoedia* he proclaimed Madame Colette Willy not only a mime and an actress but "a true writer." Her talent was "unpolished, wild, artless," and perhaps *En Camarades* was not her best effort, but Blum believed it deserved success.[5] The play opened at the Théâtre des Arts in Paris in January 1909, with Colette appearing as Fanchette. One reviewer commented that the author would not have objected to a bad review of her play provided that her performance was praised; however, he continued, "our mission as a critic demanding implacable truths, we are obliged despite everything to report that Madame Colette's play is excellent and that Madame Colette is a writer of the first rank."[6] The critic for *Le Temps* was more specific: her voice was not melodious, and her diction was unnatural; she rolled her *r*'s like an old actor in melodrama; and further, "her bearing is stiff, her face inexpressive."[7] ("But isn't that just what I told you when you announced that you wanted to be an actress?" asked Sido, wishing to be helpful.)[8]

It was only now that Colette learned what had happened to the Claudine books, nearly a year and a half after Willy had sold the rights. "He wanted not merely to obtain very little money for them,"

The house in Saint-Sauveur (Colette's room at top right)

Captain Jules Colette

Colette's mother ("Sido")

Colette at thirteen

Colette at twenty

The Colette family in Châtillon (Colette in foreground, between her brothers, Léo and Achille)

Willy and Colette at home with the Gauthier-Villarses (circa 1893)

WILLY ET COLETTE

Ch. Gerschel, phot. — Paris

A Willy postcard of the Willy-Colette couple

Willy and Colette at their apartment on Rue de Courcelles

Polaire, Willy, and Colette

Colette and Toby-Chien

Colette in *Egyptian Dream*

Colette explained to her confidant Léon Hamel, "but also to make sure that even after his death I could not take possession of these works, which are mine."[9] The publishers held her to their deal with Willy, and two world wars would come and go before Colette could begin to receive royalties on the books that had made her a writer. But in the interim she was able to do something about her "moral" rights. New editions of the novels were to be prefaced with the following confession:

> The Willy-Colette collaboration having come to an end, it became necessary to render to each his part, and to replace the single signature on these volumes with that of
>   Willy and Colette Willy
> For purely typographical reasons my name appears before that of Colette Willy, though there is every reason, literary and otherwise, to put her name first.
>
>   Willy

Later on his name disappeared from the title pages of the novels; later still, after both Willy's death and Colette's, his son insisted that it appear alongside Colette's again, and sometimes it does.[10]

Now more than ever she needed Missy. "Really," agreed Sido, "Missy is just too good to take care of you like that. She makes the distance that separates us less painful for me, and it also does her good."[11] It was a married life of sorts, only less conventional than most others. Missy continued to spoil her with little gifts, some of them as practical as a fountain pen and notebooks to help her to pursue her writing.[12]

They dined out every night, and their preferred bistro was Chez Palmyre on Place Blanche, whose owner "covers us with maternal care," as Colette told Léon Hamel.[13] She later stood up for their bistro when proper friends dismissed it as disreputable, a den of long-haired boys and short-haired girls. It was a place where homosexuals of all sorts could relax, sheltered from a brutal world; Palmyre was their protector.[14]

It seems to have been her eternal éminence grise, Willy, who set her up on another theatrical tour; this time she was to go everywhere.[15] The caricaturist Sem did a poster of Colette Willy looking provocative, though her mother missed the point: "It looks like you," she assured her daughter, "and he even caught the way you stand, the way you throw out your left buttock and offer your pretty bust."[16] Still, as the day of Colette's departure approached, Sido began to worry about her being exposed to "a thousand dangers." When Colette informed her that Missy would be coming along, Sido was relieved that "you have with you someone who loves you truly."[17]

Not only was Colette to play in *Claudine,* she was to do it in Auxerre, the district capital in which she had passed her final school exams. One anonymous reviewer was not ignorant of the significance of the event (possibly because the anonymous reviewer was Willy). "I know this play that I've seen so many times," he told his readers, "but whether it was the emotion of her own lingering memories of Auxerre or those of men of Renaud's age who recall the delicious girl from Saint-Sauveur, it seemed that Colette had never given herself so completely to this role that she loves." She was so tender, so passionate in the last act, he said, that one wished she were reciting lyric poetry. Or she could have played Cleopatra, which she would have done differently but no less movingly than "the great Sarah" (Sarah Bernhardt, of course).[18]

"Things are going admirably well," Colette promised her mother, "and I adapt to this way of life easily. Thanks to . . . you know who, you've seen her at work. I'm not even tired."[19] The presence of you-know-who meant staying in better hotels and having someone to help in checking in and out; it also meant seeing a friendly face between acts. Postcards sent to Sido told of trials (such as a heat wave) and triumphs. There were cards from Avignon, Marseilles, Toulon, Nîmes, Bordeaux, Rennes, and many other places — thirty-two cities in all, and thirty-three performances (there were two in Bordeaux). In Toulon, Captain Colette's town, there were cries from the audience of *"Vive Colette!"* In Marseilles she had a full house and a rousing success. In Brest Missy took up her pen to reassure Sido: "The child is fine, quite fine, don't worry." From Rennes, ten days before the end of the tour, Colette herself wrote, "Missy continues to surround me with a silent vigilance that is so touching. If ever that horror of a Willy seeks to harm her I swear I'll tear his eyes out." For she was receiving "neurotic letters" from her former husband, who claimed that he could not sleep or eat and was deathly ill, though one of Willy's old secretaries who was now on Colette's side let her know that he slept "like a chest," ate heartily, and saw all of his women regularly. "So much the worse," concluded Colette. "One pays for everything, and he'll pay, I promise you."[20]

She kept a diary, capturing events, recording anecdotes, and adding personal reflections — unremarkable material that was to be published quietly. It may have marked the first time that such an incisive literary intelligence was set loose on what might otherwise have been considered the seamy side of show business.[21] And all the while she was touring, she was also planning — for more stage work, and next time it would be pantomime again. Back home in Paris, she and Missy tried their hand at real estate, hoping to make some extra money that way. But they ran up against the Blum family — "a ravenous horde," she informed Léon Hamel, that was striving to take control of the business away from its "goyim competitors."[22]

The warriors' rest came in July. Photographs show Colette and Missy standing beside their beachside villa, acting as if it were not the world's ugliest. The weather at Le Crotoy was disappointing, so Colette consoled herself with riding and fishing. These photographs suggest a docile and contented Colette, alongside a severe Missy in jacket and tie, with a felt hat or sailor cap; in one of them the marchioness, looking no less grim-faced, caresses a puppy.[23] The water in the bay was rough that year, and the tide came up to their door. July may have been gray, but August made up for it and more. And then, at the beginning of September, Colette was ready to disclose to Léon Hamel that she had begun to write "a kind of novel." She was not embarking on this new thing without apprehension, she admitted.

It was an effort — a first attempt — to come to terms with her maturity, the fictional equivalent of *Les Vrilles de la vigne*. It would be published as *The Vagabond*, for that was what she was now.

There was a long automobile trip with Missy, for example, to find a house for future holidays.[24] Then, late in October, she began another road tour, taking *La Chair* south and east. "It's long, when you're alone," she complained to her mother from Lyon, but in Grenoble she had to clarify things: "Don't worry, I'm not alone, I am still with Wague and [Christine] Kerf." (Kerf played the second female role in a number of Wague's pantomimes.)[25]

It may have been during this tour that a very young Maurice Chevalier found himself sharing the stage with Colette in Lyon. He would recall the shock it created each night when Wague ripped her bodice to reveal a breast — a pleasant scandal, but a scandal even so. Because she was a Parisian celebrity, "the view of Colette Willy's tit gave even more importance both to the scandal and to the tit," Chevalier would later write. It also happened to be one of the most voluptuous breasts one could hope to see, he said. "Well fleshed out," was the way he remembered her. "Large shoulders. A bit stocky, plump, without undesirable fat; she had a heavy, full, well-supported breast." He got an eyeful of it every night before his own act and actually fell in love with its owner, but he dared not approach her. Noticing that he seemed wistful, she sought to cheer him up; later, when Chevalier read *The Vagabond*, he saw himself in the character Cavaillon, a somewhat anxious person, when in truth it had been nothing more than his suppressed desire giving him that air. Later still, when he confessed to Colette how he had felt then, she replied, "You should have told me!"[26]

For her part, Colette admired the way Chevalier hypnotized his audience. Watching as his eyes swept the rows of spectators, she would recall what Wague had told her: "A singer must look at everybody; a mime must look at no one" — or he would lose his hold on the audience.[27]

In Paris the battle royal was being fought, for the moment, with slingshots. Sido's correspondence is steeped with apprehension over the way accounts were to be settled with Willy. Colette promised that she would sue him and in so doing disclose things that would make his family want to change its name. "But what will he say about you?" asked her mother.[28] In October 1909 a magazine reported that Meg Villars was going to publish a Claudine book with a music-hall background. Colette dispatched a letter to the editor: Claudine belonged to her, not to Meg Villars or Willy. She admitted that she had let Willy take the credit for the Claudine books in order "to protect the literary personality, or just the personality, of my husband." She had not simply participated in the writing of the Claudine and Minne books, she insisted; she had *written* them. Willy had merely added "some puns, some obscenities, and nasty stories designed to satisfy his personal grudges." Their joint signature on new printings of the Claudine books, she concluded, "still gives him more than he deserves."[29]

It was now that she picked up *Minne* and *Les Egarements de Minne* and, after some editing, published them as *The Innocent Libertine,* written by "Colette Willy." She eliminated some of Willy's unkind references to his peers, though the new version did retain a number of Willyisms, if that is what they were to begin with. Thus an "Oriental Jew" and "a Jewish dealer in precious stones" remain self-confessed scoundrels in the later version. And Maugis, that ubiquitous incarnation of Willy as roué, continues to be a central character, even a sympathetic one; she would have had to cut out too much to get rid of him.

Still, it was a difficult book for the clean-minded to digest, the final love scene more explicit than most others in books signed by Willy. Francis Jammes, while thanking Colette for sending him a copy, made his disapproval clear: "When one is Colette Willy, one does not have the right to trifle this way," he scolded.[30]

Her faithful half-brother, Achille, suggested that she threaten
Willy with a criminal complaint if he failed to pay back what he
had stolen from her. He promised to testify that Willy had probably
killed his mistress (the mother of Jacques Gauthier-Villars) with
morphine snatched from Achille's medical cabinet. The family down
in Châtillon worried that some harm would come to Colette if she
went around Paris unaccompanied; Sido suggested that she take her
brother, Léo, with her when she left home.[31]

THIRTEEN

The Vagabond Domesticated

COLETTE WAS TO PERFORM *La Chair* again, this time in Brussels, and a local reviewer showed that he could watch her acting as well as her flesh: "This body given and taken back, this expressive mime, the gesture especially, the admirable gesture, this violent ripping of the tunic that lets gush out the tasty fruit of the breast!"[1] There was a week's respite in garment-ripping before a journey down to Grenoble with *La Chair* again, and then the no less exotic pantomime *The Sicilian Night*. Once more she traveled with Meg Villars. "Who or what prompts Meg to go wherever you go?" an anxious Sido wished to know. "I don't like that, for she and her confederate are capable of anything. Now that they can't count on your work to help them live, they aren't interested in keeping you alive."[2]

On the eve of Colette's departure for Brussels, early in February 1910, her mother had given her some sound advice. She had read an article by Colette, she said, and it was a good one — but what about a book? "It's very flattering to be asked to write articles, but that takes a lot of time and occupies the imagination," explained Sido. "It's a bit of a waste of talent that could be devoted to a more ambitious work."[3] From her village Sido had put her finger on the dilemma that Colette would face all her life long. The need for ready cash obliged her to write for magazines; more ambitious work often had to wait. One solution, a customary one in Colette's day, was to publish novels in weekly installments. Colette learned to write quickly and not to spoil her first try. She also learned that she would have to work continuously.

But it took time for her to learn these things. In a letter to Charles Saglio at *La Vie Parisienne* she spoke frankly about the problem. She had just read over what she had written of *The Vagabond* and realized how inadequate it was. Would he please postpone publication until May 15? "I want to give you a finished manuscript, worthy of you as well as of myself."[4]

It was not a case of writer's block; it was the stage. Now, for example, she was to do another repertory tour, playing in thirty cities in a month (in two one-acters by Courteline). "Happily Missy is there," commented Sido.[5] They returned home early in May and Colette got back to writing. The first pages of *The Vagabond* appeared in *La Vie Parisienne* on May 21, announced by a cover drawing of a comely actress in her dressing room. Readers who had been following Colette's career, even if only casually, found themselves on familiar ground. Her "comrade Brague, who helped me get started in pantomime," was of course Wague. Colette herself was present under the light disguise of Renée Néré, divorced and alone, who wistfully admits, "No one is waiting for me, on a road that leads neither to glory and wealth nor to love." Renée is thirty-four years old; Colette had been thirty-six when she began to write the novel, the previous summer. In *The Vagabond* Renée's ex-husband is an artist named Adolphe Taillandy, whose real talent is lying; adultery is only one aspect of that. He is a manipulator of other people's money, and of other people: "God, was I young, and God, how I loved him . . . and how I suffered!" Renée exclaims. She has become a writer; once, she and Taillandy were the most interesting couple in Paris.

Her present existence, as The Vagabond, is a symbol of women's endurance. She is a performing dog, thinks she, but she hesitates to accept engagements in private homes for fear that she might encounter friends who knew her when she was married, and know of Taillandy's infidelities. At one of these evenings she does talk to an admirer — Max, the idle son of wealth — and indeed grows to care for him. Max becomes a counter to her lesbian relationships: "Two women entwined will never be anything more for him than naughty people, not the melancholic and touching image of two weaknesses who have perhaps taken refuge in each other's arms to sleep, to weep, to flee from men, who are so often cruel, and to taste, better than any pleasure, the bitter happiness of feeling themselves similar, lowly, forgotten. . . ."

With the novel launched more or less on schedule, these two women, Colette and Missy, could pursue their quest for a house — the house of their dreams, as Colette referred to it when writing to her mother. They found it in Brittany, on a crest dominating a cove, the cove itself protected by craggy cliffs. It gave them a patch of sand beach all their own, and an enclave of dune vegetation. Even today it is not easy to find this dream house on its twenty acres just outside the village of La Guimorais, halfway between Saint-Malo and Saint-Coulomb (to which township it belongs). They laid siege to the place until the owner agreed to sell.[6] A lot had to be done to it to make it habitable; she and Missy would have to spend one more summer in Le Crotoy.[7]

Writers who published novels serially in magazines generally enjoyed a grace period. One could begin publishing chapters, and be paid for them, even before a book was finished. Colette was still writing *The Vagabond* when its early chapters began to appear in *La Vie*. In Le Crotoy that July (1910), she was "swimming, riding — not too much, though, because the mare is too young — and above all working a lot," she reported to a friend at the end of the month. "I must, you understand, I absolutely must finish the novel in ten or twelve days!"[8]

Willy did not wait for the book to appear before becoming angry at his ex-wife's revelations (now officially ex-, for the divorce had

become final on June 21). He let it be known that he too was writing
a novel, to be called "Sidonie: Or, The Perverted Peasant." Even
Sido in her village heard about that![9] Their mutual hostility was
undisguised now, but Willy's books no longer had the power to cause
Colette harm. Reading the latest, she felt a kind of satisfaction; it
was "sweet vengeance" to see what the "old scoundrel" was producing without her.[10]

His vengeance would not be called "Sidonie" after all, but he
would publicize his feelings about Colette, and more than once.
Meanwhile, he simply offered subjects of irritation, such as the announcement that he would write an operetta based on the Claudine
books. Once again Colette had to issue a warning. The operetta went
on stage in November, and she won her half share.[11]

In the middle of August Sido traveled up to Le Crotoy, just after
celebrating her seventy-fifth birthday — a heroic effort for this weary
woman who had less than two years to live and who had had both
breasts removed at a four-year interval.[12] Colette was to remember
her mother's final years with a kind of tenderness laced with humor.
Once, confessing that she had slipped while rushing downstairs, Sido
said, "Do I have the time to descend a staircase with the gait of the
Sun King?" She did things she should not have been doing at her
age; on one occasion she burned an arm when a pot slipped from
her hands. There were days when she could not rise at her usual
early hour, and days of remission, when Achille would catch her
sawing a log.[13]

That autumn was a busy one for Colette. In Dijon she met up
with her regular partners, Georges Wague and Christine Kerf, for
the inevitable La Chair — Colette's chair (flesh), of course. On opening night they discovered that the orchestra conductor was really a
wine merchant; the public booed the musicians but cheered the performers. She described the situation to her confidant Léon Hamel,
writing from a hotel room with a famished cat on her lap; if she
could not find anyone to adopt the creature, she would keep it, she
said: "A hotel room is better with an animal in it."[14]

They did La Chair in Marseilles, La Chair in Paris; then she indulged in some private travel, this time with a new companion, a dapper young man with a comfortable income (his family owned one of the large department stores in Paris). Perhaps Auguste Hériot was in love with this peripatetic woman who bared her breast on stage. Probably Colette was not in love with him, but she enjoyed being admired and spoiled. They had an unmarried honeymoon, even dared to have it in Capri.

They traveled by night train to Naples, which then required two nights; they sailed in the bay and explored Pompeii. It took all that to make her decide that she did not really care for southern Italy.[15] "But my companion is very kind," she told her mother.[16] In fact, he was kind when he was alone with her, as she spelled things out to Hamel; otherwise he was not a happy person, but was "built on a rock of sadness."[17]

No, she did not love this new lover; Missy, who was being kept informed of her escapade, need not fear this rival. Writing to her, Colette referred to Hériot as "the little one." "I kiss you," she added. "I know that you don't like long kisses, but that's the way it is. Oh! how I'd like to be scolded!"[18]

She was back in Paris for the publication in book form of *The Vagabond,* and for that of Willy's counterblow, which took the form of a mediocre fiction called *Les Imprudences de Peggy* (Peggy's Rash Acts). The author was given as Meg Villars, and since she was ostensibly English, the jacket announced, "translated by Willy." In the novel Peggy is the daughter of an English father and a French mother who dies when she is born. She is raised by her mother's sister, Sidonie Gabrielle Anastasie Leroi. "Her face is lined with wrinkles, like a walnut shell," Peggy, or Meg, or Willy, writes. "I despise her." This time it is Peggy who engages in Claudine-ish affairs with another girl, games of nudity, and a flirtation with her drawing teacher.

In Paris Peggy visits a writer named Robert Parville and sees a photograph of a pretty woman, which she learns is an old and retouched portrait of Vivette Wailly (Colette again!). Parville shows Peggy a more accurate photograph, this one revealing a "thick neck, a face like a top, wide temples, pointed chin, half-opened mouth with an expression meant to be ingenuous, to which two calculating eyes give the lie." Parville explains to the visitor that his poor friend Taillandy (the name Colette gave Willy in *The Vagabond*) married "this little country girl both intelligent and crafty, poor as a church-mouse and impossible to marry off in her village" (once again be-cause of her affair with a music teacher). Vivette did not love Taillandy, says Parville. A selfish person, she tolerated his mistresses so that she would not become deformed by pregnancy. And she too had mistresses, some of whom Taillandy converted into "normal" women and made *his* mistresses.

Over a twelve-year period, Parville tells Peggy, Vivette ruined her husband, spending every last penny and showing herself in public with an old morphine addict, a woman who dressed as a man, "the Baroness de Louviers." (The reference to Missy is clear: Louviers is a Norman town near Elbeuf, which is close enough to Belbeuf, her married name.) But Taillandy never thought much of Vivette, and he fell in love with an adorable English girl. Vivette revenged herself by stealing Taillandy's letters as well as his furniture, accusing him of having poisoned a mistress (the reference is to the mother of Wil-ly's son, Jacques), and involving him in a scandal while profiting from it herself (more about this event later). In the end Taillandy went to Brittany, shot Vivette and the baroness, and then killed himself.

This was not the main plot of *Les Imprudences de Peggy,* only a story within the story, one that Willy must have enjoyed concocting. The present author possesses a copy of the novel autographed both by Meg Villars and by Willy, with occasional penned corrections of the printed text in Meg's hand, which does suggest that she did at least some of the writing. The real woman behind Meg Villars would go on to become a writer, and Willy certainly deserves some of the credit for that.

Colette's version of the Taillandy story was to reach a far larger audience, then and later (just try to find a copy of Meg's book now). As Sido told her daughter when *The Vagabond* appeared, she was delighted by her success, not only because of the money but because it would "shut the mouth of a lot of people who aren't worthy of licking the mud off your boots."[19] Still, *The Vagabond* contained new reasons for a mother to be anxious. "One scene haunts me," she wrote to her daughter, "that in which you are alone at night in that empty railway station. The night is cold and moonless. . . . I see you alone, your purse in hand, waiting for the train. Is all that true?"[20]

Even without Willy, Colette had the reviewers behind her novel. She was adept at handling them. "I've never in my life been so embarrassed," she wrote to one critic who had been generous with her praise. "When they say something bad about me, I know how to take it lightly, but sympathy, real sympathy — yours — makes me weak, and cowardly, and befuddled like an animal you're kind to, and above all stupid."[21]

The mysterious scandal to which *Les Imprudences de Peggy* referred was a police-court affair. It had begun during Colette's marriage to Willy, when he had managed to extract a considerable amount of money from a married woman (a woman with whom he was particularly friendly) on the pretext of investing it in his family publishing house. Of course he spent the money and was unable to return it on demand. When the lender insisted, Willy threatened to show her husband letters she had written to him, using Colette — the "outraged wife" — as intermediary.

Willy now begged his ex-wife, his outraged ex-wife, to help him defend himself. All Colette would agree to do, however, was to write to the gullible lender, imploring her to take pity on Willy. The case went to trial in December 1910. At the time of Willy's death, twenty-one years later, the plaintiff still had a lien on his royalties.

After the trial, Willy told Curnonsky that there would have to be another one — a criminal case, this time. "For after all, I must revenge myself, yes?"[22] But he never did take a shot at Colette.

Soon she was going to feel safer all the same — and *be* safer. It did not happen all at once, the transfiguration of the vagabond, but before long she was going to be able to ally her courage to the courage of Henry de Jouvenel; the vagabond would become a baroness in her own right.

Jouvenel was a titled country gentleman if you did not know him, and a self-made man if you did. Paradox it may have been, but this man with not one but two handles to his name (he was Henry de Jouvenel des Ursins), the owner of a castle on a hill, lived on his talents almost as much as Colette the déclassée did. His grandfather had inherited a title won by *his* father, and annexed the elegant "des Ursins" from another branch of the family. In that Second Empire of opportunity, the grandfather was an achiever. His son Raoul was the youngest prefect of the Third Republic, eventually retiring to his family's Castel-Novel in south-central France. On his mother's side, Henry de Jouvenel descended from Napoleon's marshal Jean Lannes and the Perier dynasty (one of whose members, Casimir, was a banker and prime minister). As was true of many public figures who claimed provincial roots, Henry was born in Paris (on April 5, 1876), went to school there, and spent most of his professional life in that city.

He attended the prestigious Collège Stanislas in Montparnasse and there met Anatole de Monzie, who was to be his lifelong friend and political mentor. He earned a bachelor's degree in philosophy at the Sorbonne. By then he had chosen a path that was to take him far from his family.

Ever since the French Revolution, political France had been divided into resentful Right and militant Left. Now the Dreyfus affair, as well as a renewed attack on Church influence by supporters of the Republic, exacerbated the schism. As a student, Henry de Jouvenel turned his back on family tradition to side with justice and Captain Dreyfus; on one occasion, after a student demonstration, he was even arrested. He worked as a volunteer assistant in the cabinet of Premier René Waldeck-Rousseau, whose government ordered a retrial of Dreyfus and at the same time reduced the powers of Catholic religious orders.[23]

But Jouvenel's true vocation was writing. It might have led him to literature; instead, he joined a newspaper. In a reminiscence he explained how he had first tried to get a job on the daily *Le Matin,* whose editor deemed him unworthy of the lowliest reporter's duties. He finally got on to the staff by starting higher up: his activity in the Dreyfus affair made an impression on Alfred Boas, an influential Radical Socialist, who put him in touch with the owner of *Le Matin,* Maurice Bunau-Varilla. Indeed, Boas was sufficiently impressed to consent to Jouvenel's marrying his daughter. The story goes that when Henry de Jouvenel journeyed down to the Corrèze to inform his father of his plans to marry, Baron Raoul asked him to describe Claire Boas. "A Jewess," he replied. Then was she rich? "No, Father." "Well, son, you can be proud of bringing into our family the two things I hate most in the world: Jews and poverty."[24] An unlikely dialogue; in truth, Alfred Boas was wealthier than Raoul de Jouvenel des Ursins. Yet for Raoul's son to marry this woman (so Henry's son Bertrand later said) was to repeat the treason he had already been committing, in his father's eyes, in his political life.[25]

Le Matin was a newspaper in the American tradition, which meant that it featured straight news under bold headlines, reducing editorial opinions to a minimum. It had actually been founded, back in 1884, by an American named Sam Chamberlain. This brand of journalism was more tempting to the adventurous Henry de Jouvenel than a government office.[26] "What he liked in journalism," his admiring but discerning schoolmate Anatole de Monzie remembered, "was the daily opportunity to squander his nobility."[27]

By the time Henry met Colette, his marriage to Claire Boas had gone sour. They had had a child, Bertrand, in 1903, but soon after that he had taken up with another strong-willed woman, the blond and beautiful Isabelle de Comminges, who was sometimes referred to (even by herself) as The Panther. She called Henry Tiger. "Handsome, elegant, loving pleasure, passionately in love with women in general and always with one in particular, he was ever ready with the right answer, which he would let drop with the careless insolence of a lord" — that from a young editor who joined *Le Matin* in Jouvenel's time. He continued, "Without great talent as a writer, he was instead a brilliant speaker, and he would fight a duel without hesitation if anyone dared to attack him."[28]

In 1907 Henry had a second son, this time with the Panther. Renaud grew up as a Comminges, which was in fact an older and thus more distinguished name than Jouvenel. That was the way families did things, Bertrand was to think as *he* grew up. One of his grandmothers had walked out on her husband; the Panther had married one man and gone off with a second before Henry became the third, if not the last. Later Bertrand would see a parallel in a passage in Colette's writings: her daughter asks if living one's life means "to go off with the gentleman," and Colette replies yes.[29]

All the same, one cannot help wondering how Jouvenel came to meet a woman who was nightly showing a naked breast on the stage. Was it, as his son Renaud thought, a suppressed plebeian instinct, or was it perhaps some sort of compensation for the hard time the Panther gave him? (Isabelle de Comminges would remind Henry that her family had three centuries of seniority over the Jouvenels, and she told him that he rode a horse badly.)[30] A young man who began working for Jouvenel some time later understood that the go-between who had brought Henry and Colette together was none other than Meg Villars.[31] That may have been the case; Meg and Henry were friends, and they would become even friendlier. Yet Meg and her Willy, who were married the following June, were not on speaking terms with Colette in 1910.

Consider Colette's fictional account of these feverish events. In *The Shackle,* the sequel to *The Vagabond,* her double, Renée Néré, is a witness to the romance of the handsome Jean and the lovely but inconsequential May, until one day Jean turns up at Renée's hotel in Switzerland to declare his love for *her.* Henry did turn up at Colette's hotel in Switzerland (in July 1911), and she had to hide to save herself from the Panther's fury, just as Renée hides from May in the novel.

The first visible product of the encounter of Henry and Colette was professional. *Le Matin* was competing with at least one other American-style daily, *Le Journal,* in the quality of its cultural content as well as in that of its news. Both news and culture were delivered in short and snappy doses. By this time Jouvenel was editor in chief of *Le Matin,* taking turns in that position with the man who had originally tried to keep him away from the paper, Stéphane Lauzanne. Each editor in chief was in full charge for half a month at a time, retiring from the scene during the other half. It was a well-deserved rest, for editing *Le Matin* meant spending long nights in the editorial and composing rooms.

As Colette tells it, this fortnightly alternation had fostered a mutual dislike, if not a deadly rivalry. When Lauzanne was informed that Colette would be contributing a weekly story, he warned one of his editors, "If this person joins the paper, I leave at once." The editor immediately bid Lauzanne adieu, with irony, because whether he liked it or not, Colette's first story was to appear the very next day.[32]

Lauzanne stayed on, and on and on; he was still editor in chief when *Le Matin* became a Nazi propaganda sheet during the German occupation of Paris, and signed his name to editorials sympathetic to collaboration with the enemy. For this he received a sentence, after the liberation, of twenty years in prison, confiscation of his property, and deprivation of his civil rights.

Possibly it was because of Lauzanne that even though Colette's name meant something both in bookstores and on the stage, her first pieces appeared in *Le Matin* anonymously. The very first, on December 2, 1910, was introduced by a note: "The story that *Le Matin* is publishing today is signed with a mask. Under it is hidden, capriciously, a woman writer who is among the best authors of our time and whose intimate talent, composed of an exquisite sensitivity, keen observation, and mischievous fantasy, has once again been confirmed in a love story that is today's best-seller." In place of the signature, there was indeed a small actor's mask. Colette had to wait until the end of January to surface, at which point one of her stories ran over the now familiar mask, followed by the words "It's me: Colette Willy." Later she revealed that her name had been banned at first so as not to offend the "chaste eyes" of *Le Matin*'s readers.[33]

FOURTEEN

The Shackle

THE INDEPENDENT Colette was packing again. "So
you're leaving with the little one?" Sido asked her, early in the
month of February 1911. "Missy will do her tree planting while
you're far away."[1] It was a shrewd summing-up of Colette's private
life at the moment. She was not in love with Auguste Hériot, but *he*
was in love, and attentive, and able to pamper her.[2] This time they
were off to the Riviera, to familiar places and others that were less
familiar. Perhaps she was not as happy as she might have been; they
went to Beaulieu on the Mediterranean coast and she did not like it,
nor did she like Nice, or Monte Carlo. She was accompanied not
only by the little one, Hériot, but by a new friend, Lily de Rème,
"and the trio we form would interest you," she confided to Léon
Hamel — for that man-about-town, now fifty-three, did appear to
be interested in what Colette revealed of her life. "These two children in love with me are uncommon," she explained, "in the very
fact that they love me." It satisfied her ego to observe their "appetite"
for her, but she simply did not care very much for the young man.
Their adventure seemed dangerous for him above all; she herself did
not feel "morally" in peril.

She had a theatrical engagement in Nice — a dancing role.[3] Then she abandoned her friends to join the patient Missy in Rozven. After that there was another theater job, this time in Tunis. "Who are you going with?" her mother asked her.[4] It was a good question, for this time not only Missy but also Auguste Hériot was left behind. She went away with Lily! "Yes, I left my little comrade quite coolly," she reported to her mother from the Tunisian capital, "determined not to be his slave." Meanwhile, he had found nothing better to do than to argue his case with Missy, but, said Colette, "when I'm fed up, I'm fed up."[5] As for Lily, she seems to have inspired the character of May in Colette's next novel, *The Shackle:* "She gives off a perishable freshness lacking character: no distinguishing features, thick, shaded blond hair. . . . Yet this absurd little creature has her twenty-five years of light-skinned beauty . . . and an idiotic and charming way of exaggerating fashions that were already insane."[6]

Tunisia was the first totally different place she had ever seen, and she did it all — the souks, the trek to Carthage. There was an excursion up a mountain, in a camel landscape, to the waters of Zaghouan, and another up to snow at Sidi-bou-Saïd dominating the sea. "If you could only see the beautiful eyes of the young Jewesses here," she wrote to her mother.[7] She did an article for *Le Matin* on her visit to a Tunisian Jewish home — mother and daughter — in her search for local color. There was plenty of that to be had, but it was all she could do to keep Lily de Rème in check, for she wanted to touch everything, including the stunning daughter of the family.[8] "I'll tell you all about my trip," Colette promised Hamel, "and about how Lily is impossible in Tunis, in Marseilles, and everywhere." And now the girl wanted Colette to go to India with her! "I'd rather drop dead."[9]

Colette had not traveled all the way to North Africa to be someone's sex object; there was a play for her to play in (*Claudine* again). She manifested both impatience and relief in a postcard that she sent to her mother on March 2, 1911: "It will soon be time to leave, and it seems a long time since I left Missy."[10]

So she hardly stopped to catch her breath in Paris — "I was in a hurry to take refuge in Missy, to be bawled out, cared for, and warmed," she confessed to a sympathetic listener, the writer Louis de Robert, Proust's friend. "I'm finally coming out of my 'crisis of vulgarity.' I've had my fill of the fake Riviera and of friends who resemble it. I look at them from a distance without charity, as if I have never met them."[11]

In Rozven she found a house that was beginning to look like a home. Missy had fixed up bedrooms for Colette and for herself, and the oil stove was working. Soon Colette was doing her share of the job; Rozven was to be a place where one could bring friends.[12] But by the time the house Missy had bought for her became truly livable, Missy was no longer part of her life.

By mid-April Colette was back in Paris so that her bodice could be ripped away in *La Chair,* and we can guess that Henry de Jouvenel was in the audience. By now something was going on between Colette and Henry; the return to Rozven would not be easy for her. She asked Georges Wague to write to her there and pretend that she was needed for rehearsals in Paris at the end of May.[13] That was for Missy to read.

On one of those Paris nights — we know this from a brief aside in a book of hers — Henry took Colette to his bachelor quarters, a silly Swiss chalet at the western edge of the city. Still, she not only returned to Rozven but made a summer of it, inviting Sacha Guitry and his wife, Charlotte Lysès, along. Even Missy seemed satisfied.[14]

For all of her wanderings, Colette never seemed to make it down to Châtillon. "If I'm not going to see you anymore I'd just as soon die," her mother wrote to her. Sido's decline came at an awkward time, just when Colette was beginning a new life. "What is this new Cherub going to be able to give you?" inquired Sido. "A villa on Lake Como?"[15] For the time being, it was Lake Geneva; she was in Switzerland in the last week of June 1911 to do *La Chair.* Sido wondered whom she was *with* in Geneva. So on a postcard showing the view she had of the lake, Colette mentioned Henry. "You're not on a bed of roses because you're loved too much," concluded Sido after letting the information sink in. "What to do? I fear a catastrophe if those two gentlemen meet, but what worries me most is that you'll be the victim, and if Cherub discovers your little fibs he'll become furious. It also seems to me that Missy is angry. . . ."[16]

In *The Shackle,* the sequel to *The Vagabond,* the man whom she calls Jean follows Renée to Geneva. Their encounter, which is founded on physical desire, begins badly and appears unlikely to last. But who cares? the wanderer asks herself. "Why not be as imprudent as Jean, who only wishes us to come together as sensual strangers?" In this novel she was writing the story of her life with Jouvenel, writing and then publishing it at the commencement of the affair. They made love fabulously, the real couple and the fictional one, so who cared about compatibility in other things? In the end Renée and Jean, and Colette and Henry, are prepared to accept each other as they are, and the men replace the women as vagabonds.

But for the moment they were together, Colette and Henry, at the Hotel du Château in Ouchy, the lakeside resort below Lausanne. The postcard she chose for her mother shows a Renaissance castle of a hotel, all spires and gables. She marked the position of her room, in a tower with views in all directions. Jouvenel had joined her there after fighting a duel with the editor of a rival newspaper, which had made a slighting reference to his. He had been wounded, but he had come to be with her all the same, "because he can no longer live without me," said Colette. "Men are terrifying! And what about women!"[17]

Jouvenel had arrived, Colette reported to Léon Hamel, "quite wounded, with his arm in a sling" — apparently each party to the duel had been cut on the forearm. As for the warrior's rest in that tower room, it was surely as physical as the tryst of Renée and Jean in *The Shackle.* It was all going "too well!," she exclaimed to a confidante.[18]

But there were scores to settle back in Paris. On his return Jouvenel called on the Panther to confess that he now loved someone else. She promised to kill the other woman, whoever she was. When Jouvenel transmitted the reply to Colette, her reaction was, "I'll go to see her." She confronted Isabelle de Comminges with the admission, "I'm the woman." The Panther broke down and begged Colette not to take Jouvenel away from her, but two days later she was a Panther again, threatening to murder her rival. She actually seems to have gone to Colette's apartment with the intention of carrying out her threat, but Colette escaped through a window.[19]

Jouvenel drove Colette to safety in Rozven, taking along a reliable deputy from the staff of *Le Matin,* Charles Sauerwein. When the two men returned to Paris, they left her under the guard of Paul Barlet, a member of the Willy circle who had chosen Colette's side after the divorce; he had a revolver in his belt. Missy, still angry, went off to Normandy; clearly events had gone beyond her control. Her candidate for Colette had been Auguste Hériot; she had even fixed up a room in Rozven and was ready to let Colette share it with him.

Then came an urgent message from Jouvenel: the Panther, also armed, was on her way to Rozven. Sauerwein returned to Brittany — no small expedition, that 450-mile round trip in a pre–World War I automobile, even if it was one of the powerful vehicles owned by the newspaper — and drove Colette back to Paris, where he, Jouvenel, and *Le Matin*'s business manager took turns watching over her. They even got the police to help.

Her release came in a manner that she described as "unexpected, providential, and magnificent!" In what seems like the improbable plot of a bad movie, the Panther ran off with Auguste Hériot — though perhaps "sailed off" would be a more accurate term, for they embarked on a yacht at Le Havre on the Channel coast. "It's done!" the Panther told a friend. "I slept with Colette's lover." By the time the elopers reached Morocco, they were finished with each other, and Isabelle de Comminges left Hériot for a Foreign Legion officer.[20]

Colette returned to Rozven at the end of July 1911, and there took the time to write up the events of this agitated period for Léon Hamel. She let him know that Jouvenel was fixing up his bachelor's house so that she could move in with him. He was not rich, she explained, having only his salary from the newspaper, but since she also earned a living, they would manage. "Must I also tell you that I love this man, who is tender, jealous, unsociable, and incurably honest?"[21]

Then she was on her way to the Jouvenel home, Castel-Novel, in the Corrèze. "Ah! You've given yourself a master," observed her mother. "Poor darling!" Colette softened her up with photographs of the Jouvenel castle, and Sido confessed that she liked this replica of the drawings of Gustave Doré.[22]

Perhaps it was indeed a fairy-tale castle. Atop a ridge, dominating the plain in all directions, round towers and a multiplicity of gables reassured the eye seeking antique splendor. In Colette's day, as in ours, only an expert could determine which elements of the mass belonged to the centuries preceding its restoration by the Jouvenels in the middle of the last century.[23]

Once again she was beginning a new life. After Monts-Boucons with Willy, and Rozven with Missy, she could re-create her rural growing-up with a new lover. Like most Frenchmen of his time, he was drawn to Paris by ambition, but the land-poor Jouvenel also loved his Castel-Novel. Colette was not about to become domesticated, however. In Paris, in August, she began rehearsing a pantomime to be performed at what was called a café-concert, the plebeian form of variety theater — at Bataclan (then and still on Boulevard Voltaire) one was as close as one could get to the little people of Paris. "Come and see me," she invited the critic André Rouveyre, for she would be "ridiculous and agreeable." The opening was a success, Colette told Christiane Mendelys, "despite the undisciplined orchestra, despite the insufficient rehearsing, despite Colette, who replaces choreographic science with a gentle fantasy and a gall she didn't get from her mother."[24]

Her nights, like Jouvenel's, were devoted to work, but they did have free time together during the day. As Colette put it to Christiane, far from neglecting physical exercise, "I just have a new method. The Sidi method. Excellent. No classes. Private lessons, devilishly private."[25] Sidi — "Sir" in Arabic — was Jouvenel's nickname; close friends also called him Pasha. Apparently both titles suited his character.

Willy, married to Meg now, fired off another round. None of his post-Claudine, post-Colette books was worth much; all of his wit and organizing skill, and even the talented ghostwriters he occasionally employed, just did not seem to make good books. Yet for this new one he drew on his best helpers, Paul-Jean Toulet (who was to make a name for himself in his own right) and Curnonsky. Willy's chief contribution to *Lélie, fumeuse d'opium* (Lélie the Opium Smoker) was the wicked portrait of his ex-wife: "I want the Baroness de Bize to be the spitting image of Madame Colette Willy, physically and in behavior," he instructed, though he preferred not to give her "the slightest literary talent, of course."[26] The baroness created by Willy and Toulet was in "her forties, as proclaimed by the bitter lines engraved in her cheeks by the constant obligatory smile; her exaggerated behind, which friends of both sexes used to praise for its arrogant curves, had fleshed out to her disadvantage."

There was more — her "sly peasant eyes," for example, and her mouth, whose "childish pout" was practiced in a mirror. She used opium and took on younger and younger gigolos. She rolled her *r*'s like a countrywoman.[27] When the novel was published, Willy asked Curnonsky to tell his ex-wife that if he had invented such a caricature, it was only because of the way she had treated *him* in *The Vagabond*. If he now hated her so much, Curnonsky was to explain, then he must have loved her deeply once.[28]

Perhaps she was heavy and had to smile for her public, but she had a public to smile for now. She followed the Bataclan stint with a revival of *La Chair,* and still she had time to arrange her love nest at 57 Rue Cortambert. Later she would recall her first impression of the Jouvenel house: she had thought of the vulgar chalet, in a neighborhood full of other fake chalets, as a trap. That fragile house, set in a garden surrounded by other gardens, possessed a massive iron gate and lock; legend had it that a jealous artist had installed this system of protection to keep other men away from his model.

The bathroom was in a shed that had been built to keep dogs in. There was an adjacent painter's studio with a leaking roof, and indeed, the house itself appeared to be ready to collapse. Patience was called for.[29]

She was quickly domesticated all the same. A young woman named Germaine, the daughter of a friend, Annie de Pène, remembered calling on Colette to drop off a message and being asked to help her clean string beans for preserves.[30]

FIFTEEN

Sido and Sidi

COLETTE'S MOTHER was not sure that her daughter was making the best use of her gifts by writing for the daily press. A story a week in *Le Matin*? "That's a lot, and I deplore it," wrote Sido, "because journalism is the death of the novelist and it's a pity in your case. Don't waste your talent, my darling; it's worth saving."[1] It was sound advice, in the last year in which Sido could help her daughter.

It is true that Colette's occasional sketches — the storylets that appeared in *Le Matin,* for example — were collected in books. The snapshots of backstage life were published as *Music-Hall Sidelights,* in 1913, and the dog and cat stories went into several collections. (All her life long Colette would add or subtract stories and sketches for successive editions of her works.) For her career, exposure in a daily newspaper could hardly be prejudicial. By 1913, when her contributions began to appear with a subtitle, "Colette's Diary," *Le Matin*'s circulation was nearly one million copies, which placed it among the capital's biggest dailies.

Colette was now also writing for the news pages. She went up in a dirigible, for instance, to describe Paris and its countryside from the sky, at a time when few readers had had that experience. Then she took a flight in a balloon and gave an account of things perceived, things felt. Her editor and lover sent her into courtrooms to cover murder trials. Leaving the raw evidence to other reporters, she would turn her attention to the behavior of defendants, witnesses, and spectators. When a man was accused of killing the husband of his mistress, she identified with the widow, seeing her less as an accomplice than as a woman capable of inspiring passion. On another assignment she was not allowed to cross a police barrier, so she described the crowd's reaction to the siege and killing of the anarchist bandit Jules Bonnot. Later she was to cover the trial of Bonnot's confederates and once again to observe courtroom behavior. One of the defendants was a young woman, and because she wore a schoolgirl's smock, a spectator was heard to exclaim, "It's Claudine!"[2]

Those were the heroic days of journalism, and Colette was not far from the center of things; Le Matin signified power. Later she remembered another assignment, which had her leaping onto a train in the middle of the night to talk to Queen Marie of Rumania, and clinging to the gate of the royal car as the train hurtled through the countryside — remembered being frightened.[3]

Her mother badly wanted to meet this Henry de Jouvenel. She was hoping to be in sufficient good health, and hoping the weather would allow her to travel. But in autumn 1911 Colette was too busy making a life with her new man (her mother aptly called it a honeymoon) to find time for a visit from Sido. Couldn't Colette come down to Châtillon with Jouvenel? her mother wondered. And they would have to hurry, she warned, for one never knew. Soon her weakened heart was to keep her confined to her room.[4]

But by the end of the year Colette was on stage again, with a week of La Chair at a music hall and then two weeks of a new pantomime — a mimodrama, it was called — entitled L'Oiseau de Nuit (Night Bird).

A moving letter exists — or does it? — from Sido to Monsieur de Jouvenel. Colette's mother had received an invitation from him to visit them in Paris. She would accept, she said, for a number of reasons, one of which was "to see the dear face of my daughter, to hear her voice." She also wished to meet and to "judge" this man with whom Colette had fallen head over heels in love. For this visit she would abandon her cat, even abandon her plants, which were about to blossom.

The letter is undated, but the reference to blooming plants indicates spring 1912. Varying drafts have come down to us — but Sido did not write drafts.[5] In Colette's novel *Break of Day,* the letter appears on the opening page, where it is presented as a *refusal* to visit. Here Sido explains that her pink cactus looks as though it is about to bloom; it is a rare plant, which she has been told will bloom only once every four years. She is old, and if she is absent when the cactus is in flower, she is certain never to see it blossom again. Did Colette rewrite this letter for dramatic effect? Or was it, as has been suggested, to mask her reluctance to see her dying mother?

At Christmas there was still no Colette, only a sketch written by her for *Le Matin* about a child's Christmas with her mother in Saint-Sauveur. Reading it took Sido back to the time when her daughter had brightened any room she entered. She did hope that Colette would hold on to the house in Saint-Sauveur, she said.

Over the New Year's holiday Sido suffered another attack and sent for Léo, who was then in town on a visit to Achille. "To think that I could die without seeing you again!" Sido wrote to her daughter. She suggested that when Colette agreed to another theater engagement she should provide for an absence due to circumstances beyond her control. In the middle of February Sido read an article in the sober *Le Temps* that accorded Colette a place apart among women writers. She was going to send fond regards to Jouvenel, but she changed her mind, saying, "He's too happy to have you with him!"[6]

In mid-March 1912 Sido had a long robe made, with lace around the collar and a hood, to be buried in.[7] The priest began to call on her. She was not about to accept the sacraments, but she found the man most pleasant.

Then, at last, after a tour of southern France with Sidi, Colette arrived. When she told her mother about all the things she was involved in, Sido advised *her* to rest.[8]

One of these was another rowdy engagement at Bataclan. And not only did this distinguished author, columnist, and live-in companion of Baron de Jouvenel perform in this brassiest of cabarets, she also dared to write about her experience. The article, published in a popular weekly called *Fantasio,* was accompanied by photographs of Colette in costume, wearing cat's whiskers. The sketch was called *She-Cat in Love,* and for each performance over the three-week run she was shut up in a box representing the base of a statue. She would spring out, an alley cat in tights, to the surprise or delight of the audience, or merely to satisfy its curiosity.[9]

And then this singular woman continued to pursue her affair with Henry de Jouvenel in public — for how else should we take her monologue to "you whom I love," printed in *Le Matin* on January 11, 1912, or, on February 1, the one titled "Sleep," alluding to the man who lay "alongside me"? Sido was particularly struck by a piece on a tomcat called Sidi, in which the "noble cat" declares, "I lead the troubled life of one created by love for its harsh duties." "At least you're not like everybody else," was her mother's comment.[10] On May 16, a column headed "Griefs" concerned a lover's quarrel, which found its way into her next novel, along with some of the other personal confessions that she made in print.

If those early quarrels were easily patched up, by the beginning of summer the crisis had come to a head. They fought a four-day battle, agreed that life together was henceforth impossible, and wondered if they could stay friends. No, decided Colette. If they were to part, it would have to be immediate and definitive. They planned to separate on July 1; she promised to tell Jouvenel, out of "simple loyalty," if she met someone who was both "sleepable and amiable." Sidi thought this was a reasonable decision, but meanwhile, he asked, couldn't they play a game of cards? They proceeded to do so, and more besides. Writing to her confessor Léon Hamel from the country house of Jean Sapène, *Le Matin*'s business manager, she hinted at the reason for their quarrel, declaring her "tremendous resentment toward the bitchy character of that man, who can't support a woman or defend her." Still, alas, "the presence of that unworthy individual is sorely missed, along with his warmth, the sound of his voice, his lies, his childishness, his ridiculous behavior."

Hamel advised her to get her own flat; she thought it was a good idea but could not afford to move. So she accepted her fate, and in her confession to Hamel there is more than a hint as to what it was that really kept her on "good terms" with Jouvenel, and vice versa. "There is even on his side (I tell you everything) a rather extraordinary carnal energy. Since I have the same weakness on my side, I must conclude that there are good moments and bad ones."[11]

She was alone in Paris in early August, with Henry down in the Corrèze. So she took charge of the rehabilitation of the chalet, she told her confidant Hamel, as if she were going to live there all her life. In order to be able to leave when she wished to, nevertheless, she borrowed against her pearls (and from none other than Auguste Hériot). She could pack her things and walk out on Henry in two hours' time, but she did not want to. That very day she was writing to the "Baron," so she ironically informed Hamel, while he "strutted and piled up debts" in his beloved Castel-Novel. On his return she found him "friendly and cautious," his egotism so naive and childish that she felt like laughing and crying all at once. "But I let myself go in an ephemeral animal happiness that has its price. You know how important it is to have, after hours and weeks of gloom, the presence of the necessary person." Jouvenel was moving furniture around as she wrote, arranging both their future and the bric-a-brac.[12]

Meanwhile, she was working on *The Shackle,* the plot of which was less compelling than the nonfiction being lived out on Rue Cortambert that year.

And Sido was dying. At the end of August Colette told Wague that she was leaving for Châtillon, "where my sainted mother is unbearable — not that she is more seriously ill, but she is having a crisis of 'I want my daughter.'" Sidi gave her three days' leave, "at the most." Her mother was not in the best of shape when she arrived, she admitted, but she would live, and that was all they were asking of her. When Colette returned to Paris, it was to a Jouvenel who was more affectionate than he had ever been.[13]

In September, when she began a new run at the Bataclan cabaret, doing *L'Oiseau de Nuit* with Wague and Kerf, she found herself performing with application rather than enthusiasm. She would give up the cabaret circuit without regret, for now everything was going well on Rue Cortambert. Then, during the run at Bataclan, Sido died. "Mama died the day before yesterday," she wrote to Hamel on September 27. "I don't want to go to the funeral. I'm telling almost no one and wearing no mourning clothes."

So she did not go to Châtillon, but soon she was down in Castel-Novel with Jouvenel. She had expected to be put up by friends in the region; instead, she was welcomed at the family castle. "My mother-in-law, as Sidi calls her, is youth itself, and gaiety," she reported to Hamel. She met Henry's sister, and his brother Robert, whom she described when she knew him better as "blond, brilliant, irritable, a hard worker who overworks in a nonchalant manner." A journalist in his own right, he would indeed have a brilliant career, writing books and managing a newspaper, before being brought down by an early death. One day they toured the countryside as far as Curemonte, a collection of castle ruins that Robert owned; later Colette would appreciate its isolation. And then it was back to Paris in the middle of October so that Henry could begin his fortnight at *Le Matin*.[14]

L'Oiseau de Nuit took her to Geneva during the same fortnight. In a letter to Hamel she speaks of her lethargy, her desire to relax, to think as little as possible; blame it on the baby, she says. For there was to be a baby, presumably conceived between the death of her mother and the end of her run at Bataclan. Yet for the moment she could continue to dance. In another letter to Hamel she describes a request she has received for a performance in a private home, doing either *L'Oiseau de Nuit* or *La Chair* (with its famous breast). Personally she would prefer *L'Oiseau de Nuit*, says she.[15]

So they were married. The date was December 19, 1912, the place their neighborhood town hall (the 16th district); Hamel was her witness. It was the simplest ceremony possible, but they were to celebrate all the way to Christmas and beyond, going from lunch to dinner to lunch, then to a Christmas Eve party that lasted until seven the next morning. Could their child help but be a party-goer? she wondered. For her part, she was growing out of her dresses: "*He* needs room, he'll wreck everything!" So she explained it to Wague's Christine. "You can see that he already resembles his father." Sidi, meanwhile, worked without a break, for war had broken out in the Balkans in October, during his fortnight on duty.[16]

SIXTEEN

Baby Colette

LATER ON Colette would remember that she had been worried that she would not make a proper mother; she also knew that it was not a good idea "to start a baby in thinking about it." In the early months of her pregnancy she tried to carry on as if nothing was happening. At *Le Matin* Charles Sauerwein, himself a father, warned her that she was having "a man's pregnancy." She also recalled that when she announced her condition to Georges Wague and Christine Kerf, they were distressed at the thought that a Geneva theater engagement would have to be canceled. Colette made sure that it was not. Still, each day saw her giving up another aspect of her life, though on the other hand there was the euphoria, the "sweet animality" of the mother-to-be.[1]

She was not about to be bedridden, in any case, nor even houseridden. She planned a January holiday. Castel-Novel seemed too far away, and Rozven lacked furnishings; in the end they opted for the Mediterranean, which was even farther south than Castel-Novel, and this at a time when automobiles and the roads they traveled were not as we know them today. She promised herself that she would work on *The Shackle* during the holiday.

On February 6, 1913, she wrote to Hamel from Nice: so far it had not been the restful trip that had been planned for her. "Everything drives us on: the crisp, cloudless weather, . . . Sidi's young appetite for life." Without her, he had attended the Opera ball that concluded the Mardi Gras festivities, staying until five in the morning, "delighted and satiated with having fondled so many anonymous buttocks." Meanwhile, the baby inside her was jumping about; would he, or she, be a goat?[2]

March brought some minor triumphs. Her friend Paul Barlet, who owned a small publishing house, produced a limited printing on fine paper of her animal sketches. Then *Music-Hall Sidelights* appeared, with its depiction of show business, the grim side that audiences never see. *La Vie Parisienne* began to publish *The Shackle* in installments. Not only had she not finished the novel when these first chapters appeared — that was normal practice — but she was still living the life that she revealed to her readers, for of course the real heroine was still in the clutches of the virile hero, and she was still a vagabond at heart.[3]

One young critic, however, decided that Colette hid as much as she disclosed: "Madame Colette Willy is quite ready to show us her almost-naked body, but she only lets us guess at her deepest wounds, veiled by modesty and a proud restraint." This René Gillouin found too much lamentation in her work all the same; she could be using her talent on better material, he said. Her novels contained much observation and sensitivity, but they lacked the novelist's most important quality, objective imagination. He had a point, but it would be some time before Colette would be able to set a stage and not put herself at its center. She was, wrote René Gillouin, one of her time's leading women writers, and he was sorry that her financial needs, or some craving to keep her name before the public, or a desire to enjoy herself, led her to produce "book after book."[4]

Pregnancy or no, when Sidi had his next free fortnight they drove off to Castel-Novel, doing the three hundred miles in a twelve-hour stint. It was a rainy May, and then suddenly it was June-in-May, with blooming roses. Then it was really June. "How heavy I am!" she wrote to Georges Wague.[5]

She could no longer dance on stage with him, but she could watch him dance. So she went to Bataclan to review a pantomime mounted by Wague, this time with Christine Kerf as the half-naked heroine. Kerf, Colette told her readers, had succeeded in this "most difficult enterprise of her brilliant career," and Wague was "gripping, unrecognizable and yet faithful to himself. . . ."[6]

But now she had something quite different to write about. In a sketch called "Maternity" we follow a woman "whose customary life at that time was to travel by rail or auto to mime and dance." She was feeling so good at the moment when she was ready to give birth that the event surprised her while she was watering the garden on Rue Cortambert. She woke to find Sidi nearby and hardly believed him when he said that they now had a little girl. He thought the infant looked like her mother; she saw Jouvenel in her face. From then on, unsure of her own maternal love, she loved in the baby what she found in her of him.[7]

So Colette de Jouvenel des Ursins came into the world, born on the third of July 1913, the daughter of Henry de Jouvenel des Ursins and another Colette de Jouvenel des Ursins. For this was now Colette's name, even if her books were still coming out under the signature of "Colette Willy" or simply that of "Colette."

Actually childbirth may not have been as easy as she made it out to be in "Maternity." "I've got a little mouse," she declared to Wague, "and I paid for it: thirty hours without respite, chloroform and forceps. She is well made and pretty, with elongated eyes and a shock of hair."[8] Still, Colette was back in the garden eleven days after the delivery, and three days after that she took a car ride out to Versailles for a dinner party.[9]

She had not finished *The Shackle* before the baby arrived. Its serial publication ceased abruptly with the July 5 issue of *La Vie,* whose editor informed readers that "a serious but happy event" had prevented Colette from doing that week's chapter. In their wisdom the Jouvenels decided that the new mother should spend the rest of the summer with the baby in Castel-Novel. "My daughter is already a month and two days old, and she is pretty, sunburned, and vigorous;

imagine that she raises herself in her cradle . . ." — this to Sacha
Guitry's wife, Charlotte. As for the mother, "It is truly very pleasant
to feel oneself light, flat, fit for tennis or driving, and to find that
one hasn't had the slightest bit of damage." She hoped that her friend
would like little Colette and agree that she was worth Mother Colette's having been ugly for so long. Meanwhile, they were living
with repairmen, with plaster, with rats alive and dead. The wheat
harvest had been poor, but the bat harvest was better than anyone
could have predicted.[10] Castel-Novel was not a luxury palace.

Later Colette admitted that maternal feelings had come to her
gradually. Her admiration for her daughter was not yet love; it was
to take an accumulation of feelings, "and the pride of disposing of a
life of which I was the humble creditor," for her to become "an
ordinary mother." Still, she never became soft in the head; her "touch
of virility" saved her from that, and saved her for writing. Her own
mother, when watching Colette sew, had once told her, "You'll never
seem like anything but a boy sewing." If her mother could have seen
her now, Colette thought, she would have said, "You'll never be
anything but a writer who gave birth."[11]

Perhaps she need not have felt guilty. The evidence is that little
Colette was raised just the way most children were in those times
and circumstances. Both parents had careers that demanded travel
and evenings out when they were not traveling. So Colette's daughter
was brought up by a nurse, until she was eight and ready for boarding school.[12] There was no religious nonsense. As Colette later explained it, Sidi did not wish his daughter to be baptized, preferring
that she choose her religion for herself when she was old enough to
do so.[13]

"My daughter is charming," Colette told Léon Hamel; she was "a
bit of a nuisance, but so bright for her age." Her age was one month
and seven days.[14]

The interruption for childbirth did not help the novel. She worked
on it through the summer; on her next-to-last day at Castel-Novel
she spent six hours at her desk, on the final day eleven hours. By the
middle of September she could announce to Hamel that she was

done. "I rejoice with relief, but I vomit that book and despise it" —
and indeed, the final pages do seem an unnecessary dragging-out of
what should have been a tight narrative.

There had been other distractions from the writing chore. Raymond Poincaré, then the president of France, had come to their
region on an official visit, and Jouvenel had served as his local host.
She had "the pleasure of hearing Jouvenel acclaimed by the crowd
as much as Poincaré," so she wrote to Hamel. She herself was involved in the festivities, putting up arches of triumph, even giving a
dinner for eighty-seven guests, all while trying to finish her book.
She returned to Paris at the beginning of autumn in time for its
publication.[15]

She need not have worried about the reviews for *The Shackle*.
Rachilde, who had perceived Colette behind *Claudine*, reassured her
readers: "Whatever she does, whatever she says, one is safe with her.
Madame Colette is a demigod."[16] Having fulfilled her authorial duties, Colette returned to Castel-Novel to rediscover her infant, "a
bronze little Sidi, bossy, with a lively little body. . . ." She confessed
to Hamel, "I walk in calmly, I find this little thing in the drawing
room — and I burst into tears!"[17]

If cabarets and touring companies were out of the question now,
she could still pursue her writing career. She contributed regularly
to *Le Matin,* her subjects the stuff of everyday life, people odd or
ordinary whom she met. And if she had abandoned the stage, she
could go before an audience all the same. On February 7, 1914, she
lectured on Molière to introduce a performance of *The School of
Wives,* revealing (according to a report in *Le Matin*) "how Molière
satisfied her intelligence and her taste, while disappointing her sensitivity." "Nuts to Molière!" was her own summing-up of the lecture
for her actress friend Marguerite Moreno. "I hate talking about
something I don't know."[18]

One skeptical witness to Colette's life as a married woman was
Natalie Barney, the American perennial in Paris, who had long since
transferred her Sapphic colony from the garden in Neuilly to another
on Rue Jacob, where she had rented a small house with a large

drawing room. Only later did she reveal her apprehensions. Colette and Jouvenel may have shared pleasures — food and bed — and they may even have shared a newspaper career, Natalie conceded. But how to keep this tall, dark man — in the prime of life, intelligent and vain both, and so pleasing to the ladies — how to keep him tied to one woman?

Natalie Barney even claimed to have been present at one of their first scenes. She was in Colette's office at *Le Matin* one day when Henry walked in. In obvious good humor, he informed his wife in an offhand and somewhat cocky way that she need not wait for him for dinner. But would he return soon after? she asked. His reply, in the opinion of the observer, was a declaration of independence. Natalie could see that Colette was hurt.[19]

For Easter 1914 the Jouvenels traveled not to the Corrèze but to Brittany, sleeping in the barn at Rozven; there was still much to do there. "But the sea is quite moved in," Colette assured Marguerite Moreno.[20] Then in May she visited Castel-Novel to confirm what she noticed each time she saw her child: she looked so much like her father. But when the infant shouted, she had Colette's lungs, and when undressed she showed that she also had her mother's behind.[21]

Perhaps Rozven was not quite livable, but Sidi was nonetheless addicted to it now. He liked the sea, liked swimming naked in it and fishing for shrimp. The actress Musidora, then twenty-five and already a star of the silent screen, was with them that summer (not overdressed herself, according to Colette's report to Hamel). On July 15 Sidi was back in Paris for his fortnightly duty at the paper, intending to join his wife in Rozven on August 1. He wrote to her, at the end of July, that peace was still possible. Paris was worried but confident.

So she could continue to enjoy Rozven and its changeable but seldom extreme climate. She exercised by working on the house, polishing floors. And she was becoming a better swimmer.[22]

It seems astonishing that the Great War could have sneaked up on them like that, so that even an editor close to the seat of power could underestimate the danger, as Henry de Jouvenel appears to have done at the end of July 1914. The belligerents had been making faces at each other for some time; even the wartime alliances were in place. In hindsight we know that the trigger had in fact been pulled on June 28, with the murder of the heir to the Austro-Hungarian throne, Archduke Francis Ferdinand, during his visit to Sarajevo. The killer was a Serbian nationalist; on July 28 Austria-Hungary went to war against Serbia. Britain and Russia, as well as France, took Serbia's side; Germany stood with Austria-Hungary. France called up its troops on the first of August, and Germany declared war on Russia the same day and on France two days after that.

Of course Sidi did not return to Rozven. Colette was stunned: "Perhaps, yes, far away, on the other side of the earth, but not here. . . . " And if the war would not come as far as Brittany, she would go out for news of it, to the urban Saint-Malo, with her house-guest Musidora. There they saw posters announcing the draft of all able-bodied men. They learned how war came to the shops, in hoarding, in a suspicion of paper money. . . .

In a sketch called "The News" she re-created the atmosphere of that instant, *the* instant, "when in the middle of the city all the uproar broke out at once: the alarm bell, the drum, the cries of the mob, children crying. . . ." In those days important news was read out on the street by a drummer. But no one listened, because everyone already knew.

The two women drove back to the calm that was calm no longer; Colette knew that her place was in Paris. They packed so as to be ready to leave the following day; it was a long night.[23]

The thirteen-month-old Colette was left in Rozven, the hope being to recruit a couple of friends — women who were alone and in need of money — to take care of her. Sidi, a reservist, had been called up; this meant there would be no income from *Le Matin* other than what Colette herself could earn. She worried that as the Germans advanced on Paris, newspapers would suspend publication.[24]

SEVENTEEN

Verdun

AT THE AGE of thirty-eight Henry de Jouvenel was all of a second lieutenant, assigned to a territorial regiment (for reservists who were no longer young and not to be sent to the front). By the end of August he was in Verdun, virtually a frontier post in that time when Alsace and Lorraine were German. And then in August 1914, when the Germans marched toward Paris and were stopped in the Marne Valley, Verdun became the eastern pivot of French strategy, withstanding repeated attacks of an army commanded by the Imperial Crown Prince himself. Verdun's resistance then and later was equivalent to victory, the only kind of victory France was to know until the final offensive of 1918.

"I'm leaving," Sidi had announced to his best friend, Anatole de Monzie. "I do intend to return. But you never know. If by chance I remain over there, please take care of my loved ones."[1]

Marguerite Moreno kept a diary in that first month of the war. She and Colette decided to pool their resources, which would be modest enough even in combination; at the very least they would take their meals together. She recorded the departure of Jouvenel, equipped for the front and "joyous." Colette pretended not to mind, "a relaxed attitude which is painful to see. . . ." On August 13, the day after Jouvenel's departure, Marguerite wrote, "Colette holds her head high. Women are behaving well just now." On August 17 Colette had a brief note from her husband — brief but tender. He was in Verdun, in good spirits, and loved his wife. "She rejoices."[2]

The petite and provocative Musidora slept on a cot at Rue Cortambert and did the shopping and cooking; Colette swept and washed. Other women joined them, including Annie de Pène, who worked at *L'Oeuvre,* the paper edited by Robert de Jouvenel. She would survive the war by only a few weeks, a victim of the Spanish influenza that killed more Europeans than the war itself. They were a commune, Colette would say; they kept each other company and cheered each other up, providing material as well as moral support.[3]

Although he was not actually attached to a fighting unit, Henry soon found himself in the thick of battle all the same, as Verdun came under attack. On one occasion an ordnance officer standing alongside him was killed by a shell; jumping away to avoid shrapnel, Henry fell into a ditch and injured a foot. Colette got the news because the mail worked and in those days soldiers could say almost anything in their letters home.

She suggested, in one of her letters to him, that his duty might lie at *Le Matin,* which for a time seemed to be in danger of closing down. He replied with "a patriotic scolding," she reported to Lèon Hamel. (Hamel, who was older than any of them, was in Brittany.) Shells fell on Paris — smallish ones, she told her correspondent, just big enough to be frightening. One of them had come down near the chalet.

In October she began to help with wounded soldiers, taking night duty at a makeshift hospital set up in a high school not far from their home — "*every* nursing chore to do," she spelled it out to Hamel. After a time male nurses took over the night watch.[4] She had fresh material for her newspaper column, which became a kind of war diary. The tone was usually inspirational: the home front was doing its duty. Two of her columns were combined to form a moving sketch called "A Zouave," an ode to patriotism and to her father.

Verdun, we have seen, was in the front line; Colette should not have gone there, but she did, as did many soldiers' women. She got to Châlons-sur-Marne easily enough, going on from there in a blacked-out train. Once in Verdun she lived as a stowaway, and she was there when a French offensive was launched just before Christmas in that first year of war. The cannons fired continuously; her windows rattled, and the door trembled. At nightfall she climbed to the citadel to watch the shells bursting. She wished she could return in daylight, with field glasses, but *that* was forbidden; she would quickly be expelled. "At night," she told Hamel, "Sidi returns to his harem." She knew that behind other closed blinds there were other cloistered women waiting for their men. No one was supposed to know they were there, and their men left them to report to duty each dawn "with an air of indifference."[5]

Stowaway she might be, but she was to publish stories from this battlefield, and publish them immediately, in one of the country's biggest newspapers. The account of her personal experience, describing her presence in Verdun under a false name and with borrowed papers, would wait for book publication in *Les Heures longues* (The Long Hours).

In early February 1915 she was still in Verdun, recounting (to Hamel) an air combat witnessed from beneath a bridge. Shell fragments fell within ten feet of where she was standing, and she knew that if she received the slightest scratch she would be confined to quarters or sent back to Paris. She walked home past bomb craters. "Sidi is well, extremely well, and so happy when I'm here that I wouldn't have the heart to leave," she said. So she would journey to Paris and then come back again — to the countryside, as she would say prudently. She was a prisoner, spoiled, overfed, overwhelmed by comforts and by aerial bombs, she wrote gaily to Georges Wague: "Twenty-three of them six days ago, thirty-one yesterday." Bombs, she meant.[6]

A letter has come down to us from Sidi, written to Colette during one of the periods when she was not in the "harem." He was then riding horseback, practicing swordsmanship. He did it to keep healthy, he explained. There were times when it was better to be deaf to the rest of the world, because it was the only way to make life supportable. "This parade of sobbing wives and mothers, these fathers who come to plead for the bodies of their sons, which we can't give them, these refugees who write letters begging to be allowed, even under cannon fire, to return to their villages, and whom I'm not allowed to help — all this creates a frightful atmosphere." Did Colette still love him? he wished to know. There was that, happily, and the daughter they called Bel-Gazou.[7]

The child was now snug in Castel-Novel, with an English nurse who had been recruited soon after her birth. Later Colette paid tribute to this severe woman — "a sour-faced stranger, a scolder, rough with everyone and with herself" — who served as her daughter's guardian and also as cook, gardener, and doctor in that remote and uncomfortable castle in the Corrèze, refusing all wages for the duration of the war.[8]

As for Colette, she won a more restful, recreational journey. Italy had at last joined the war, on the side of France, and Colette was assigned to cover that nation from a human-interest angle. She would write not of war but of the people's determination to *win* the war.[9] She traveled, as she had a right to, as the Baroness de Jouvenel. But another Baroness de Jouvenel had preceded her to Rome; Henry's first wife, Claire Boas, was a notable figure in her own right, active in social and political causes. Just then she was facilitating contacts that would lead to the creation of an independent Czechoslovakia, with an army of its own that would be prepared to join the Allies in 1917.

So in Rome, where the Baroness Claire had made a conspicuous entry only a short while earlier, the Baroness Colette was treated with suspicion — even as an adventuress — when she presented herself at the reception desk of the elegant Hotel Excelsior on the Via Veneto. When the Excelsior would not give her a room, she found shelter just across the street, at the Hotel Regina, but the incident made her wonder whether she had been too indulgent in allowing the first Madame de Jouvenel to continue to flaunt the title that now belonged to *her*.

One good thing did come out of the contretemps, however. At the Hotel Regina she had an exceptional neighbor in the soldier-poet Gabriele D'Annunzio, a larger-than-life personality ten years her senior who was to end the war with his own army of volunteers, seizing the contested port of Fiume from Yugoslavia in 1919.

He was also a famous seducer, though Colette later volunteered the information that he had not touched her. When one explained that one was a visiting journalist of whom nothing could be expected, said she, D'Annunzio became a "delicious companion."[10] So they talked about other things, such as her father's heroism in Italy.[11] According to D'Annunzio, she took her daughter's photograph out of her handbag four times, each time saying, "You don't know my lovely baby?" Despite this sentimentality, and despite her adoration of a cruel husband (D'Annunzio is talking here), Colette had genuine talent.[12]

He was certainly right about her love for Sidi. We can believe that she talked about him, just as she thought about him, during her Italian stay. As she walked through an overgrown churchyard one day in the summer heat, the "voluptuous" setting led her to dream of her husband and lover: "One wish, in touching the hot stone: to return here, to this very spot, with him."[13]

As edited for publication, her Italian diary (in which this thought appears) consisted of inspirational pieces suitable for a newspaper that was to see its circulation rise, with the hunger for war news, to one and a half million copies by 1917. Meanwhile Colette was also collecting her short pieces on household pets for a little book called *Creatures Great and Small,* maintaining, in an ingenuous preface, "At a time when men are tearing other men apart, it seems that a singular pity inclines them toward their pets. . . . Innocent animals alone have the right to ignore the war." At times in this volume men and animals are thrown together, and there is a suggestion of the animal's moral, if not physical, superiority.

In September 1916 she got what she had dreamed of: a second honeymoon with Sidi, and in Italy. They chose Cernobbio, on Lake Como. "Ah! Hamel, how happy we are in this place!" her first postcard began. "Sidi, the lake, the red sage, the morning glory, the water stairways, the ripe figs. . . ."[14] She found the material for another patriotic piece right there in the lobby of the Grand Hotel Villa d'Este: a fashion show from Paris. She even managed to redeem the idle rich who composed the audience: "You have to look at them more carefully to recognize the deep thought, the only thought, that of all women in war: waiting. But neither laughter nor elegance and music are banished from this place; telegrams and newspapers bring news of success in battle. . . ."[15]

The real adventure would come in Paris: the inevitable departure from the Swiss chalet, their love nest — but one that had not been built to endure. One day she had the feeling that it was raining in the bathroom, and indeed it was; a side of the house had collapsed into the garden. The landlord found it easier to let his tenants go than to pay for repairs. She found a little house in Auteuil facing some disarmed fortifications, with a forest of vegetation covering the moat; the Bois de Boulogne was close by. This house too seemed fragile, and it took three years to make it a pleasant dwelling place.[16]

This was Boulevard Suchet number 69, which was to remain Colette's home long after it had ceased to be Henry's.

Italy again: at the beginning of January 1917 the Jouvenels were together once more, each with a job. He was assigned to a conference at which the powers allied against Germany were to agree upon their war aims, prior to the entry of the United States into combat in April. It was a secret meeting; when the French premier, Aristide Briand, and Britain's prime minister, David Lloyd George, turned up in Rome, *Le Matin*'s correspondent told readers that it would be unpatriotic to say why they were there.[17]

Of course *Colette* could write what she wanted to, wherever she happened to be. Just then she entered a world that was new to her: the cinema. Motion pictures were simple and silent then, but they did require scenarios, and who better to write a screen treatment of *The Vagabond* than its author? The star would be her sexually provocative comrade Musidora — they called her The Vamp then —

with "her courageous spirit, gorgeous eyes, perfect long legs, her striking black-and-white beauty. . . ." Colette remarked with amusement that Italian directors found the dark girl *troppo italiana*; they would have preferred a blonde. The stint gave Colette four winter months in Rome, more than Sidi got.

For her, Rome had an extravagant beauty, though she soon tired of living in a country and not knowing its language. Despite food shortages, she found a small restaurant, the Basilica Ulpia, facing Trajan's Forum, where spaghetti was generously served and so were fried artichokes. What was more, she had left a gray and rainy Paris to find sun in Rome on Christmas Eve day.[18] She could tell Hamel that her life in Rome was not all that different from her life on Boulevard Suchet; instead of walking her dog in the Bois, here she had the Borghese Gardens. Sidi would join Colette and the dog for lunch when he could spare the time.[19]

Afternoons she found refuge atop the Palatine; there was not another soul there on weekdays. She plucked spring flowers. All of these things were reported to Hamel; she also asked him to visit her in Castel-Novel that summer. He was quite ill, and would die in a month's time; this is the last known letter that Colette wrote to him.[20]

A byproduct of making movies was writing about making movies. She was soon contributing to three different magazines, two of them specialized (*Le Film* and *Filma*). This was not quite the birth of the cinema, but rather its early adolescence. She was to concern herself with the medium for only a short time, writing about audiences as well as what they saw on the screen — but that was always Colette's way.

She also set down her observations on the making of the film version of *The Vagabond*. The sun is blasting away outdoors, but she is indoors, in a stifling studio, under skylights. At lunchtime the smells and sounds of cooking emanate from the porter's cottage, but they must go on working while the sun is high, as Musidora roasts under the glass roof. On the previous day the star changed clothes eleven times; tomorrow she would be up at dawn for snow scenes

in the nearby hills. Colette offers a close-up of how silent movies
were made, stepping out of her role as observer at least once to advise
an actor on how he should play a music-hall singer. The film opened
in Paris in March 1918.[21]

In July 1917 Sidi came home again, again a temporary civilian, having been appointed assistant to his friend Anatole de Monzie, who,
lame and exempt from service, was now undersecretary of the merchant marine. Of course the couple found time to go to Castel-Novel.
"The weather is good and I have Bel-Gazou's hand in mine," she
wrote in a piece for publication. Her daughter was now four, and a
true "fruit of the earth," having spent four summers and three win-
ters in that province — which meant that she behaved like a farmer's
daughter, and had the accent.[22]

Her daughter was to remember that her mother's arrival brought
"tenderness and warmth." Once, when she fell down and cut her
forehead and nose, her mother slapped her, scolding, "Just let me
catch you again spoiling what I created!" Both mother and father
were severe educators. On another occasion Colette stood by as her
daughter picked up a dog's bone and got bitten, wanting her to learn
the hard way.[23]

Renaud, Henry's son with the Panther, was just ten years old in
1917. He remembered the old pink-stone castle in his own way. His
stepmother had a large bedroom on the highest floor, with a huge
bed — made to order, he thought. The walls of her room were covered in a pink cretonne. His father had a smaller room whose walls
illustrated La Fontaine's fables. The gas lamps projected "disquieting
shadows in the corridors" and gave the rooms "mysterious corners."
Aunt Colette would call the children to meals the same way one
called dogs; indeed, it was Renaud's recollection that the animals got
priority. He remembered that once, when Bel-Gazou was stung by
a wasp, Aunt Colette blamed her for having excited the insect.[24]

EIGHTEEN

Mitsou

IN PARIS in August 1917, Colette sat down to her first work of fiction in a long while, one of her first wholly invented books, which is to say that it was not based on her own life. *Mitsou* is a sentimental tale designed to soften the hearts of *La Vie Parisienne's* readers. That its author did not take it terribly seriously is suggested by her decision not to sign her name to it. She wrote this little book during a period of depression, and before she got over it she lost the manuscript on the subway; she did not even have an extra copy. So she went home and hid under a blanket on a torrid summer day. Sidi found her there, shivering, a hot-water bottle at her feet. The next day she was up and ready to begin writing the book all over again.

When she was finished, in September, she left for the Corrèze "to rejoin my superb daughter" — not without apprehension, for there was a cabinet crisis, and if the government fell, Sidi might be called back to the army.[1]

Why would they send a gifted organizer back to service in the territorials, doing what was essentially a clerk's job? Because, a political comrade later revealed, the man in charge of manpower, who had "the narrowest mind in Parliament," insisted on it. For his part, Sidi did not want to make a fuss.

When the minister of maritime transportation, his friend Henry Lémery, accompanied him to receive his assignment, Jouvenel made a request (or so Lémery chose to remember): "If I am killed, you won't have a lot to say about me. Talk about my love life. I'll give you the title: 'From The Wandering Jew to The Vagabond.' " [2]

Mitsou appeared in five issues of *La Vie Parisienne* in November and December 1917. In this magazine version, the affair between a light-headed variety performer and a young officer begins in the tawdry atmosphere of a music hall. Later the lovers exchange letters, and in these letters the frivolous Mitsou becomes a woman, and flirtation becomes love. In the longer version, published as a book in 1919 — this time signed by Colette — the transformation of flirters into lovers is even more central to the story.

Les Heures longues (The Long Hours), published at the end of 1917, was denigrated by Colette herself as a collection of "poor journalistic things." [3] Nonetheless, the sensitive Marcel Proust felt that he had to respond when she sent him a copy (as she did to so many authors, following the custom). He was then composing his multi-volume masterpiece, *Remembrance of Things Past,* and was writing and reading both with failing eyes. "And despite that I read your book, almost the whole thing, in a single sitting," he told her. This sedentary man had never been to Rome, "but your Rome is not less marvelous for that." One of her descriptions had made him think of the elegant seventeenth-century prose of Bossuet. [4] If Colette really doubted the value of her work, or the durability of her journalism, this tribute should have made her feel better.

Musidora asked Colette to write another movie for her, this time an original. By now the Vamp had made fifty-four films, both dramas and comedies, all in a period of 104 weeks. (Her nickname was apparently derived from *Les Vampires,* a film series in which she played a bewitching bandit.) So Colette wrote *The Hidden Flame,* in which Musidora is a student who marries a wealthy schoolmate instead of the poor boy whom she really loves. Wishing to return to her true love, she ruins her husband, hoping to drive him to suicide. Instead, she is the one who dies, in an explosion.[5]

The war continued. In January 1918 the western allies were held to a defensive strategy while the Germans launched a series of attacks in an attempt to obtain a decisive victory before the Americans were ready. From the middle of March to the middle of July, the order was to contain the enemy onslaught.

Having been promoted to full lieutenant, Jouvenel was in the thick of it in northeastern Picardy. "My love," Colette wrote to him, "you don't receive my letters either. We are poor beasts. . . . I'm keeping up the morale of my creatures at home; they are quite helpful. But nothing can prevent us from long preposterous discussions of the fate of our armies and of Paris, in the kitchen, and we all know that you can't work while talking about the war." That was early in April; before the end of May, the enemy would get as far as Château-Thierry, less than sixty miles from Paris.

There were painful nights in June. Now, as Colette told Wague, Sidi was at the most "feverish" point of the front. She feared he had been killed or taken prisoner; she learned that he had been brave. Proudly, he sent her the citation (because, he said as an excuse, the daughter of a soldier cared about such things). Of Jouvenel, Henry, lieutenant in the 10th company of the 29th Regiment of Territorial Infantry, it noted:

> Courageous officer, devoted and remarkably cool, distinguished himself particularly on 11 June 1918 in going out alone, under fire, to meet an enemy patrol expected to surrender, an example to all of total unconcern for danger.

"Well, my love, I'm rather pleased to be copying this for you," he added — pleased not only for her sake, but also about showing up someone who had called him a coward. On hearing that insult he had said to Colette, "I've got to have a citation." He reminded her that on his next leave he would have two extra days; let that be a warning to her![6]

To Francis Carco, a fellow writer who could understand, she confessed in July that she was not working. By that time Sidi had come home and then left again for the front; his departure had the expected effect (she called it "inevitable cowardice" on her part). Early in August he was home again, complaining that the territorials were being withdrawn from combat to perform less noble tasks (surely because of the arrival of fresh troops from the United States).[7]

In October — with Jouvenel on leave again — they traveled down to Castel-Novel. Colette described it as his "farm leave," and we can guess that Sidi had been authorized to supervise his harvest. Perhaps it was now that Colette took her daughter to Paris, for in a sketch she says that baby Colette was five when she snatched her from her English nurse for an orgy of circus-going and movies. The child seemed restless throughout the trip; Colette discovered why on their return to Castel-Novel. For there the little Colette burst into tears, crying, "Nursie-Dear . . . Oh, Nursie-Dear . . . Nursie. . . ." In this way did she learn that a child, like a lover, could weep for joy.[8]

It was now also that the pandemic Spanish flu set its sights on Colette's beloved comrade Annie de Pène, who had shared her war-widowhood. A diary exists in which Colette inscribed, for each day of the week, "Go to see Annie." On the page for Thursday she added, "and that, until the end of my days, is the grace I wish for myself." She was in Castel-Novel when the bad news came, and she did not look forward to returning to a Paris where she would not see her friend again. Later she found some solace in Annie's daughter, Germaine Beaumont.

The armistice put Henry de Jouvenel back in the driver's seat at *Le Matin*. Now there would be a renewed battle for circulation, as each of the Big Five papers recomposed its team of star reporters and famous bylines. Colette's charter was henceforth to extend to drama criticism, reviews that were short and crisp, appropriate to the newspaper for which she was laboring.[9]

When *Mitsou* was published as a book it was accompanied — to fatten the volume — by her play *En Camarades*. Of the latter one reviewer noted, with unusual frankness, that it was "an unsuccessful work, weak and insignificant";[10] but sooner or later Colette published nearly everything she wrote.

She was to say, later on, that *Mitsou* was an operetta, the Great War dressed up for the stage. She did have to eat![11] Again Marcel Proust was there to set her right. "I wept a little this evening," he wrote, "for the first time in a long while, and yet for some time I have been overwhelmed by grief, suffering, and miseries." He had wept because of the letter that Mitsou sent to her fair lieutenant. These letters at the conclusion of the novella — the lieutenant's to Mitsou, announcing his departure for the front, and hers to him, ingenuous and sincere, promising that she will wait for him — were, for Proust, the "masterpiece" of the book. He preferred a scene of hers, in a restaurant, to those he himself was writing about his character Swann (he was now publishing *Within a Budding Grove*).[12]

She moved so easily between her milieus, between *La Vie Parisienne* and Proust, between her backstage comrades and the dignitaries that a Baroness de Jouvenel received. Certainly her talent commanded respect now. The director of the Paris Opera asked her to do a libretto for a ballet; the music was to be written by a composer whom she had met in her days with Willy, Maurice Ravel, who in 1919 was at the height of his reputation. In fact, as we shall see, Ravel took his time in completing the score. *L'Enfant et les Sortilèges* would not go before the public until 1925.

NINETEEN

Chéri

IN THE FIRST full year of peace, Colette was sufficiently at peace with herself to contemplate a more ambitious work, a story that, like *Mitsou,* was more than a simple transposition of her own experience. In *Chéri* she gave the world two types: the older woman at the close of her love life and the young man at the beginning of his. Neither of her protagonists was a role model, and neither was a horror.

A story called "Chéri" had appeared in *Le Matin* as early as January 25, 1912. It opened, as the novel would, with the nonchalant young Chéri playing with the pearls of his aging mistress, Léa, while announcing that he is going to marry. This little story was the novel in a nutshell. When Colette wrote it she was thirty-eight, not much older than the men in her life then; whether or not she herself was the model for Léa, *Chéri,* fiction when it was written, anticipated the fears she might have felt later.

Dialogue carries the novel; in fact, it was first conceived as a play. She did much of the writing in Rozven in the summer of 1919. In a letter to her colleague Francis Carco from her "incomparable" Breton retreat, she proclaims herself ecstatic about the beach and the swimming (her own). Then she adds, "Imagine that my play is going to be a novel. . . ." Germaine Beaumont, Annie de Pène's daughter, was with her, and so was a resuscitated Meg Villars. Willy's wife, now thirty-four years old, was in the process of getting a divorce; she was once again Colette's friend and possibly her rival, as any woman who spent much time near Jouvenel was likely to be. Meg was now working as a correspondent for the London magazine *The Tatler*.[1]

Colette kept on writing in Castel-Novel in the fall. "I've been working quite hard on *Chéri* since yesterday," she reported to Hélène Picard, a divorcée of Colette's age who was a poet and now her assistant at *Le Matin*. "It has to be not only finished, but polished." Then, in the last hours before packing, she could exclaim, "Imagine, *Chéri* is finished! And Sidi listened to me read it and liked it! I can't get over having finished it. You'll see my hands and arms, for I celebrated my freedom by attacking rosebushes and nettles!"[2]

The new novel began to appear in installments in *La Vie Parisienne* in January 1920 and then went from magazine to book with scarcely discernible changes. In a sense it was Colette's first original work. "The others," she explained to Proust, "were rewrites — that is to say, the 'vagabonds' and 'shackles' always resembled vague claudines."[3] There is a brutal realism in this novel, a loss of illusion in these women who were made for love but are now in the twilight of their lives, passing the time remaining to them with other redundant women. Chéri, whose real name is Fred Peloux, ponders Léa's wrinkles. She finds him ugly when he laughs. She is fifty, twenty-four years older than he; their liaison has been going on for half a dozen years. Léa thinks that her breasts will hold up until he marries someone else.

When they first met, Chéri proved disappointing as a lover. She got him to gain weight and improve his physical condition. Now, when he informs her of his plan to marry a proper young lady, she is upset. For his part, he says that although he realizes he was not her first lover, he should have liked to be her last.

He marries and leaves on his honeymoon; Léa also travels. They miss each other. When the newlyweds quarrel, Chéri walks out and returns to Léa. She is pleased that he is back and begins to make plans with him, but in the end she sends him home to his young wife.

We can catch glimpses of Colette at this pivotal moment in her life, the publication of the book that was to establish her as an author. She continued to be a good hostess at the Jouvenel home on Boulevard Suchet, serving her guests by candlelight. But now and then she might take an evening off to wander with Francis Carco (so Carco testified) through neighborhoods of bad repute, meeting characters of equally bad repute, in a quest for new sensations. They might end up at a bistro in the central markets at three in the morning.[4]

Such things may well have upset her husband. We know that in January 1920 Colette appealed to Philippe Berthelot, who had first met her when she was a young writer and he a young foreign-service officer (he was to end his career as the most important man at the Quai d'Orsay). She asked for his help in handling Sidi, who had come upon a letter written to her by a senator, expressing regret that he could not join her at an "intimate luncheon." This sounded suspicious to Henry de Jouvenel, sufficiently so to raise questions in his mind not only about their present life together but about their past. Sidi, said Colette, had gone so far as to compare a portrait of the senator with one of their daughter, in an attempt to detect a resemblance. . . .[5] We can take Colette's request at face value, or read false naïveté, even a touch of hypocrisy, into it. Or we can assume that Colette had not been unfaithful to Henry before this time, whatever he may have been doing.

Liane de Pougy, a demimondaine who had become increasingly mondaine over the years, recounted an exchange of gossip between herself and the writer Rachilde (this in a diary entry for February 1920): "We have . . . the same opinion of Colette Willy," she wrote, "of her insincerity, her affected airs, but also of her talent — and her infernal spitefulness."[6]

"It's whispered that she isn't very happy, is cheated on, rejected, badly treated," Liane noted in another entry. "Perhaps she still loves Willy, who was her first victim and whose sad fate exacerbates her resentment. . . . Poor, poor Colette . . . bloated with fat, blown up with malice, envy, ambition. They say she's after the red ribbon."[7] On that point the diarist was not wrong: Colette did want to be appointed to the Legion of Honor.

But Colette also had her worshipers, one of them the starry-eyed Claude Chauvière, an aspiring author who served her heroine as secretary, companion, and early biographer. She did see and record much; among other things, she described the house on Boulevard Suchet, which Colette had rescued (said she) from the previous tenant's bad taste. Thanks to the trees on neighboring properties, the garden resembled a park, and branches touched the windows of the living room. By preference Colette received in her upstairs boudoir, facing the Bois; she worked at a small, cluttered desk. She would often lose her pen, her glasses, her watch (her father's gold watch); she would lose her money as well. Pauline, a teenage housemaid from the Corrèze who would attend Colette to her death and beyond, would find all the lost things eventually. Claude Chauvière was there to take dictation, after which she might accompany Colette on urgent errands. Colette usually lost the notes she had made to remind herself what the errands were, so she would have to improvise.

The world lined up to meet Colette, in boudoir or in living room; visitors would come from as far away as the United States and Japan. Some were autograph hounds, others impresarios, fellow authors, painters, musicians — odd ducks and perfectly normal people. There were famous actors who had roles in her plays, political leaders, fashion designers, and "a couple of frightfully tender and wrinkled women. . . ." Chauvière might find Colette at the piano, and she guessed that she was playing music she had composed herself. Colette told her that she could have become a musician, even a painter; her secretary saw pastels and watercolors by her, and even a penciled self-portrait.[8]

Mornings, she would ride to *Le Matin* with Sidi in his chauffeured

Citroën coupé, returning with him in the evening. During the day she would have her own appointments, some of them at home. When he was in charge of the paper, Jouvenel would return to his office after dinner, staying until the next day's edition was sent to press, at two in the morning. In the meantime, Colette might go to the theater, after which the chauffeur would pick her up and then collect Jouvenel.[9]

In April 1920, with the help of a lawyer, Colette drew up a complaint against Henry's first wife. Although they had divorced in 1909 and Henry had married Colette in 1912, the first Madame de Jouvenel continued to use his name. The confusion was such that Colette received bills for hats purchased by the first Madame de Jouvenel, newspaper reporters were sent to the wrong address, and mutual friends got mixed up when they made appointments. And when Claire Boas invited friends to her home, they would often turn up at the house of Henry and Colette, which obliged the latter two to play host at a perpetual feast. Of course the complaint also includes an account of the embarrassment suffered by Colette when she tried to check in at the Hotel Excelsior in Rome.[10] The affair may or may not have reached the courtroom; all we know for sure is that it did no good. The first baroness would use the title all her life long.

Over Easter Colette was in Castel-Novel, annoyed that Sidi had spent only a single night with her before rushing off to a conference. "If he doesn't return immediately after the meeting I'm getting the hell out of here and back to Paris," she told a friend.[11]

"Besides my daughter, who is bursting out of her skin, who is florid, proud, goes out by herself, goes to school, comes back, goes out again . . . there is a family here that you'd love," she reported to Marguerite Moreno. Even Claire Boas — she who was still calling herself Baroness — was supposed to be there, for complaint or no, she and Colette had become fast friends within instants after they met. Claire did not come, in the end, but she sent them Bertrand, the son she had had with Henry de Jouvenel.[12]

As Bertrand was to remember it, he met Colette for the first time at Boulevard Suchet, where he had gone on a mission for his mother. If the young man trembled — he was sixteen and a half at the time — it was not because of Colette's status as a celebrity but simply because he feared this woman who had been described to him as formidable. He had to explain that his mother wished to continue to call herself Jouvenel. She was utilizing the name in a good cause, to work for an independent Czechoslovakia. Colette, as we know, objected violently to the idea. Claire was hurt; after all, she had facilitated Henry's divorce so that he could marry Colette before their child was born.

Bertrand was "a studious and bookish adolescent," by his own account. He had enrolled in a Versailles high school in September 1918, less than two years before he was to graduate. That and the final year, in which he was now engaged, were almost the only ones this privileged young man had ever spent in a classroom, the rest of his education having been conducted by private tutors. He lived near school and spent his time off in Paris, at his mother's apartment. Madame Boas de Jouvenel ran a proper salon, bringing together the greats of the time, but Bertrand did not appreciate the private dancing evenings that his mother insisted he attend.

But now he was visiting Colette, sometime during the spring of 1920, with a bouquet of flowers gripped in his fist. He waited in a dark corner of the living room, so that when Colette barged in, she cried out, "But where *is* that child!"

He remembered her then as being "smallish, stocky, rapid, and powerful." When she raised her head to size him up — for he was somewhat taller than she — he remarked the "majesty" of her forehead and her nose. What struck him most, however, was her energy. It did not put him off. He was a docile youngster; from that time on, he decided, he would place himself under Colette's wing.[13]

Portrait photographs of Bertrand at this time show a strong-featured young man with wavy blond hair, looking no older than he was.

Of course Bertrand was not Chéri. Colette's novel was already written when they met, and most of it had been published in *La Vie Parisienne*. For the first time, with this book, she had written something concerning which she had no doubts, of which she need not feel ashamed. Women saw themselves in Léa, and readers were always thinking they had discovered the living model for Chéri.[14]

She was now being recognized by the makers of modern literature, such as André Gide. "I shall wager that you didn't expect to receive praise from me," he wrote to her. But he wanted her to know that he had devoured her novel in a single breath. What a subject, done "with such intelligence, such mastery, such an understanding of the most deeply kept secrets of the flesh!" He praised the keen descriptions, the natural dialogue, the spareness, the "nudity" of the text, wondering why it had not yet been compared to Benjamin Constant's *Adolphe* (an earlier century's incisive portrait of a young man and an older woman). Gide's reaction was all the more valuable to Colette, and all the more convincing, because he was not a friend or a friend of a friend, not beholden to her, not expecting her to review one of *his* books favorably.

Conservatives did not share Gide's views on *Chéri*. In the humorless *Journal des Débats,* Jean de Pierrefeu complained that Colette's "art of the senses" led to "the definitive impoverishment of the human person, reduced to the rank of animal." The author's genius was not in question, nor her gift for language; it was just regrettable that she used them to write about vulgar things. Colette asked this reviewer why he and others like him were so anxious to save her — was it beneath her dignity, or theirs, to care about helpless souls such as Léa and Chéri?[15]

A critic in charge of "Feminine Literature" managed to praise the novel while condemning its author. Apart from *Chéri* and *Mitsou,* said Henriette Charasson, Colette had never written about anything other than herself. "Besides, she has often spoiled her lucid analytical talent by writing to please, chewing over her memories, flirting with her reader; she whips up — with no concern for bitter psychological truths — a mixture of false modesty, crafty sensuality, and sentimentality, whose charm is immediate but which . . . doesn't endure."[16]

Did Henry de Jouvenel really like the book? Later, when there was no longer a Sidi, Colette would remember that "one of my husbands" had asked her, "But can't you write a book that isn't about love, adultery, half-incestuous combinations, or breaking up? Is there nothing else in life?" If he had not been in such a hurry to rush off, she said, "for he was handsome and charming, to some romantic rendezvous, he would perhaps have taught me how to deal with love in fiction and out of fiction. . . ."[17]

TWENTY

Bertrand

ROZVEN, the old house guarding its cove, was Colette's personal domain. At times it appeared to be a matriarchy, for she shared her reign with woman friends, either writers or would-be writers. Germaine Beaumont remembered collective dining in the large room facing the sea, and the rocky trail that they called "the end of the world." For distraction they would explore the antiques shops of the region or wander among the streets and stores within the ramparts of Saint-Malo.[1]

Then the women were joined by children. The younger Jouvenels had Castel-Novel, of course, but now they could have seaside vacations as well. A photograph survives of a Rozven summer: alongside Germaine Beaumont and Hélène Picard and Francis Carco's wife, Germaine, there are Colette, her daughter, and her stepson Bertrand. It may have been taken in 1920.

Bertrand de Jouvenel's sentimental education, as he himself was to refer to it, began that summer in Rozven. He went there with his father; Sidi had insisted that his ex-wife, Bertrand's mother, allow the boy to go to Brittany when he was there. But almost at once, Sidi left to return to Paris, and suddenly Bertrand found himself all alone with a group of women much older than he. Never having liked the company of strangers, he was intimidated. And he had another reason to be unhappy: he had done badly on his school exams.[2] As Colette explained it to Marguerite Moreno, she was providing hospitality to the young Jouvenel, "whose mother had turned him over to me, for his hygiene and his misfortune. I rub him down, stuff him, scrub him with sand, and burn him in the sun."[3]

He remembered learning to swim, or beginning to learn. But his stepmother also got him to read books he would not otherwise have read, books by Marcel Schwob, Marcel Proust. She gave him a copy of *Chéri* and called him *chéri* (darling) in the inscription. Recalling this a long time after the fact, he was prompted to think that it was, in a way, a premonition of a legend that it would be hard for him to live down — the legend that *he* had been the model for Chéri. At the time, he felt himself the very opposite of Fred Peloux.

When he arrived in Rozven, only Germaine Beaumont and Hélène Picard were with Colette. Colette asked him which of the two young women he found more attractive. (They were not all that young; Germaine was thirty, and Hélène exactly Colette's age, forty-seven.) He stammered out an answer, not quite understanding what Colette was getting at. She insisted, saying, "You must become a man." She would help him do that.

One thing was certain from the start: she taught him that there was a world beyond the printed page. She got him involved with nature, even with the food he ate, and made him aware of colors and other sensations. He followed her around Saint-Malo chasing antiques and went fishing with her for shrimp along the coast. Colette perceived the change in him and was amused by it; he was now her "adopted son." But the same change alarmed his mother, who warned Sidi that Bertrand was being corrupted. In Paris that autumn he was not to be allowed to see Colette often, except on Sundays, when he would join her for lunch with his father.[4]

"A thousand things to tell you!" Colette announced to her perennial confidante Marguerite Moreno.[5] We can guess at a few of these, for in addition to the Jouvenels young and old and the Carcos, Germaine, and Hélène, a new guest had turned up, in the person of Meg

Villars. She was very much part of the family circle now. Colette may have been gracious toward her, but she let off steam with Sidi: "Won't I have a few days with you (your sons don't bother me) without Mamita [his mother] and without Meg? Think about it. I'd be so happy! This is the second time that we've brought Meg back and forth with us to Castel-Novel, and twice here. That rejuvenates me *too* much."[6]

The writer Pierre Benoit advised her confidentially that she would soon be hearing something she had been waiting to hear. And he congratulated her.[7] She was going to be decorated with that symbol which every Frenchman with ambition longs for, and which those close to power obtain with relative facility. The Legion of Honor is given for outstanding achievement, both to soldiers in uniform and to civilians. It was the intention of the founder of the order, Napoleon Bonaparte, that its holders should form a national elite. Colette's third husband was to say that if Colette actively solicited such awards, it was because she was her military father's daughter.

She received more than four hundred congratulatory letters (Henry's son Renaud counted them). She did not find that an unmixed blessing, however, for she planned to reply to every one of them.[8]

Chéri and the ribbon: fame had arrived. The novel had gone through sixty-two printings by September 1920 (although, as she hastened to point out, that represented only 31,000 copies).[9] Theatrical producers hoped to stage it as a play. She was courted by young writers and by editors who wanted her byline in their newspapers or magazines; she began to appear in histories of literature. Her name rose to the top in popularity polls. In 1921 she was a close runner-up to the romantic poet and novelist Anna de Noailles in a contest to determine the "Queen of Letters," and again in 1923 in one for the "Princess of Letters."[10]

She was also somewhat concerned about her appearance now. She was a bit portly for the dashing Sidi, but there seemed to be little she could do about that, or little she wished to do.[11] She may have had a face-lift in January 1921; that was the rumor, at least, when she failed to attend a dinner party.[12] (We do know that she went to

Nice with the Carcos for what she described as a period of convalescence after an attack of bronchial emphysema.)[13]

Sidi also accepted fame, though perhaps with more reticence. In
January he finally took the leap, put forth his name, and was elected
senator of his district.

French senators, then and now, are chosen not by popular vote
but by the endorsement of elected local officials. It appears that Jouvenel could have won election to the lower house as early as 1914
had he been willing to confront the electorate; he had a second
chance in 1919 and again shied away. It may have been simple non-
conformism that stopped him, or he may have worried that his life-
style — his life with Colette — would become an issue for debate.[14]
"Let me remark," he declared to an interviewer later in that decade,
"that it was characteristic of people of my generation to lack ambition."[15]

In springtime 1921 Colette was in Castel-Novel, where "everything
is magnificent," as she informed Marguerite Moreno. "My daughter
is a kind of elegant Cupid, robust and toothless. . . ."[16] She had
gone to the Corrèze with a mission: to write a draft of the stage
adaptation of *Chéri*. This time she had a collaborator. Fifteen years
her junior, Léopold Marchand was at the beginning of what would
be a fruitful career as a playwright. Along the way he was also to
become the special sort of friend to Colette that Léon Hamel had
been a decade earlier, a masculine confidant who would never be
her lover. In Colette's letters, he was "My child Léo," and she was
no less taken by his adorable companion, Misz Hertz, later to be
Misz Marchand.

Early in May she was able to report to her "child Léo" that her
draft was done. She read the third act to Sidi, who claimed to be
moved by it. Indeed, she had rewritten the end of that act three
times, "grumbling, swearing, and blaspheming all the while."[17]

Whenever she wrote to friends from Castel-Novel, she could not help
mentioning her daughter, now a peasant girl who spoke the local

dialect, led the cows home, and talked of marrying a farmer. These letters tell us something about Colette, too, of course — something that needs to be remembered.[18] Legend has it that Colette de Jouvenel grew up with an adoring father but was cast aside by her mother. In fact her country childhood, with a governess, was the expected choice for parents who lived as the Jouvenels did. Later, when the growing girl was brought to Paris, she was put out to pasture once again, in boarding schools as far away as Versailles. But Bertrand de Jouvenel, the apple of his mother's eye, was also sent to school in Versailles.

Colette's daughter told an interviewer — this when she herself was sixty — that her mother had been like a cat who after a time tells her little one to manage for itself.[19] Certainly the Corrèze was very far away, and the governess efficient but not tender. The younger Colette portrayed herself as having been shy and overwhelmed by her mother's personality; it was her contention that Colette was afraid of becoming "involved."[20]

Much later, Bertrand de Jouvenel would remember the summer of 1921 in Rozven as the time when he and his stepmother were "joined."[21]

At the outset he felt somewhat estranged from Colette; her young friend Léopold Marchand seemed to him more fun as a vacation companion. Nonetheless, Bertrand shared things with Colette: a sensitivity toward nature, of course, but also writing. He was soon composing his own stories, though when she wanted to submit one of them to *Le Matin* he worried that his mother might find out about it. Eventually he took a pen name, and Colette was able to publish several contributions by him in her story column.[22]

"Bertrand is quite fine this year," Colette reported to Marguerite Moreno. He swam like an eel, and Renaud also swam, while little Colette sank right to the bottom.[23]

There was time, in Rozven, to catch up on obligations. She wrote to Marcel Proust, who had sent her his latest work, the second part of *The Guermantes Way,* with *Sodom and Gomorrah.* She explained why she had been so tardy in acknowledging his gift: she had been doing assignments for *Le Matin,* accompanying her husband to political banquets in his home province, and selecting stories to publish in her column. She would have liked to be able to tell Proust that she had finished his book, but she had not; she continued to dig into it each night in bed, she said, so that Sidi had to rescue the volume and her reading glasses from under her. She was dazzled, all the same, by what she had read of *Sodom and Gomorrah;* no one had ever written that way before about "Inverts" (she capitalized the *I*).[24]

TWENTY-ONE

My Mother's House

LATE IN AUGUST Colette was in Paris. In a way it was a stopover before the continuation of the summer holidays in Castel-Novel. Maurice Martin du Gard was hoping to convince her to contribute a piece to a magazine he published, and he called on her at *Le Matin.* The porter denied that Colette had returned from her vacation, until he was persuaded that the young man really did have an appointment. Martin du Gard walked in on her while she was on the telephone, her mouth filled with chocolate. He caught a rustic Burgundy accent as her voice became more excited; Colette was obviously speaking to one of *Le Matin*'s editors, complaining about censorship. You couldn't mention coal merchants, she said, or perfume salesmen, profiteers, Bolsheviks, pregnant women — what *could* you write about? She would nevertheless do the desired cutting, she promised, for she did not want to lose the author and his story.

After hanging up, she collapsed on the desk, defeated. But then her face lit up with what her visitor took to be mischievousness. She grabbed her handbag and removed her powder case, makeup, lipstick, and key chain in order to retrieve a photograph of her daughter — "the best thing I ever did!" Then she could not find her comb, so she rooted around under a pile of manuscripts, letters, proofs, and bills. While he waited, she made up her face using a small mirror.

He thought her garrulous, but she did tell him about her latest enterprise. She was writing a book about her childhood, to be composed of individual sketches that she would publish as they were written; Martin du Gard would be given one of them for his magazine. Colette said that she hoped to dig deeply enough to find her true childhood and adolescence; she would sweep away Claudine's recollections to recover her own.[1]

That autumn she returned to her birthplace in a pilgrimage. At his own request, she took Bertrand de Jouvenel along.[2] He was with her in Castel-Novel, too, as were Renaud and little Colette; she managed to get all three youngsters into one of the episodes of *My Mother's House* (the old castle seems to be haunted, until Colette discovers that the intruder is only an owl).[3] "The children are superb, and sweet," she wrote to Marguerite Moreno, "and Bertrand follows me like a puppy."[4] He remembered the day Colette fell from her horse and the animal nearly trampled her; he was deeply affected by the incident.[5] Yet there was a restraint in their relationship that is reflected in his reminiscence.

As a senator's wife, she did more than her share of socializing — hosting a dinner for a dozen guests, for example.[6] She would have to wait until her return to Paris to sit down to work again. She wrote *My Mother's House* the way she preferred to write, and as she had told Martin du Gard she would: in the form of sketches first published — and paid for — by magazines. She was reliving her childhood, making her parents warmer than they had been in her earlier work. Her mother, around whose memory Colette was creating a myth, comes into her own in these sketches, written eight years after the funeral that Colette did not attend.

Chéri opened at the Théâtre Michel in Paris on December 13, 1921. The adaptation, said the critical critics, lacked the moving qualities of the novel.[7] Yet it ran for more than a hundred nights — the criterion for success in France — and was revived later and taken on road tours. Before that year was over, there was talk of a movie version; she had not yet received a specific offer, Colette told her actress friend Musidora, but there were plenty of candidates for the part of Chéri.[8]

Bertrand de Jouvenel went along with her to theater openings. He would then accompany her to Boulevard Suchet, which gave him the opportunity to watch her work late into the night. She would wrap herself in a blanket and begin to scribble on blue manuscript paper, the blue that she now used for all her work. Words gushed forth: there would be four or five acceptable pages, then one that had to be thrown away, then four or five more good ones.[9] All of this was instructive for the young man, who was to produce a full shelf of his own books.

Bertrand was with her in Castel-Novel for the New Year's holiday. She had had to stay in Paris over Christmas to attend the final rehearsal of a new play; Christmas Eve was free, however, and she celebrated until four in the morning. And then on December 26 she was ready to travel.[10] "The big boy is fine," Colette dutifully wrote to Bertrand's mother. In truth, he had not been fine the first day; she found it outrageous that he was not hungry for breakfast! But now he was sitting down at eight in the morning to cold meat or fried bits of duck or goose skin. He was not working, she assured Claire Boas, "except for such frivolities as a five-act play, social novels, and such things. . . ." They were hearing from Sidi by telephone, but he had not yet been able to join them, for parliament was rushing the budget to a vote before the first of the year. "My daughter is a rural cherub with fat cheeks and uneven teeth," she told Claire before returning to the subject of Claire's son. "Bertrand is dotted with pimples, heightened by dabs of iodine; that's another privilege of youth. But he is a good companion, and usually of a wonderful intelligence. At eighteen they are often so serious, or so brutal!" As for herself, she was working, trying to get ahead of her deadlines.[11]

For the hundredth performance of *Chéri,* on February 26, 1922, she mounted the stage to play Léa. Although there was no longer a full house every evening, she had hopes of seeing the play open at another Paris theater when it finished its run there.[12] In any case, she would take time off now. She was going to Algeria, and with Bertrand. We know that this escapade was one of the "false steps" that alarmed Bertrand's mother,[13] but we cannot be sure of precisely what it was that she suspected. Colette's log of the journey does suggest that Bertrand was being introduced to an exotic side of life for which Boulevard Saint-Germain had not prepared him. They went to see Zorah, who danced naked save for a silver belt, and Colette — if not Bertrand — was delighted by her "boyish buttocks, her little pointed breasts. . . ." They looked at the desert scenery, took a trek out to the Roman ruins of Tipasa, and toured the Casbah with a police officer. There was more naked dancing, and then some properly clothed dancers at the governor general's palace, where five hundred guests in formal attire greeted the visiting French president, Alexandre Millerand.[14] Colette came out of the experience with a touch of dysentery, which she blamed on the "unpure waters" of Algeria. "I lost six pounds, so there's a good side to it," she reported to Bertrand's half-brother, Renaud.[15]

In May, back home in Paris, her car was smashed up by a truck. "Did you read in *Le Matin* that a woman of letters miraculously escaped death?" she asked Marguerite Moreno. "I was the woman." The automobile really was a wreck, and her escape without injury a miracle. While checking her over, her doctor informed her that she was unlikely to have any more menstrual periods; she seemed more concerned, however, by what she found when he stood her on the scale: she now weighed 178 pounds.[16]

She also had another examination just then, this one unsolicited. Arthur Mugnier was a phenomenon even in an eccentric society, a country priest who was invited to the finest homes. He would walk in wearing peasant shoes and a well-worn cassock and proceed to match wits with the best of the guests. What his hosts could not have guessed was that he was putting all of them, and their friends, into his diary.

Actually, despite his appearance, this Benedictine presided over one of the loftiest congregations in Paris. He met Colette for the first time in June 1922, when they were fellow guests at a dinner party. After they were introduced, he said that he had prepared for her by reading the nightingale passage in *Les Vrilles de la vigne.* To that she responded, "And I didn't prepare myself at all!" Clearly she had won the first round, but he said what he had to say in his diary: "Dressed all in white, in a Moroccan crepe, she seems like a child who has been badly brought up, who doesn't know how to behave, lacks all reserve, and is amusing all the same and perhaps a good girl at bottom." She had talked that night about her journey to Algeria — talked about everything in sight, including the food and the wine and the furniture. "If her husband holds to propriety, I pity him," the abbot summed up. After dinner, while speaking with one of the other guests, Colette had patted the woman's breasts, complimenting her on her good health.

In spite of all this, or perhaps because of it, the churchman accepted an invitation to lunch at the Jouvenels' — "that is," he explained, "at the home of Monsieur Henry de Jouvenel and Colette." He allows us a look at the house on Boulevard Suchet in its finest hour, at the zenith of Colette's reputation (if not of Monsieur de Jouvenel's): "A small ground-floor reception area, with a little drawing room covered with tapestries and a garden that is not large but that the July sun rendered delightful, with its geraniums and crimson roses." The guests that day included André Maginot, then the minister of war, and Princess Marthe Bibesco, about whom there will be more to say later (unhappily, for Colette). Colette had the cabinet minister at her right and her dog, called Pati-Pati, at her left; beside the dog sat Abbot Mugnier. He remarked that Colette adored plants that smelled. She gathered up leaves from the garden and pressed them so that her guests could appreciate their odors; the diarist and Marthe Bibesco were given some as keepsakes. "Colette has painted lashes and sea-green eyes. . . . Monsieur de Jouvenel is not merry. He seems concerned about something." Mugnier decided that there was something harsh about Colette herself, something "not joyful." [17]

TWENTY-TWO

The Ripening Seed

JULY, OF COURSE, meant Rozven. Once again there would be a full house. She traveled there with Bertrand, having sent her daughter down first with the maid. Then Henry arrived in the company of Germaine Patat, a winsome young businesswoman who was to become the couple's go-between, Colette's friend as well as Henry's. She was "blond, rosy, and . . . as if by magic packed forty dresses into a cookie box," Colette reported to a friend.[1]

And still Colette was ready for more guests — Léopold Marchand and Misz Hertz, for example. In a letter that may date from this moment, Colette paints the scene: "The children are delirious; my daughter, dirty and hearty, is once again colored like fruit and varnished pottery. Bertrand, still listless, spreads out on mother earth to come to life again; as for myself, since my arrival, I have taken the measure of my humiliation of these past weeks and feel hopeful again." If her husband's peccadilloes — with Germaine Patat, perhaps, if not with Meg Villars or Princess Bibesco or someone else — had finally gotten to her, she was now able to shrug them off, for there was Bertrand, and the sea. Its presence calmed her, she told Hélène Picard — referring to the sea.[2]

After the July 14 holiday, Bertrand had to return to Paris for school examinations. "Will he come back?" she wondered aloud. "I can't remake his health in two weeks' time." Sidi and Germaine Patat spent a fortnight in Rozven, and then they were gone. Colette stayed on with her daughter and "my great greyhound of a boy" (this to Marguerite Moreno).[3] For he *had* come back.

Colette's *The Ripening Seed,* written in Rozven, features a young man of sixteen and a half and a girl of fifteen and a half, whose families share a vacation house at Cancale (which happens to be near Rozven). Philippe wishes to be older than he is; Vinca, to be more attractive. Then a Lady in White enters the story, to instruct and then seduce Philippe. Summer draws to a close; will Philippe and the Lady in White continue to see each other back in Paris? But the older woman vanishes without saying good-bye. Vinca, who knows what has happened, will offer herself to the young man, whom she would not give up for anything.

Bertrand de Jouvenel would later say that the novel had been inspired by a story he had told Colette about an innocent flirtation in summers past.[4] On her side Colette would explain that she had wanted to write a one-act play: "The curtain rises, the stage is dark, two invisible characters talk about love, with considerable knowledge and experience. Toward the close of their dialogue, the lights go up and the surprised audience discovers that the two characters are fifteen and sixteen years old. I wanted to show that passionate love has no age. . . ."[5] It is interesting to note that Colette, like Bertrand, seemed to overlook the fact that *The Ripening Seed* is not only a story of young love; there is also the Lady in White. Philippe guesses that she is thirty or thirty-two, which makes her nearly twice his age but still not very old. Her last name, Dalleray, is revelatory. Bertrand had a small flat on Rue d'Alleray in Paris, the rent for which was paid by Colette; she would go there to meet him.

Once again this astounding woman could not only make a book of her life as she was living it but also undertake the challenge of composing the novel in short segments. *The Ripening Seed* began to appear in *Le Matin* in July 1922, with further sections being published through the following March. The prudish management of the paper called a halt to publication just at the moment when Philippe was about to yield to Madame Dalleray; later readers, including Colette's third husband, decided that the novel benefited from this censorship, for the final section did not have to be written in short takes and thus shows a greater unity.[6]

That autumn Henry de Jouvenel, as a member of the French senate's foreign-affairs committee, was in Geneva at the head of his country's delegation to the international disarmament conference. "Our Sidi-in-chief is in Geneva, as you know, and I myself haven't heard much from him for the past month," Colette wrote to Renaud de Comminges, then fifteen and lonely, exiled to a Catholic boarding school in far-off Pau. "Your sister will also be locked up Sunday, at the Saint-Germain Lycée, for I can't watch her sufficiently here. . . . Everybody here below has his 'cell,' my dear boy. It's not your father's fault if he owes himself to Europe more than to his family." In retrospect, Renaud wondered whether Colette was not simply protecting her husband out of conjugal loyalty, for she was in fact being abandoned.[7]

The script of *Chéri* — the play version, written with Léopold Marchand — was published in October, and the partners pursued their collaboration with a stage adaptation of *The Vagabond*. They worked well together and seemed to share the same opinions on the choice of actors and settings. Concerning an actress who was asking for a considerable amount of money, Colette growled, "She must be a sordid Jew who doesn't wash" — a remark that was certainly made without reflection, not least because Marchand's companion, who was to become his wife and a friend of Colette's for as long as she lived, was Jewish and would suffer for it when the Nazis came.[8]

Before the end of the year Colette summed up her life for the exiled Renaud: she was now writing the fourth act of *The Vagabond* and pursuing her work at *Le Matin,* and she had recently agreed to be the editor of a series of novels to be called the Colette Collection.[9] And although it was not a proper subject for her letters to Renaud, by now she and Bertrand had organized their relationship, and she would go to see him at his bachelor's flat on Rue d'Alleray (it happened to be in the same building as Hélène Picard's apartment). In a memoir of those years, Bertrand took pains to point out that he had never been unfaithful to Colette. The time came when the young woman who was the real-life inspiration for Vinca in *The Ripening Seed* asked him to take her to his apartment; he agreed, but on the way there he decided that this was something he must not do to her. To her? And to Colette? [10]

She was editing the Colette Collection for Ferenczi, the publisher who had brought out *My Mother's House*. Clearly Colette's was a good name to place at the top of a series of modestly priced novels by relatively unknown authors, and she was both a good editor and a good publicist, since she knew the reviewers. Some of her authors were true finds, such as Emmanuel Bove, whose first novel was a serious contender for a prestigious literary prize. She also published Philippe Soupault, best known as a Surrealist poet, and her friend Hélène Picard. The Colette Collection was not an unmitigated success, however: a scholar of our own day who wanted to track down the books edited by Colette discovered that six of the twenty could not be found even in a library. [11]

And then the stage adaptation of *The Vagabond* was in production. As the author of the novel, a coauthor of the play, and a veteran of the theater world herself, she was obviously going to follow the production right up to the opening curtain. A drama critic who visited a rehearsal found Colette on stage, playing a male part, in an attempt to show the actor how it should be done. The visitor concluded that Colette had not changed; she had retained her sharpness, her liveliness, and her good cheer as well. She was getting little sleep, she told him, but she admitted to dozing at her desk at *Le Matin*. Inevitably she would wake up hungry, and she was gobbling down food like a monster, she said; after the play was launched, she would definitely go on a diet. And then, the interview over, she returned to center stage to play the actors' parts for them. [12]

It was at about this time that Willy wrote to a friend, "She's got —

and it must dismay her, but it delights me — an ass like the rear of a stagecoach . . . which doesn't tempt me to take a ride in it."[13] Not that anyone was asking Willy to take such a ride.

For the final week of rehearsals, work began right after lunch, continuing until three or four the next morning, with only an hour's break for dinner. Then came the first performance, for the press only, and another just for insiders, and then finally the first public performance — each of them a triumph. Colette was called to the stage four times to receive applause.[14] "In my opinion," she told an interviewer, "as the situation becomes more dramatic, and violent, the language must in compensation become simpler. The modern theater has no place for pompous discourse in the classic style."[15] Working with her own fiction — which itself avoided bombast in favor of dialogue that was spare and descriptions that could offer flowers without being flowery — she could more easily write sparely for the stage. In that she was at least a generation ahead of her time.

She was soon back on stage before an audience, playing Léa in *Chéri* to full houses along the Riviera. That was in March 1923. She returned to Paris in time to put her daughter and Bertrand on the train for Castel-Novel, where they were to spend the Easter holiday. Before joining them she had to correct proofs for the play version of *The Vagabond,* for publication in a prestigious illustrated weekly.

She stayed in the Corrèze beyond Easter. "Sidi still isn't here," she confided to Hélène Picard. "But I learned that he'd gone away for a week, returned to Paris, and then left again. Youth is a wonderful time!" In another letter Colette sent regards from "the big little boy," who "kisses your hands, your cheeks, and who knows what else?"[16]

She was working on the final pages of *The Ripening Seed,* that long last section which did not have to be broken up for newspaper publication. The process was "not without torment," she told Marguerite Moreno; the very last page took an entire day. "It was maintaining proper proportion that gave me trouble," she explained to her Marguerite. "I have such a horror of the closing grandiloquence."

Soon, she said, she would be able to see Marguerite in Paris; she would walk in with her "79 kilos [174 pounds] and my false air of confidence, also with cigarettes, some alfajores [Spanish pastries], a liter of port, Bertrand, Pati-Pati [her dog] — in short, my material possessions." [17]

After some investigation, she discovered that Sidi had left Paris immediately after her departure for the South, though he had never turned up in Castel-Novel. She retained her sense of humor, at least when writing to Marguerite: "Amour, amour . . . an anagram of *amour* is *rouma*; add *nia,* and you discover a woman built like a horse who turns out books in two volumes. Our Sidi just isn't lucky. . . ." [18]

Marthe Lahovary, born thirty-seven years earlier to a family of Rumanian aristocrats, was perhaps less an author than a personality. At the age of sixteen she had been married off to Prince Georges-Valentin Bibesco, whose family belonged to high society in Paris. (Among their number was the writer Anna de Noailles.) In the spring of 1923, while Colette was waiting for Sidi to show up at Castel-Novel, Marthe Bibesco was publishing a novel on the glory of the Rumanian peasantry.

She first met Henry de Jouvenel through a cousin, and he led the attack (now it can be told, for Marthe's biographer got hold of her diary). Aware of his reputation as a lady-chaser, she let herself be chased. "The manners of the senator from the Corrèze are captivating," she confessed to her diary. "He excites feelings in me that I have never experienced before."

Henry dashed off a letter thanking her for existing. He kept up his "ardent courtship" all that spring, with letters and flowers, some of the former six pages long, some of the latter as big as bushes. Coming back from a visit to Nice, Marthe met up with Henry in Nîmes (he was coming from Castel-Novel, for he had turned up there at last). They promised each other eternal love, and divorces on both sides. . . . [19]

She worried about Sidi, Colette told his son Renaud (and seemingly without irony): he had a sudden fever, severe back pains, a headache. It was all due to overexertion. He was soon back on his feet, ready for more overexertion.[20]

The Ripening Seed was published in July 1923. André Billy, who was later to sit with Colette on the Goncourt Academy jury, praised the author's "deftness with the dubious," regretting all the same that Vinca gave herself to Philippe in the end.[21] The influential critic Benjamin Crémieux spoke of a "Colette school," which he said had "opened up new possibilities" for style.[22]

Meanwhile, the author was where she thought she belonged in July. "Rozven, crackling with heat, is a dazzling place, and we have toads here as big as my behind!" That was to Hélène Picard, with a trace of confession afterward: "The first swim was icy, then tepid, and the dry sand is a bandage for all my moral and physical wounds."[23] Here is evidence that Sidi's roaming could not be ignored. This time he had himself sent on a mission to Rumania, where he joined Marthe Bibesco at her castle in the Carpathian mountains and then sailed with her down the Danube.[24]

All Colette got was a telegram from Sofia: "All goes well." Indeed. Even Bertrand had to leave, to meet his mother in Saint-Moritz. When he came back to her, he was exhausted — "wrecked," in Colette's expression, due to "the excessive altitude, tennis, dancing, nights at costume balls — in other words, everything that a maternal presence, and one of the worst kind, encouraged."[25]

In *Break of Day,* which is made up of a bit of fiction and a great deal of autobiography, Colette seems to be alluding to such a situation in a passage concerning a still-young mother and a mature mistress who are engaged in a rivalry over a young man — a rivalry that becomes hatred. "Sons who are loved too much!" the author cries. "You can't go from one mother to another without committing treason, despite yourself."

TWENTY-THREE

Ruptures

COLETTE MET UP with Sidi in Paris anyway, and together they traveled down to Fontainebleau to pick up their daughter, who had been riding horses there. But it was only to escort her
to her "jail" — Colette's nickname for her daughter's boarding
school at Saint-Germain, outside of Paris. Then it was off to Castel-
Novel — for Colette, at least, who needed to get away from Paris to
prepare for a lecture tour. With some amusement, and surely some
bitterness, she decided to abandon her first lecture topic, "Problems
of the Couple." She had already written thirty pages of her talk
before she realized that it was something she simply could not deal
with just then. The new topic would be painless: "What I Saw of
the Stage from the Audience, and of the Audience from the Stage."
She asked Léopold Marchand to join her in Castel-Novel and help
her draft the lecture.

Sidi should have been there, too; letters forwarded "naively" from
Paris made it obvious that he had left home soon after she did.[1] But
Bertrand was close at hand. "He is not in the best of shape," Colette
confided to Marguerite, "and yet I swear that he is as careful as he
can be." That winter he would have a holiday in the mountains,

"and without his sainted mother."[2] He celebrated his twentieth birthday with his stepmother *and* his father.

For Sidi had turned up at last, as had Germaine Patat, "with her pretty smile and charming good humor." (So Colette wrote to Léopold Marchand.) But the arrival of Raymond Poincaré, then the premier of France, made it less of a vacation, and shortly after that it was time to leave again.[3] Colette began her sweep through southern France, with the lecture that had been so difficult to write, and soon found that without a manager to handle travel and hotel bookings, touring was a hardship. She would pack in haste and make a dash for a railway station, she told Marguerite, and rush from stations to unheated theaters. Winter had come early, and she discovered a South "all powdered in white chalk."[4]

On the other hand, she knew what she would find when she returned to Paris, and she proclaimed, "I'm fighting it off by a deliberate appetite, directed especially toward seafood."[5]

There was more warmth in Marseilles, and there was also Bertrand. "He is acting in a way that calls for considerable gratitude on my part," she informed Germaine Patat. "For you can well understand, my child, everything I don't talk about in this letter — that is, the state of mind I find myself in now that distance and reflection have done their job. I am obliged to consider that I'm being led along a trail prepared in advance, one that horrifies me. I also know that the house I am returning to will be empty."

Her daughter, she added, had gotten high marks when reciting in class because, according to little Colette, "I weighed my words carefully." "Let her continue to weigh them carefully in life," Colette commented to Germaine Patat. "Her mother never did enough of that, and often regretted it."[6]

On her return to Paris, she was able to confirm what she had already guessed: the house on Boulevard Suchet was empty. Jouvenel let her know that he was prepared to have her sue for divorce. But she wished for no battle.

She had been right to fear an empty house. It had taken three years to make a home of it; overnight it slipped back into what it had been before, damp and sad. She shunned the dining room and took a tray upstairs for the "snack of solitary women." She kept her bicycle in the dressing room. The garden did not change, but she herself had changed; she no longer thought that she could heal her wounds simply by looking out at trees and flowers.[7]

Distraction came in the form of another lecture tour, with the same script: theater versus reality. She went to Nantes, in southern Brittany, down the Atlantic coast to Bordeaux and Bayonne, then across the border to San Sebastián. She was being introduced as *Mademoiselle* Colette de Jouvenel, she reported to Marguerite; "It's a way of pleasing everybody. . . ."[8]

Bertrand de Jouvenel did not think it was Princess Bibesco who broke up the marriage, nor Germaine Patat; he believed *he* was the cause of the rupture. Later on he revealed a crucial moment in the affair: his mother asked his father to take Colette away from him. Colette and Henry had a "violent" discussion; it ended with Sidi's walking out.[9]

There was also a rumor to the effect that Sidi actually found Colette in bed with his son.

Jouvenel's young assistant Jean-Louis Aujol was at *Le Matin* on the day he stormed in after learning of his wife's shenanigans. The next day Jouvenel stopped in at Boulevard Suchet to remove his personal belongings.[10]

Clearly Sidi saw himself as the wronged party. On her side, Colette obviously believed that she and her husband had granted each other certain liberties, and now he was no longer playing the game. She was surprised at his surprise. When she told Germaine Patat about the situation, she was also sending a signal to Henry; Germaine and Henry were close enough for that.

In any event, she was once again a vagabond. "Don't worry," she told another friend, "I'm dealing with my unhappiness with energy."[11] That included hard work. One day in January 1924 she began writing at 8:30 in the morning and did not stop until an hour after midnight. She talked to publishers and magazine editors, though she was still working for her husband's *Le Matin*. She also tried on a snowsuit and was eager to begin packing for a winter holiday.[12]

Perched between the Bernese and Vaudois Alps, Gstaad was, and still is, a resort for royalty and for celebrities. A literary colleague who ran into Colette there found her "robust, agreeable, and generally quite merry," which suggests that she was able to put her anxieties aside. She explained that she was taking care of Bertrand, whose mother had turned him over to her.[13]

At Gstaad she had the first skiing lesson of her life. In truth, she had never been to the mountains in winter and was astonished by the heat of the sun. One day she went off to ski by herself, fell, and was unable to get up without the help of passersby.[14] To her confidante and intermediary Germaine Patat, she claimed that she was learning to ski in order to prevent "my little companion" from skiing too much.

Colette had not forgotten her material concerns, and Germaine, practical women that she was, suggested that she go into business for herself. If Germaine had an idea for her, Colette said, she would give herself to it entirely. She pointed out that *Le Matin* had not published her last story on the day it was scheduled to run; Henry had pledged to get her a job on the competing daily, *Le Journal*.

The weather changed. Fog and thaw kept them indoors. Bertrand sat down with a ream of paper, Colette reported proudly to Germaine, and began to turn out political articles that were not bad at all.[15] She was encouraging the debut of what was to be a brilliant career indeed.

She promised herself — and surely Bertrand — that there would be more winter sports.[16] Before the Gstaad holiday was over she was dreaming of another one at Montreux, where friends of hers were staying. The friends came to Gstaad for lunch and brought along the owner of their hotel, who beseeched Colette to come to her place![17]

But first there was some business for her to see to. She was talking to the editors of *Le Journal* about doing two weekly columns for their front page, as well as one short story a month; the same paper would also publish her next novel in installments. She related all of this in a note to Bertrand, adding that she was sending him money to allow him some freedom of movement. (He should not keep her letter, she advised.) Colette wanted him to stay "well and courageous, if only to help me keep all my courage. . . ." When Henry telephoned her to talk about the negotiations with *Le Journal,* she begged him not to add financial disaster to her morale problems; he assured her that he would do what he could for her. Meanwhile, she gave the chauffeur his notice and returned the car to *Le Matin.*[18]

Before leaving for her second round of winter sports, in Montreux, she wrote to Hélène Picard: no, she had not been able to see her during her brief return to Paris. On the one day when she might have met her, she had not seen anyone, "for everything I stood on seemed a rotted plank." She had gone to bed for twenty-four hours, and the warmth of her bed, the immobility, had helped her to recover — "On the following day I went out to a thousand combats." A friend had lost her job on a newspaper, she remarked; "How many women there are like us who are tormented by worries about their future!"[19]

Les Avants, above Montreux, was a less prestigious address than Gstaad, but it had snow and sun all the same. Bertrand joined Colette there in mid-February; he was in good health, she told Germaine Patat, though he could have been sturdier. In this note to her go-between she offered to work for Germaine's fashion house, her qualifications being "physical soundness" and "a good head that is not silly," in addition to a desire to accomplish something.[20]

It was still not clear, she explained to Anatole de Monzie, Henry's friend and the family's legal adviser, whether she would be kept on at *Le Matin.* If she moved to a competing newspaper, for ethical reasons she would have to stop writing for three months and would require a source of income in the intervening period. She had saved no money during her marriage and was now almost broke. Jouvenel could and should help her, she insisted. Once he had promised her a car; now he was not even talking to her. Was he counting on her committing suicide?[21]

Still, there was the snow. When she arrived at Les Avants she was sick as a dog, she told Léopold Marchand, both "physically and morally poisoned," but within twenty-four hours she was on her feet, on skis, on a sled, and often "on backside."[22] She had gone to Switzerland with plans for a novel and found herself working on a different one. She was even making progress, she informed Francis Carco. "But it's terrible to think, as I do every time I begin a novel, that I have no more talent, never had any talent."[23] We cannot be certain that the novel in progress was *The Last of Chéri,* which she seems to have been working on by the end of that year, but it would be a neat irony if she were now plotting Fred Peloux's final renunciation of Léa.

For a way had been found at last to take Bertrand away from her. Thanks to his mother's connections as well as Henry's, he was to go to Prague to work with Edvard Beneš, the foreign minister of the newly independent Czechoslovakia. His parents had tried to pry him loose from Colette earlier, but he had refused, even though he knew it would appear monstrous for him to stay on at Boulevard Suchet after his father had walked out. He felt, however — and so he admitted to his uncle Robert — that since he was responsible for the breakup of Colette's marriage to his father, he could not abandon her.[24]

She put the best face she could on it. He was right to go; his career would begin with this mission. She knew that on the whole she had not been a bad counselor to the young man.[25] For his part, he felt that he had given his stepmother the pleasure of creating something; in return, he had received the advantages of an opening to the wide world. He owed her all of that.[26]

Indeed. Her Bertrand was to become an influential political scientist and diplomatic correspondent, eventually going on to teach at some of the world's great universities, including Yale, Chicago, and Berkeley as well as Oxford and Cambridge.

*　　*　　*

The devilish Abbot Mugnier observed Colette not long after that, in May 1924, when they were once again guests at the same table. She wore a print dress whose dominant color was red; she had strong, bare arms. She looked at everything, touched everything. When mushrooms in cream were served, she exclaimed, "They'll go down easily!" He remarked that a traveling salesman would not have expressed himself otherwise.[27]

Early in July, Robert de Jouvenel died. It was an unexpected death, a hospital accident; Henry was at his brother's bedside in the final moments. Robert had been — "alas," confided Colette to a friend — "the *only* great and deep affection of his life." She sent a letter of condolence, certain that no one would open it.

Marguerite Moreno invited her down to her home in the southwest Lot district, but she could not accept, for Bertrand would have to remain close to his father now. And when Bertrand returned from his uncle's funeral in Castel-Novel, he was able to report "a human gesture" on Sidi's part — for his father had murmured to him, "Your health above all . . . I don't want you to be unhappy." Bertrand decided to interpret this in his own way. Since her daughter's school had informed Colette that she needed to be at the seaside, mother and daughter would go to Rozven that month; Bertrand would follow. He was free until late September, when he was to meet up with Beneš in Geneva.[28]

In spite of family pressures, Bertrand did join her, and so did the Marchands. Early in August Bertrand had to leave, "the idiot" — as Colette tenderly referred to him in a letter to Marguerite. He was to preside over a youth congress in Geneva. Although he had promised to return to Rozven before the end of the summer, she was upset because he was compromising her achievement: she had helped him to put on nearly five pounds in a fortnight. As for herself, she was working badly, but swimming well.[29]

TWENTY-FOUR

The Last of Chéri

BERTRAND DID COME BACK, briefly. They met up at Mont-Saint-Michel, she driving there in her own little car; she wanted to witness the famous spectacle of the dramatic tides that rapidly surround "that curious comic bazaar," as she called the site.[1] The Marchands had gone back to Paris some days earlier, leaving "a great emptiness," Colette confessed to Hélène Picard. "The more one knows Miche [Misz Marchand], the more one holds her in esteem. What a perfect equilibrium in this Slav, and how well she hides her intelligence so as not to wound Léo."[2]

Bertrand returned to Paris, and so did she, for several busy days — casting *Chéri* for the Théâtre de Monte-Carlo, seeing publishers. She had to see Monzie as well, for the eternal negotiations concerning the divorce.[3] Then there was a surprise: Bertrand was getting married — or rather, was being married off. It was her own fault, she told Marguerite Moreno, for in a moment of exasperation she had thrown him out. The family had obviously been waiting for something like that to happen; they even had a fiancée ready. Bertrand came back to Colette to tell her all of this. She agreed that he had been trapped, but attempting to get out of it now would only create a scandal.[4]

The young couple went so far as to have an engagement party. On his way there, Bertrand stopped off to see Colette. "Why go?" she asked him; then, "Don't go." But he had to go. As he left the house on Boulevard Suchet, he saw a scrap of paper floating down to the street. "I love you," it read. Colette had never said that before. He turned and went back to her. End of engagement.

But it was hardly the end of his family's efforts. In the spring they sent him to Cannes, supposedly for his health but actually in order to place a delightful young woman in his path. Colette arrived; she and Bertrand talked, and talked, and she invited him to take up life with her again. But then they talked some more and agreed that it could not work. He left the next morning; she wrote to him, but he never got the letter. His new fiancée had intercepted it. She confessed to that, and recited the letter to him, long afterward.[5]

It was time for Colette to write *The Last of Chéri*. She picked it up as soon as she got back from Monte Carlo, where she had played Léa once again.[6] "I'm working on my novel with a desperate courage," she reported to Marguerite in December 1924. "It will be in an unfunny genre," she warned Germaine Patat. "Perhaps it will not please people, but I promise you that it won't be indifferent!"[7]

Again the fiction is remarkably close to the real story, and the time elapsed between the two remarkably brief. In *The Last of Chéri* Fred Peloux is thirty, a war hero, bored with his efficient and still-young wife. He goes to see Léa but fails to recognize the stout, sexless creature who was once his mistress; when she alludes to the past, he wants to cry out a denial. But he begins to spend time with an odd old lady who is able to talk to him about Léa. Then even this confidante abandons him; in the end he shoots himself in front of a portrait of his impossible love.

She had to put the novel aside after all; there were shorter pieces to produce, bringing quicker returns. She agreed to do a page each month in the French edition of *Vogue*, writing about practical matters such as formal visits, Christmas gifts, winter sports, and fashion shows. Her real contribution, of course, was her personality. In this Bible of elegance, she stressed elegance on the cheap, advising readers, for example, to change not their clothing but only their makeup for the dinner hour.[8]

In February 1925 she was Léa again, on the stage of the Théâtre Daunou in Paris, with thirty guaranteed performances. Again she participated in the casting and direction, even as she was attending the opening of everybody else's new play for review in *Le Quotidien*.[9]

The magazine *Fantasio* published an unkind caricature of a stout Colette holding a miniature Chéri in her arms. The caption scolded her for taking the place of a good actress who had previously appeared as Léa. "She writes remarkable books, and in that role no actress could replace her," read *Fantasio*'s attack. "Let her continue to do that and leave acting to actors. The character of Léa must be played by a beautiful, elegant woman, for otherwise Chéri becomes ignoble, inexcusable, a soulless gigolo." Another writer, Marie de Régnier, who used the pen name Gérard d'Houville, felt otherwise: "Anyone who has not seen Colette playing in *Chéri* has deprived himself not only of an immense pleasure but of the total understanding of this famous work. . . ." The critic made the additional point that the subject could indeed create anxieties in women who had sons, but not if they watched Colette performing the role, which she did "with a kind of curious majesty, that of nature, of an outlaw innocence, that of instinctive and maternal animals. . . ."[10]

She was still doing Léa when *L'Enfant et les Sortilèges* was presented, for the first time anywhere, at the Théâtre de Monte-Carlo on March 21, 1925. This was the fantasy ballet written for her daughter, set to music (at long last) by Maurice Ravel. The scene is a country house; a boy of six or seven (Colette's daughter's age when she wrote the sketch) has been punished for misbehaving. Far from worrying about that, however, he wanders away from home, deliberately hurts a pet squirrel, and pulls the tail of a cat. First the furniture revolts, and then the teakettle and cup turn on the child; finally the animals decide to punish him for his cruelty. But in the struggle the squirrel is wounded, and the boy cares for it. So the animals will bring him back to his mother.

Colette missed the Monte-Carlo opening, but as soon as her Paris theater engagement ended she was off to the Riviera all the same. Her destination was the Eden Grand Hotel, only a short distance west of Monte Carlo, at Cap d'Ail; her companion was Marguerite Moreno.

This Easter was going to change her life. She could not have been freer than she was; the divorce was decreed on April 10, 1925, and would become definitive on August 11. Henry, for his part, seemed to be dividing his time between the enterprising Germaine Patat (who would remain a confidante of Colette's) and Marthe Bibesco. When he became the French High Commissioner to Syria that autumn, both women would manage to slip away to visit him there.[11]

Maurice Goudeket, at thirty-five, was a debonair fellow. He had hoped to become a writer and once even published a slim volume of poetry. He also had a great talent for talking to women, so he used it to sell them pearls, which before the invention of the artificial kind was a fine business. He got into the best homes and at a party at one of them had even met Colette. She had come with Marguerite, whom he knew, but he was not sure that he was going to like the famous writer. She was stretched out on a sofa, lying on her stomach, when he walked in. Almost as soon as they were seated for dinner, Colette grabbed an apple from the fruit basket and bit into it. He thought that she exaggerated her gestures, was playing the part of someone called Colette. But she fascinated him in the end, and when he poured wine into her glass, she turned to look at him with something more than indulgence.

This Easter he had booked a room at the Eden and invited Marguerite to drive south with him in his chauffeured automobile. When Marguerite told him that Colette was going to join them, he was not overjoyed at the prospect of another enounter with her. But in fact, she remained out of sight most of the day, working in her room, then later slipping out on her own. They would all meet for dinner and cards. The game required keeping a poker face, and Goudeket was good at that — "Like a covered flame," Colette commented of that face.[12]

What did not get into Goudeket's memoirs of the holiday was an account of the visit they made together to Cannes. One person who remembered their sudden appearance there was Bertrand de Jouvenel, for it was now that she put the question to him: would he like to return to her? And they agreed that such a thing could not happen.[13]

She was totally free after that. Later she would tell a friend that she was "monogamous"; when she desired X, she had to "liquidate the other thing first." She could not make love to one person if the previous person was still in her life. Women, she said, did not have dual controls.[14]

The day after Colette made her appraisal of Maurice Goudeket as a covered flame, a telegram summoned him back to Paris on business. He decided to leave that very evening by sleeper and gallantly offered to have his chauffeur drive Colette to Paris later. After saying his good-byes, he left for Monte Carlo to board the night train, only to discover that he could not get a berth. So he returned to their Eden hotel, feeling somewhat foolish. He had invited her to use his car and could not withdraw the offer; now he was asking for her hospitality. "I'm coming home by way of a magnificent automobile ride," she told Hélène Picard.[15] To the Carcos, she wrote, "I'll take three days . . . or eternity."[16]

He drove the car, with her alongside him and the chauffeur comfortably settled in the back.[17] No doubt he told her part of his story then, and part during their long evenings of conversation at Boulevard Suchet. Goudeket had been born in Paris on August 3, 1889, sixteen years and six months after Colette. His father was a Dutch diamond merchant, his mother French. Business called the family to Amsterdam when the child was three; he spent his growing-up years there. The Goudekets were Jews, but though they had returned to France in the wake of the Dreyfus hysteria, Maurice could not recall their having any difficulties then; he was to find out what it meant to be a Jew only during the German occupation of France in 1940. When war broke out in 1914 he tried to enlist and was directed to the Foreign Legion.[18]

He had never been married and never felt the need to be. To suppress what he felt was an infantile romanticism, he cultivated an exterior coolness, what he himself called a "starched manner."[19] Those who approached him, including the present writer, could testify to the truth of that assessment.

When Goudeket later wanted to describe Colette, he began with her eyes, blue or sea-green as the Mediterranean (the French term for them is *pers*). She always made up her eyes with kohl, an Oriental powder that was in fashion in her time; she believed it was good for her eyesight, and he thought she might have been right. He saw something provincial in her, a shyness that was almost an inferiority complex. Like a cat, she was both a homebody and an adventuress. And he observed another contradiction: this woman who had stripped off much of her clothing on the stage was in fact terribly modest.[20]

Perhaps she *was* shy, for there would be a long courtship. In his homages to Colette, which take the form of memoirs, Goudeket evokes long evenings of talk about everything (save literature), evenings that were "orgies of mineral water, oranges, and grapefruit, and of cigarettes." Apparently she was still being cautious, as Marguerite wished her to be. One day she rowed alone on a lake in the Bois de Boulogne, chanting to herself, "Hygiene, hygiene, turn me away from thoughts . . . that might excite a big girl like me, who emits fire from her nostrils and who is beginning to find the worries of recent months quite insignificant. . . ."

She was falling in love again and could say so. For the second time she had a handsome man (Sidi had been the first) and was prepared to fight to keep him.

After nights at Boulevard Suchet, they spent days in the country. In mid-June they drove — Maurice and Colette — as far as Saint-Sauveur, to see the roses in her old garden; they went back at midnight to look at the house of her birth again. Until now the watchword had been caution, but now, at the start of summer, "Ah! la la, and again la la! And never enough *la la*s!" she exclaimed to Marguerite. "She's a clean girl, your friend. She's in a fine mess, an

agreeable one, up to her eyes, to her lips, and beyond! Oh, the sa-
tanism of quiet people — I'm talking about the Maurice fellow.
. . ." Marguerite replied, "Can't you manage to live in peace, unhappy woman! You're given a servant, and bang! you make him a
master." "Don't think I'm crazy," Colette pleaded with her, pointing
out that Maurice was accepted in the best circles. Anna de Noailles
was "crazy" about him, the Princess Edmond de Polignac (born
Winnaretta Singer) invited him to see her regularly, Hélène de Chi-
may (the sister of Anna de Noailles) quoted him. They *all* liked
Maurice, said Colette, "But I moved faster."[21]

Later Goudeket reflected that a man had to take a new conquest
away from her past. He told her, "You adore Brittany; henceforth
you'll love southern France." So she shared his little rented house on
a slope at Beauvallon, near Sainte-Maxime, on the Mediterranean.[22]
"This region is incomparable," she told Léopold Marchand. "We're
surrounded by wooded hills, and the sea, and let ourselves roll down
to it. Do you know where I slept last night? Outdoors, on a mat-
tress."[23] It was her first taste of the South in summer, and she was
convinced. "Let's retire to Saint-Tropez, land of the handsome fish-
ermen," she teased Hélène Picard.[24]

Goudeket accompanied her on her tour as she played Léa in *Chéri*
at fifteen different watering places, one each day. She was going to
die of the heat and exhaustion, she informed Hélène, but she would
bring her some of the gold she had picked up along the way. Hélène
Picard was now an invalid, and a recluse.[25]

Even before her summer tour began, Colette had been asking
friends to help her find an old farmhouse near Saint-Tropez, and
now she came across one. "The seashore and sandy beaches are my
native elements, and love too," she proclaimed shamelessly to Marguerite. She confessed that she was in love. Hadn't Marguerite herself
predicted the previous winter that Colette would meet a man during
a trip, and that he would change her life?[26]

In 1925 Saint-Tropez could still appear to be a sleepy fishing town.
She found the house of her dreams a mile from the old harbor, on
a side road, behind a gate smothered in oleander. It stood on five

acres of ground, with its own vineyard, orange trees, and fig trees. . . . The small house itself counted less for her than its terrace covered with wisteria and bignonia and mimosa trees.[27] It was a humble dwelling, she admitted, but who would notice that amid all that luxuriant vegetation? For Colette and Maurice, Saint-Tropez was to be the scene of their "blooming together, of our exultation," as the dapper young man was to remember when he was a dapper old gentleman.[28] Now she had to make a decision: Rozven would have to go.

Back home in Paris at the beginning of autumn, she went back to *The Last of Chéri*. "This *Last of Chéri* will be the last of me, it's such a pain," she told Marguerite. But still she labored on. Meanwhile, she added, "Maurice is Maurice, often silent, full of activity and nonchalance, and I'm so happy when he relaxes at my place in the evening."[29]

TWENTY-FIVE

La Treille Muscate

DIVORCE, and then a new life with the man whom she was calling her dark Satan, would not make it easier for Colette to bring up her daughter. That summer (little Colette turned twelve in July) Germaine Patat had taken the child to her country house in Touraine. "I gave you this little girl whom you love with the feeling of having deposited her in a safe place," the grateful mother wrote. "After that I was able to play my hand of the moment — this year's game."[1] Actually, she was playing for higher stakes than that: the rest of her life.

In retrospect Goudeket proclaimed that Colette had been a good mother, and insisted that his own arrival on the scene had nothing to do with her decision to send her daughter to boarding school. But he also admitted that the child herself might have felt otherwise, might have felt unloved. Both Colettes were happy when they were together, he affirmed, even if both were slow to express their feelings. Once together, they would invariably seek a still closer contact, though they never quite succeeded in establishing it.[2]

Revolt was not long in coming. The younger Colette did what she could to exasperate her teachers, to the point of getting herself expelled from school. Later she would say that when she realized who her mother was — when someone remarked how lucky she was to be the daughter of a famous writer — she became the world champion of laziness overnight.[3]

Boarding school seemed to be the only answer; certainly it was impossible for her mother to keep her at home. In September 1925, for example, Colette met with an impresario to work out another strenuous itinerary, this one to start the following January. And then there was *The Last of Chéri*. "This novel," Colette warned Marguerite, "will be quite gloomy, and bare. . . . I'm astonished myself to see how much I now detest decoration."[4]

She had someone to watch her now. Goudeket may not have been the first to see her at work, but he was the first to record what he saw. He noted that the essence of what she wished to say appeared in her first draft; she would worry about the rhythm later on. She was incapable of dictating and had to set everything down with her own pen. She could still work quickly; some of her best prose, he said, was dashed off while a newspaper messenger waited in the kitchen. She wrote a lot; to the fifty published volumes one must add newspaper and magazine pieces that were never collected in book form, as well as stage adaptations, film dialogue, lectures, and five or six daily letters with no words crossed out.

She worked afternoons, from three to six; mornings were for walking the dog. Goudeket also remembered that she was so busy, and so active in her movements (this despite her weight problem), that when she finally sat down to write, it was with a sigh of relief, for then she knew she would not have to budge again.[5]

"Much success," she reported to her coauthor, Léopold Marchand, from Brussels, after the first performance of a new run of *Chéri*. Once again she was starring as Léa. "Friday at midnight, as I dragged my feet toward the hotel, destroyed by fatigue and after having acted well, I found Maurice Goudeket on the sidewalk, can you imagine. Léo, this lad is such a nice man."[6]

Back in Paris, she set aside her own rules and worked evenings on the novel. It was midnight; Goudeket had been with her and finally left for his own apartment, and now she returned to the manuscript. "My God, it's difficult!" she complained to the faithful Marguerite.[7] In mid-November she wrote to Hélène Picard, "Oh, shit on *The Last of Chéri*. Let him fall dead!" She completed the novel not in Paris but in Rozven, leaving from there for a Christmas engagement in Marseilles.[8]

Her dark Satan joined her for the New Year's holiday at the Golf Hotel in Beauvallon, near his old house and her new one. "There's nothing like Saint-Tropez, my Hélène," she wrote to her stay-at-home friend. Then she was off to Paris for a hasty reading of the proofs of *The Last of Chéri* before going back on the road. The first stops, though in France's deep south (Tarascon and Saint-Raphaël) were "a nightmare of uninterrupted cold. . . ." Everything changed for the better in Nice, where she found a hotel room flooded with sunshine and a heated theater. More, she was getting letters from Maurice, letters (she told Hélène) "filled with young love. What cannibalism on my part to accept it."[9]

More warming news greeted her in Paris. The previous year, the heirs of her half-brother, Achille, had sold the house in which she had been born. The buyer was a silk merchant whom she did not know but who had promptly put up a plaque to commemorate her residence there. Now he went a step further, granting her free use of the house during her lifetime.[10] She decided to leave it unoccupied for possible visits; later, more realistically, she rented it out.[11]

She returned to the stage in Paris, once again as Léa, directing her own rehearsals (while autographing copies of *The Last of Chéri* for what she hoped would be friendly reviewers).[12] A critic who visited her in her dressing room judged that she had "eyes *made* for the stage, turned up at the tips to offer, under heavy lashes, an expression of youth, joy, a ray of light so bright it appears artificial." The visitor watched, as Maurice Goudeket might have, as she put the final touches on her makeup; all the while, people wandered in and out of the dressing room and were introduced to each other. His description continued: "Her gaiety has something of the flavor of the flesh of this woman. Her laugh is loaded with *vitamins,* to employ a new word." She told the journalist that she was about to go off to Morocco, exclaiming, "What I'm not going to eat in Marrakesh!" But in the end he perceived a "fleeting expression" of melancholy. He thought he had discovered the same thing in her acting: there was "another creature" hiding behind the merry, robust exterior.[13]

There was indeed a schoolgirl's delight in the way Colette looked forward to Morocco. She was going with Maurice, of course, and they would be the guests of Al-Glâwi, the Pasha of Marrakesh, who in those days of the French protectorate exercised considerable authority in his wondrous fief. "It's still an ostentatious medieval era," she explained to Renaud, Henry's son, "and I wish to contemplate something dazzling, under a Moroccan sky, before becoming a completely old lady. I want feasts out of the *Thousand and One Nights,* and almond milk instead of wine, and enclosed gardens. . . ." She had heard that Al-Glâwi touched only materials that had been woven especially for him, and that he had eighty cooks.[14]

It was conceivable that Morocco would not live up to this buildup, but in fact it did. In her log of the journey, Colette described their host, with his deep eyes, and that little chin characteristic of capricious or violent souls. . . . He served as their guide on a tour through long rooms furnished with divans, smelling of cedar and vanilla. But the true luxury was the slave labor; seven or eight women served at table, "beautiful Negresses smoother than fruit. . . ." Other slaves danced for the guests.[15]

And as if this were not enough, the pasha also lent them his palace in Fez. He did not accompany the travelers there, but instead placed them in the care of a retinue of slaves, within walls of colored tile and perfume gardens (gardens of roses and mint and yellow jasmin and more). At last the pasha's chauffeur drove them on to Rabat. "Between the sea and the hotel there is only an old Arab cemetery . . . and closer by, old reddish ramparts covered with storks," she wrote to Hélène.[16] She could have stayed there forever — or so her enthusiasm suggests — but Maurice had to get back to his business.

In *Mercure de France,* a seasoned critic, André Rouveyre, used the occasion of another run of *Chéri* to size up the abilities of its author as an actress. He had not liked her when she did pantomime and had said so at the time. Now he decided that she was *still* an amateur: "In her stubborn efforts she is there, before us, quite inferior to herself. . . . She would appear childish alongside an intelligent and skilled actress." Her writing was a "wild fruit," he condeded, but she lacked the talent to bring it to life on the stage. "Let Madame Colette not fool herself: the spectator comes out of curiosity for the writer." Even so, he pointed out, not all of her readers were tempted to see her in the flesh; she drew smaller numbers to the theater than she had book buyers. The real pleasure lay in reading her, he concluded, and it was cheaper.[17]

Colette now went to Rozven, not for a summer holiday but to arrange to move her belongings to Saint-Tropez. "I'm in such a hurry to sell Rozven, but nobody wants it," she complained to Hélène. For she had to pay for the new house, and intended to do it out of the proceeds from the sale of the old one.[18] After packing her daughter off to Castel-Novel, she drove with Maurice to Saint-Tropez, where they camped in the house he had rented the previous summer in nearby Beauvallon. They were waiting for the movers. One morning Colette hastily finished off a note to Marguerite so she could stand at the roadside and wait for a delivery truck, which was coming from a Nice department store with bedding, heating equipment, and kitchen supplies.[19]

The crates arrived at last, and within forty-eight hours she and Maurice and her faithful servant Pauline had made a home of the house she would call La Treille Muscate (The Muscat Vine). In early August her daughter was driven down by a member of the staff of *Le Matin.*[20] Then Colette had to leave for Bordeaux to play in *Chéri* at the beginning of September; what to do with her daughter? "She's like a fruit on the branch, a sheep in the pasture," she described the thirteen-year-old to Germaine Patat. "A little too pretty, as I always say, with just too much strength and sensuality in her magnificent person." Could Germaine take her for a while? she wondered. And what to do about school that fall? "Where can we lock her up? Paris? That would not be my ideal."[21]

So Germaine took the girl to her country house in the Loiret district; Colette and Maurice even came for a visit. In October they were all in Paris together, with Colette planning another theater tour and Maurice scrambling to keep his business going, something that it was becoming harder and harder to do. "My charming cats keep me company," Colette told Marguerite. "You'll see what beauties they are. . . . My daughter is locked up in Versailles, but with evil thoughts. . . . The magnificent little brute likes the countryside, swimming, luxury automobiles, phonographs, dancing . . . a child of her times, in other words. And I'm in a bad position to punish her, for it's to me that the child gives her most sincere and secret tenderness, and her best humor."[22]

Some letters piously saved by her daughter date from this unhappy time. "You tend to treat your teachers a bit lightly, and your fellow pupils, too," her mother scolded her. "You think of yourself as a young demon who from the lofty heights of your thirteen years judges, appreciates, likes, or dislikes." Colette added that she, too, could have made fun of the children of farm families with whom she went to school, but she had been careful not to do anything like that. "It's thanks to my scruples that I have been able to make a name for myself in literature, darling," she explained.[23]

TWENTY-SIX

Break of Day

IN NOVEMBER 1926 there was a new production of *The Vagabond* in Brussels. Colette, at the age of fifty-three, played her alter ego Renée Néré for the first time. "I think you'll like me in it," she allowed herself to say to Hélène Picard. She had worked hard to make a success of it, rehearsing in Paris at first and then, in eleven-hour days, in Brussels.[1] And it *was* a success, though one critic suggested that that was less a triumph of theater than a tribute to the power of curiosity. Soon after the Brussels run, Natalie Barney invited Colette to do a scene from the play in her drawing room on Rue Jacob. Privately, Barney was pitiless, describing "Colette, indeed a vagabond, a walking pedestal topped by a little triangle, with her fat solidly implanted and the tanned complexion of Alexandre Dumas *père,* looking for all the world like a screech owl surprised by daylight. Colette, squat so as to be nearer her aromatic plants and more able to fill her pockets with them, walks or stands on the legs of a sportsman."[2]

It was at this time that Colette moved at last from the house on Boulevard Suchet, into an odd suite of rooms at 9 Rue de Beaujolais, in the Palais-Royal quadrangle, just north of the Louvre. It was a mezzanine servant's flat with impossibly low ceilings and half-moon windows that opened onto not the gracious fountains and regal gardens but the somber arcade. It was not exactly what she had wanted, but by now she was desperate, and there were not many competitors for such accommodations. Later she was to have her chance at a high-ceilinged apartment just a floor above, with a proper view.

She referred to her new quarters as "the tunnel." It was a sublease, and she would learn to love the place; imagine, she exclaimed, she could hang curtains without needing a ladder! But it received only reflected light, and she could see the sky only on the street side of the building. Beneath her floor, a passageway ran from the street to the garden; she and her pets had to learn to ignore the sounds of dogs, children, newspaper vendors, and guards who slammed the gates closed at night. The thump-thump of a nearby printing press made her feel as though she was on a ship at sea.[3]

In 1927 the first serious account of her work was published. The author, Jean Larnac, brought to bear some original research on her childhood in Saint-Sauveur; he also stressed her acute psychological approach — apparently to confound those critics who were blind to it — and compared her writing to etching.[4] Meanwhile, in a lecture on the contemporary novel, the Catholic writer François Mauriac had high praise for the morality of Colette's work. The characters in her Chéri novels might be down-and-out, he said, but the books themselves "do not diminish us," for Colette made the reader see "the tragic side of those poor beings who place all their hopes in a love as perishable and corruptible as its very object: the flesh." He concluded in a manner that was certain to comfort her readers: "This pagan and sensual woman leads us irresistibly to God."[5]

Soon the pagan herself was seated beside Mauriac at dinner, at the home of the playwright Henry Bernstein. Abbot Mugnier was also there. "Colette talked of cooking, of Château d'Yquem and dishes she likes," the priest wrote in his diary. "She brings everything back to gluttony; there is culinary gluttony, voluptuous, etc. Several times she made the point that purity is a temptation, like the other ones, and not more noble than they."[6]

If there was one question for which Colette had no ready answer, however, it was how to deal with her almost-grown-up daughter. "Firmness is necessary with you, my darling," she explained to the younger Colette. "The proof is the affection you have for me, even though I'm the one who spoils you least."[7]

When her daughter was caught smoking, Colette chided her, "If I have avoided the smoking habit" — she could take a cigarette or leave it — "it's not because of the harm that tobacco, smoked with moderation, could do to me, but because during a long life I have seen friends *devastated* by the tyranny of habit." Habit made one a coward and a liar, she said, and "I have so much ambition for you, darling! Ambition not as to career but as to character. Do you understand me? I can blossom now only through you."[8]

A buyer was found for Rozven at last. Henceforth summer holidays — with Maurice, with her daughter — would mean the house called La Treille Muscate, on the bay of Saint-Tropez. This year she took along a batch of research material for a new book: her mother's letters.[9] This was to be *Break of Day,* another book that was not merely a novel, though it was constructed like one, and not quite autobiography. She began to write it during this holiday at La Treille Muscate, which itself is described in the book. She also used the real names of friends and analyzed her feelings with seeming frankness. But then she went on to proclaim a calmed sensuality on her part, a renouncement of love — and this just after she had embarked on a new and very intense affair.[10]

As the book opens, the writer is settled in her new house. Is it the last she will own? she asks herself. She details her life there, simplicity itself; her companion is not a threat. One of her husbands suggested that perhaps at fifty she would write a handbook on living in peace with a man; this book may be it, as well as a tribute to her mother.

In quasi-diary form, she talks of a young lover, of her own aging, of the elements of a Saint-Tropez summer: plants, her faithful dog, cats — including *the* cat, the third she has possessed, if one counts "only she-cats of true character." Yet she no longer writes about animals, she says, aware that this only served to distance her from other human beings.

There is a fiction, all the same, in *Break of Day*. The heroine is courted by a younger man; a friend desires him, so Colette (or the narrator) chooses not to stand in the way. The young man has considered the difference in their ages and dismissed it; for her part, she wants him to understand that for the first time since the age of sixteen she has decided to live without passion. She remembers how her mother once liked to play chess but resolved to stop before age made her seem ridiculous: a lesson.

The writing went slowly. Surely it was a tour de force to transform daily life into fable. Why aren't we all rich? she wondered out loud to Léopold Marchand, implying that if she had not needed the money she would have given up writing altogether.[11] But she would never be rich. Her wealth, she told Marguerite, consisted of friends, a bit of soil, an automobile in working order, health, the freedom not to work when she did not wish to.

With her daughter and Maurice she helped with the grape harvest. When the two of them left, she stayed on, writing. She confessed to the Marchands that if she had not had a man in Paris, she would have stayed in Saint-Tropez forever.[12]

Indeed, after spending the autumn in Paris she was back on the Mediterranean coast at the end of the year to pursue her writing — not at La Treille Muscate, for it lacked heating, but in a hotel in the wooded landscape of La Croix. "Am I working?" she wrote to Marguerite. "Yes, if working is tearing up what I did the previous week and beginning again." She had gone there with Pauline and the cats, and Maurice joined them for the holidays.[13] "My novel is fighting me off like a demon," she complained to Léopold Marchand.[14] "I've begun the scene with the man *eight* times," she told Marguerite. The "man" is described as a Saint-Tropez neighbor; he is Colette's lover in the book, though not in real life. He is obviously not Maurice Goudeket, for she chases this other man away.

She stayed on for another ten days after New Year's; when she got home to the Palais-Royal, the book was far from finished, but she thought she had done the hardest part.[15] Then she was able to announce to a friend, "I still have sixty pages to produce"[16] — for this writer-journalist was always keenly aware of the number of pages required for magazine publication.[17]

As for her renouncement of love, the clearest message of *Break of Day,* Goudeket's presence offered irrefutable evidence that Colette herself had made no such resolution, whatever anguish this may have caused her. "Another summer, another summer gone," she wrote to Maurice. "They are more and more precious, more and more poignant, these summers with you. A more reasonable person than myself would take herself in hand and decide something. Thanks to God, thanks to the devil, I'm not a more reasonable person than myself."[18]

She finished the book in January 1928 and treated herself to another winter holiday. She and a neighbor, Alba Crosbie, went to Saint-Moritz, where once again she was a beginner on skis. Snow did something for her, though — more than alcohol or coffee or pep pills could, more even than the climate of Saint-Tropez. While on holiday she received the first proofs of *Break of Day,* along with word that her publisher loved it. She herself was not satisfied with the book, however, so she cut and revised on the proofs. She would go through three sets before she was done, and still she would worry that her novel was "full of negligence and loose threads and breadcrumbs, but that's the way it is," she told Renaud de Comminges, her "dear Kid" (using the English term).[19]

Home in the tunnel, she sat down to . . . another novel. "Yes. You can't believe your eyes?" she asked Marguerite, to whom she revealed this. It was just that she did not want to break the habit, she said, and after giving her previous book to one of her publishers

(Flammarion) she had to fulfill a promise to another (the faithful Ferenczi). She was writing *The Other One*.

Meanwhile, there was a pile of finished copies of *Break of Day* on her table. She spent two days signing copies for reviewers and friends before leaving for Saint-Tropez for a spring holiday and to supervise some work that was being done on the house.[20] She was still there when the first reviews of the novel appeared. In *L'Oeuvre,* André Billy hailed "something extremely new and courageous, something that has no precedent, I believe, in literature . . . , which is that the novel's heroine is none other than its author." Instead of transposing real-life situations to fiction, she had reproduced them. "Dear friend," Colette wrote to Billy in acknowledgment, "one can hide nothing from your sharp eyes; you have discovered that in this novel the novel doesn't exist."[21] Whatever her original intentions may have been, Colette now seems to have been using the book as a means of protecting her private life — life with her dark Satan.

TWENTY-SEVEN

The Other One

*I*N THIS NEW NOVEL that was not about its author, we meet Farou, a successful if tiresomely egocentric playwright, and Fanny, his wife of a dozen years. Earlier, when Farou had an affair with an actress, Fanny accepted it with resignation, but now she is startled to discover that her husband's assistant, Jane, has become his mistress. Is it just a fling, Fanny wonders, or a good reason for breaking up the marriage? They are all going through a difficult time, for Farou's latest play is about to go on the stage. Fanny finds herself protecting Jane from her irritable husband.

When at last the women have it out, it becomes clear that Jane truly cares about Fanny; for her, Farou is quite an ordinary person, while Fanny is special. And Fanny realizes that she is happy to have Jane there as a buffer. So an arrangement seems possible, though when Farou learns of their entente, he slips out to avoid a confrontation.

Later Colette would conclude that if her earlier heroes had been mere skin and bones — Renaud, for example, whom she had eventually killed off out of boredom, or Maxime in *The Vagabond* and Jean in *The Shackle,* who were simply male leads — in Farou she had fleshed out a genuine character, even if he did draw some of his warmth from the friendly female rivals who shared him.[1] And of course there was a bit of Colette and Henry and Germaine Patat in *The Other One*. "Not love you?" Colette wrote to Germaine while she was working on *The Other One*. "You are not only a concerned witness to my life, a tender confidante," Colette assured her. "How many times have you jumped the barriers to place yourself on my side?"[2]

The book was still in rough draft when she transferred her office to Saint-Tropez that summer, but the condition of the house was such that she would not be able to complete the novel by the deadline she had set for it. She arrived with Colette II (as she now referred to her daughter)[3] to find an unpleasant surprise: the workers had gotten the dates mixed up, so they said, and had not yet finished the renovations. The cook would have to use a stove in the garage, the toilets had not been installed, the furniture was piled up in the bath-room, and the shutters had all been taken down.[4] This crisis never-theless brought out the best in her daughter, who never backed away from anything that she could do with her hands.[5]

In any event, Colette's writing did not go well, and the editor of the magazine to which she had promised her novel began pleading for chapters. But still, there was the grape harvest, and the late sum-mer was divine. "If Maurice wasn't in my life," she said again (to Marguerite this time), "I swear I wouldn't return."[6]

She still dreamed of honors, but sometimes she seemed to be in too much of a hurry for them. Her friend Louis Barthou, the minister of justice in the Poincaré government, advised her that she could not get what she wanted — promotion to the rank of officer in the Le-gion of Honor — because she lacked seniority. Then, smack in the middle of a cabinet crisis in November 1928, Barthou telephoned to let her know that her promotion had been approved.[7]

Anna de Noailles reacted with a joke: "Instead of a ribbon, they should have given you a bellyband." Colette replied, "You mean a G-string." "Colette," said the countess, "you're so glorious you have nothing to hide." Born Princess Anna-Elisabeth de Brancovan,

Countess Mathieu de Noailles was a classical poet as well as a novelist. The source for this sampling of her table talk is none other than Abbot Mugnier, who had it from a confidante.[8]

The parish priest was seated with Colette again that autumn, and we will take advantage of his reportorial skill to observe Colette dressed all in black, with a long red scarf. She scrutinized everything, as usual, analyzing the contents of the dishes they were served. She said that she adored garlic and consumed lots of it, and that her eyes were rotten but she retained the senses of taste and smell. She mentioned the nudity of men and women on Riviera beaches. Some of the bathers were Americans; the sight of them, she added, did not arouse her sexual instincts.[9]

She had to leave Paris to finish her book, but by then Christmas trips had become something of a tradition. This time the site was remote: a castle-hotel in the Belgian Ardennes Forest. "A frightful castle, a good hotel," she summed it up for Marguerite. "In the silence you can hear the blood in your veins. A bit of snow, immense forests, everything hilly and rather Swiss, in the best sense of the word." They had driven there through fog, which had added nearly a day to the trip; she intended to rest for another day before sitting down to her manuscript.[10] "It's raining a soft rain, quite pleasant for the face and eyes," she told Anna de Noailles. She was working fastidiously, "and I hate what I am doing." Later she would admit that she had imposed "an awful Belgian existence" on poor Maurice, with silences that lasted for nine hours.[11] She dramatized the last moments for Hélène Picard: "I finished — a little before the twelve strokes of midnight, on December 31!"[12]

She was calling the book "The Last of the Last"; she pardoned it, she confessed to Louis Barthou, only because it was done.[13] But Goudeket remembered that she counted *The Other One* among her best novels, though she knew that with its latent drama it did not appeal to readers as much as her other books.[14] Reviewing it, André Billy declared its author "a writer . . . who, all things considered, has had an exciting and refreshing influence on French prose, equivalent to that of a Rousseau, a Chateaubriand, a Flaubert. . . . No one until now has presented the new sexual morality in such a sad and true light."[15]

Over Easter 1929 she and Maurice took the train to Madrid, their first stop on a long trip through Andalusia and across the strait to Tangier. Madrid meant Goya first of all, but they found the Prado closed for Easter. When they were unable to get seats on a train for Seville and Algeciras, they hired a taxi to take them.[16] Colette jotted down her impressions, as she occasionally did, beginning with Holy Week in Seville, but her liveliest prose was reserved for letters written to friends during this "idiotic and charming journey."[17] "Hélène, you'd love this climate, this land, the mountain crossed at twilight, the burning bushes carried in procession in Seville, fat Andalusia, emaciated Castile, and the domain of the Pasha of Marrakesh, where everything swarms, even the little gray and black snakes." This last was a reference to their friend the pasha's estate in Tangier — nearly two hundred acres of Eden, as she gushingly described it. They saw none of the things that tourists were supposed to see, only what common mortals never did.[18]

Back home again, at her writing table, she would use Tangier as the background for an eerie tale that she called "The Rendezvous." After the exoticism of that city, Paris with its "entanglements" could only seem sinister.[19] But no matter, for she was soon off again, this time on one of her oddest assignments. She was to write about the animals in the famous Antwerp zoo for a book to be published in a deluxe edition. "I died of boredom because of the rain," she had to tell Hélène, "and of aggravation because of the captive animals."[20] Although she managed to control her outrage, it did come through in the finished book, for all the edition's elegance.[21]

Rozven was no longer hers, but she and Maurice went to Brittany all the same. They were guests of the Marchands at their feudal-style castle at Ploumanach, on a jutting peninsula that featured some of the most rugged scenery she had ever encountered; even the former mistress of Rozven could be dazzled. In ten days she and her friends caught twenty-one lobsters, nineteen giant crabs, and countless fish. She adored the seascape, moonlight over the cliffs. If she had such an island, she said — for it was completely surrounded by water at high tide — she would never leave. And yet . . . Maurice, who had gone back to Paris early, was coming to pick her up for the drive down to Saint-Tropez.[22]

"To visit Colette one must, by a road all white and usually pitted . . . leave the town in the direction of the vineyards on a slope" — thus André Billy recounted the experience for his readers. "Suddenly, enveloped in foliage, a red roof, white walls, a small wooden gate supported by two plaster columns: it's the house of Colette. . . ." Pauline greets him but insists that her mistress is not at home, until he convinces her that Colette is expecting him. "One reaches the house by a shaded lane, then a flight of steps that forms a terrace," he continued. Colette's room was a huge cement cube constructed behind the main house. He sees Breton furniture, a worktable, a large divan and its mosquito net. The beach is a surprise: a tiny, private strip of sand just a hundred yards from the house.[23]

Her painter neighbor André Dunoyer de Segonzac, who was to illustrate Colette's impressionistic account of life at La Treille Muscate with his own graphic art, remembered spending lazy days there with friends such as his fellow artist Luc-Albert Moreau and his Hélène, the actor Pierre Renoir, the actress Valentine Tessier. He also recalled a procession of cats following Colette on her walks. Then, "suddenly, and resolutely, she would sit down at her table to begin writing. Her fine and powerful arms served as buttresses on the writing stand. She remained there, as if frozen, for hours. . . . Only the rustling of a page, as she threw it off with controlled rage, broke the silence from time to time."[24] This was a rare portrait of the writer writing. "Her heart and her senses satisfied by Maurice," observed the sharp Natalie Barney, "with her Pauline taking good care of her and sparing her the household chores, she could give herself to her work. . . ."[25]

TWENTY-EIGHT

Claridge's

ABUNDANT CORRESPONDENCE survives attesting to Colette's adoration of her Maurice. He himself published extracts of her tender letters from Saint-Tropez. "Hearing your voice makes me angry," she declares in one of them. "Within reach and out of reach at the same time. Oh, how I detest the telephone. Don't forget to telephone on Wednesday. I'm being unreasonable, but it's hard to live without you in so lovely a place."[1] He never stopped being the model lover, quiet and sauve, in prime physical condition. His career as a dealer in expensive jewelry had taught him when to be discreet and when to use his charm. Uncharitable observers tended to focus on the sexual side of their relationship; Paul Valéry was supposed to have said that the name Goudeket was derived from "Good *quequette*" — that is, good organ.[2]

One thing that strikes readers of her letters is that Colette could talk about her pets or not, depending on whom she was writing to. Friends who loved cats were spared no details. Willy had been a coconspirator with her in the animal line; Jouvenel had not. Goudeket seemed to enjoy the antics of the little beasts, and so Colette's letters to him often contained cat-talk.

Clearly Colette's dark Satan was a necessary part of her life as she approached her sixties. He was always nearby, or seemed to be. After the collapse of his jewelry business, which coincided with the collapse of the stock market, in 1929, he spent more time at home. Sharing work and leisure hours, they were not often separated, day or night.[3]

Raising her daughter remained Colette's chief concern. In this summer of 1929 one aspect of the worry was relieved, for Colette II received a generous legacy from an aunt on the Jouvenel side. "My daughter has arrived," Colette announced to Marguerite (in September, from Saint-Tropez). "A twenty-five-pound phonograph in a case follows her like her shadow. She has the shirts of a boy and the breasts of a young Negress — the prettiest, in other words." She had turned fourteen in July. As for Colette *mère,* she was fine: "Nothing but this physical existence, which suits me so well." She had harvested her grapes, some 1,500 liters of them, and they promised to be "suave."[4]

Perhaps there had been *too* much physical labor. "I come home with empty hands and bent shoulders," she complained to Hélène Picard, "bent under the work I didn't do. It's going to be some winter!"[5]

Soon enough she was back on the road, this time traveling all the way to Berlin to lecture. There were news photographers at the station, and interviewers at her hotel; at a banquet in her honor, which brought together the elite of the German capital, she sat to the right of the French ambassador. It was the kind of reception that she would get on her every trip abroad from now on.

That year, seventeen years after her mother's death, she sat down to write *Sido.* It was another journey home to Saint-Sauveur. Once again she read her mother's letters, using them to create dialogue. We discover a Sido who abides no nonsense and is ready with an answer to every question, a remedy for every ill. She is often funny, but Colette never lets us know whether or not the humor is intentional on her mother's part. Sido speaks for village life but keeps a sharp eye on Paris all the while. Upon publication of *Sido,* Janet Flanner, writing in *The New Yorker,* observed that Colette had been the first to give the French what Flanner called "news of nature"; in so doing, she said, "she has the strangeness of a traveler who tells them of an unknown land."[6]

Colette finished the writing at La Gerbière, a house that Goudeket had acquired during his good years, located at Montfort-l'Amaury, just twenty-two miles west of Paris. One of the attractions of the spot for her was the proximity of Luc-Albert Moreau and his companion (later his wife), Hélène Jourdan-Morhange, both fellow lovers of nature and of cats.

And, too, Saint-Tropez was not what it had been. "You find here the people whose pictures appear in *Vogue*," she grumbled to Marguerite Moreno. One summer day she had gone to the old harbor quay to buy toilet paper and some canvas to line a cupboard with, only to find three rows of elegant automobiles blocking the waterfront. A crowd gathered just to watch her come out of the store. If the town was spoiled, however, there was still the tranquillity of La Treille Muscate. She would learn to avoid the harbor area, now a summer Montparnasse.[7]

In a book that she published in 1930, the critic Rachilde devoted an essay to Willy, titling it "The Almost Great Man." She described him as "the most naive and mildest of men," recalling the "delicious critic who distorted his erudition for fun."[8] But by now Willy was no longer in a mood to amuse. He lived alone, was ill, and had no regular source of income; he would die in debt. His old friends tried to help, but his former secretary Marcel Boulestin — Claudine's Marcel — remembered Colette's reacting negatively to such appeals. When told that Willy's right arm was paralyzed, preventing him from writing, she supposedly replied, "You really wouldn't want him to begin now, at his age!"[9] Even his defender Sylvain Bonmariage said that by the time Willy died, on January 12, 1931, he had lost all of his friends because of his sharp tongue and his lack of gratitude. When Bonmariage paid him a last visit, Willy was bitter. He was being allowed to die like a derelict, he lamented. He had written a hundred books, but he was going to disappear into a void.[10]

Later Colette would say that it was on her doctor's orders that she gave up the Palais-Royal tunnel; the dampness was responsible for her repeated attacks of bronchitis. Her solution was novel. She and Maurice (who for obvious financial reasons had given up his own flat) found rooms in a hotel on the Champs-Elysées. The Claridge — or Claridge's Hotel, as it called itself — was in the highest luxury category, but its attic floor was not terribly luxe, and Colette had been offered a reasonable rate. "Two small connecting rooms under the roof, a bathtub, two small twin balconies at the edge of the rain pipe, red geraniums and strawberry plants in pots, most of my own furniture, and all my books stuck on the walls" — that was the way she described the new accommodations in a little book of hers devoted to apartments she had known, *Trois . . . Six . . . Neuf . . .* (published in London as *Places*). A dressing closet served as kitchenette for simple meals; fancier dishes were ordered up from the hotel restaurant. The manager made everything easy, and the house carpenter even fixed up a table so she could work in bed, refusing to accept payment for it.

If she so desired, she said, she could be alone with her cat and dog (and with Maurice, of course, though he is not mentioned in her little book), or down in the lobby she could meet the world: dressed-up English ladies; Hindu princes who reserved entire floors for their wives, children, servitors, and private orchestras; candidates for Miss Universe; politicians banqueting in private dining rooms. The hotel porter helped to protect her privacy (by lying for her).[11]

She did not think she would live there forever. What she *really* wanted, she informed a friend, was a proper apartment in the Palais-Royal.[12]

TWENTY-NINE

These Pleasures

COLETTE'S FAITHFUL DISCIPLE Claude Chauvière described a day at Claridge's. Colette has decorated the suite with her own wallpaper (dotted with roses), and everything else — including the cats — is familiar. Colette says she enjoys the privacy she has there (Chauvière wonders about that). There is a rap on the door: the maître d'hôtel with a menu. The telephone rings constantly, and "Colette picks up the receiver, puts it down, replies, refuses, accepts, changes her voice, her mood, her desires." A Rumanian journalist drops by to invite her to lecture in his country, and they discuss the details. Colette's daughter turns up, all "mystery and beauty." A messenger enters with a box of fruit and vegetables, and Colette, her daughter, Pauline, and the dog and cat set about examining the harvest sent up from Saint-Tropez.[1]

Chauvière's book on Colette was published that very year, 1931. Goudeket said that the young woman never hid the fact that she had gone to work for Colette as a secretary so that she could one day write about her.[2] And it was not all hagiography. She showed Colette greedily munching on chocolate éclairs, keeping friends apart so that she could have them to herself, and craving material possessions. "Colette loves money," observed Chauvière, "as she loves everything that serves for enjoyment." She was without apparent method but in fact knew precisely what she possessed and when she was being overcharged. She was drawn to beauty even when it was not accompanied by good character. Not understanding politics, she would take on her husband's opinions for the duration of their marriage.

Once, in an attempt at rejuvenation — and Chauvière claimed to have actually witnessed this — Colette had a series of blood transfusions; the donor was an attractive young woman. Afterward Colette insisted that her eyesight and breathing had improved.[3]

A year and a half earlier Colette had accepted an advance for a movie adaptation of *The Vagabond,* and now came the time for her to write it.[4] There was another check, a big one (Chauvière saw it), for the Rumanian trip — Colette got the amount she asked for. Once again it was a triumphal tour, beginning in Vienna, where photographers were at the station to greet her, and there were twenty interviews. She autographed copies of German translations of her books and paid a call on her publisher there, Zsolnay.[5] In Bucharest she was received by the king.[6] She calculated that by the time she saw her own bed again, she would have spent six nights in sleeping cars.[7] She could not wait to see her two little rooms, she wrote to Marguerite Moreno, with "my friends, my animals — and Maurice."[8]

But these trips paid well. Soon after her return from Rumania she was off on another round of lectures, traveling to southwest France in March and then to Tunisia and Algeria in April. "This year has been bad, and both Maurice and I lack money," she explained to Hélène Picard. One of the necessary consequences of the liquidation of Goudeket's business was the sale of his country house, La Gerbière; they had to move out in a hurry, for the purchaser — Coco Chanel — wanted to start renovations at once.[9]

Then she could begin serious work on a book that would represent a return to her wilder years — a compendium of sexual variations, in which she adopts the role of discreet observer, never expressing more than mild astonishment at the activities of the other characters.

In the opening sketch, an experienced woman feigns pleasure in the sexual act out of sympathy for the young man, who is ill. Next, an aging Don Juan confesses that he desired quick conquests, only to discover that women demanded permanence. This Don Juan charges that Colette is not really a woman, and she admits to suffering from "mental hermaphroditism," though she believes this had nothing to do with her lesbian experiences. Later on she makes it clear that even when she dressed as a boy, she remained a woman, and the other women knew it.

She then tells the terrifying story of Renée Vivien, Natalie Barney's lover, whose sexual excesses and drinking killed her. Colette goes on to discuss the more sensible relations that are possible between women, since each partner understands the other's preference. Finally, there is her friend Marcel, who taught her (with his circle of young men) that one sex could do away with the other by ignoring it.

Other writers treated the topic quite differently. Her friend Radclyffe Hall, for example, in her novel *The Well of Loneliness,* painted lesbian love as an often harrowing experience. Writing to Una Troubridge, Hall's companion, Colette explained why she disagreed with the novel's conception of abnormality: for her, "an abnormal man or woman should never feel abnormal; quite the contrary."[10]

She would call her own little book *Ces Plaisirs* . . . (These Pleasures). The reference was to a line in *The Ripening Seed:* "These pleasures which are thoughtlessly called physical. . . ." Ten years later a new edition would bear the more sober title *The Pure and the Impure.*

She worked against a deadline, having committed herself to serial publication in a brash weekly called *Gringoire.* "I'm working like an ant," she reported to Marguerite from Saint-Tropez that summer. "I hoist something up, then I let it drop and start all over again." When the time came for her to return to Paris, the book was still unfinished. "I'm going home next week," she told Marguerite, "poor but not discouraged — but damn it all, Maurice and I are going through a bad time. . . ."[11]

Just at this bad time, she lost her footing while taking a walk and fell into a ditch along the road; she might easily have broken a hip, but in fact only the fibula of her right leg was affected, and it was a clean break. It was not particularly serious, and could have been much worse, but at the time it was high drama: she screamed with pain until she began to faint, and then she was taken to the hospital in an ambulance. She managed to get back to Paris in a sleeping car.[12]

Bedridden or not, she completed *Ces Plaisirs* . . . in November 1931. "I vomit it up, of course," she declared to her fellow writer Lucie Delarue-Mardrus.[13] She finished it "over nights and days of despair, as is customary," she amplified for Hélène Picard. Meanwhile, her fracture had mended, though she still suffered from torn ligaments. And because she had to place all her weight on a cane, she had strained the hand she used for writing.[14]

She took advantage of her forced leisure to make plans for what was to be the business venture of her life. She had begun to talk about it that summer, when it had become clear that all of Maurice's best efforts were producing meager results. Why not capitalize on her own name and prestige, she reasoned — why not make Colette a trademark? Women used her books to help them resolve problems in their lives; might they not follow her beauty tips as well? She would sell a line of beauty products named after herself.[15]

Goudeket advised her that if she went ahead with the scheme, she would actually have to make up her customers; she liked the idea. She had been writing for a long time and needed a change. The new business would give her greater contact with the outside world, something she had enjoyed as a performer and then, later, in a newspaper office.[16]

So that autumn in Paris, with the troublesome book behind her, she began a new life — meeting potential backers, for instance. "I have one perfume ready," she reported to Hélène Picard, "another that soon will be, a splendid toilet water. . . . The other poisons, rouges and creams, etc., are running late." The paradox is that this woman who cultivated rusticity, who henceforth would wear sandals even on formal occasions, who still rolled her *r*'s as if she could not help it, was to take the business of elegance seriously. We have an unkind portrait of her at this moment, by a pert and pretty American of Paris named Bettina Bergery (née Elizabeth Shaw Jones), for whom Colette was "a squat neckless woman with toes like bunches of muddy carrots and a forehead like a Greek temple, concealed by a shrubbery of frizzled hair — though the old cat eyes were piercing."[17]

She was still using a cane when she called on suppliers, such as a perfume and soap factory out in the suburbs.[18] She seemed driven to do things that she would have preferred not to do, to see people whom she scorned. "It's Maurice's torment that torments me above all," she explained.[19]

The first blow came from an unexpected quarter. At that time *Gringoire* claimed a circulation of nearly a quarter of a million copies, a figure that would triple before the decade was over. It published the first installment of *Ces Plaisirs* . . . at the top of its front page on December 4, 1931, and then published three more, ending the last of these (on December 25) with a thunderous "The End." But it was far from the end of the book that Colette had submitted to *Gringoire*.

It is true that she had been warned that the magazine's readership would not go for her subject or for the way she had treated it. Without thinking, she had given the editors permission to deal with the text as they saw fit, and deal with it they did. The last published installment concerned lesbians and featured a masculine woman of noble blood; it was cut off in the middle of a sentence. There should have been five more installments after that one.[20]

Her revenge would be the publication of *Ces Plaisirs* . . . as a book; the book would endure. Besides, in the early weeks of 1932 she had other things on her mind. She was adding to the list of backers for her cosmetics business, and they had found a good location for a shop, just off Rue du Faubourg Saint-Honoré, opposite the presidential palace. The invitation for the opening was printed in a facsimile of Colette's handwriting:

I will inaugurate my beauty-products shop on Wednesday, June 1, and the following two days. I should be happy, Madame, to greet you personally . . . and to counsel you on the most becoming makeup, for the stage or for daily life.[21]

A surviving photograph shows Colette holding a ladder for a worker who is decorating the storefront. It was not the face powder that women came for, of course; it was Colette, who made up her customers personally. There are photographs that show her doing that, too.

Another relic has survived from that period in the form of a booklet titled *Colette,* written by Colette for her Colette business, containing her beauty secrets. About kohl, her constant companion, she wrote, "If you live in the sun in the daytime, and in artificial light in the evening, use kohl, even *during the night.*" In a list of products at the end of the booklet, she said again, "Kohl saved my bad eyes. I use it in the daytime, and then put more on at night."[22]

She did what had to be done; five afternoons a week she was in the shop, standing all the while. (She wore elastic bandages to protect her still-fragile leg.) "This business I'm engaged in with Maurice," she told Hélène Picard, "will flop or succeed, but my own hands and my obstinateness will be involved in it until the end."[23] In retrospect Goudeket judged that she had enjoyed every minute of it, including the inspecting of laboratories, the designing of packages, and the writing of prospectuses. Not only was the opening of the shop an event, but newly beautified customers would regularly hold out copies of her books to be autographed.[24]

THIRTY

The Cat

SHE LONGED to get away for the summer. The Léopold Marchands, after a stint in Hollywood, were back in France and hoping to lure her to their enchanted Breton castle on the sea. Then one of her publishers, Ferenczi, bore down on her, for she was to deliver another book, this one consisting of previously published articles that needed to be edited, shortened, or otherwise improved. And she continued to work in her shop. "Yesterday [July 11] was a remarkable Monday, with six or seven makeup jobs and customers who made purchases," she noted. One of that day's visitors was Renaud's mother, the ex-Panther.[1]

Before her departure for Saint-Tropez, she had a new book to sign for reviewers: *Prisons et paradis* (Prisons and Paradises) contained her zoo sketches, a tender account of life at La Treille Muscate, and some travel notes. Then she was off, but this summer at La Treille Muscate was going to afford her even less of a rest than the prior ones. She had lent her name to a group of local businessmen who were opening a shop to sell her products on the old harbor of Saint-Tropez; in fact, she had not only lent them her name and supplied them with her cosmetics but also promised to help. She was present for the shop's inauguration, on August 6, and after that stopped in regularly to make up customers. Soon there would be Colette products in tourist centers as far apart as Biarritz and Vichy, and in proper cities such as Bordeaux.[2]

And Saint-Tropez itself was becoming more and more like . . . Saint-Tropez. Paris had literally colonized the fishing village. As Colette described the scene to Maurice, she went into town with Hélène Morhange, picked up her mail, and dropped in at the beauty shop to chat with a friend who was having her nails done. Then, while she was shopping, "two hands were placed over my eyes, an agreeable body leaned against my back. . . ." It was Misia Sert. Along the waterfront the wife of Henry Bernstein greeted her and invited her to dinner at Robert de Rothschild's home. A little further on, she continued, "two hands delicate and cool covered my eyes: it was Coco Chanel." That led to another dinner invitation, this time at a tavern on the harbor.[3]

Goudeket spent much of his time in their Paris store, but soon he too was in Saint-Tropez, to join Colette on her first cosmetics tour, to Montpellier, Tarbes, Biarritz, Saint-Jean-de-Luz, and Bayonne, calling on beauty shops and hairdressers that handled their products. And so to Paris. "I spent the afternoon in the laboratory," she explained to Hélène Morhange, "where I selected, banished, modified, and redid thirty-four face powders (keeping fifteen of them), and let me tell you, it was a tough job." Then she was off to Marseilles, to make an appearance at a Colette stand at an international exhibition of perfume and beauty products. There was a banquet with the district prefect, and she lectured. On the second day she went to a lunch attended by all of the city's important hairdressers.[4]

In between these trips, when she might have been resting, she was instead writing — writing a jewel of a book. The protagonist was a character who was already familiar to Colette's friends: the she-cat named The Cat. In this novel, to be called *The Cat,* the nineteen-year-old Camille is to marry the blond and handsome Alain, twenty-four. But Alain is far more amorous toward his family's cat, Saha, "chartreuse, purebred, small, and perfect." If he marries Camille, what will happen to Saha? But he does marry her, and at the outset his young wife appears to be sympathetic, less inflexible than Alain himself (he is shocked when she walks around their apartment naked). He blushes when he has to tell her that he is going to visit his mother's house; she says that he only wants to see her rival, the Cat.

When Saha loses weight and appears listless, Alain brings her to the apartment that he shares with Camille. He insists on dining at home in order to be with his cat. In other ways — sexually, for instance — the marriage is fine.

Camille takes matters into her own hands and pushes his pet off their ninth-floor balcony, but Saha survives. When Alain realizes what his wife has done, he leaves her. "Camille doesn't like Saha very much," he tells his mother. "That's very serious!" she responds. "Yes, for Camille," Alain says, meanness in his eyes.

While getting over a severe case of flu in January 1933, Colette took time off to do another film job, writing subtitles for an American movie. "It's a delicate, boring, all but mathematical job," she commented to Hélène Picard.[5] In *No Greater Love* (directed by Lewis Seiler), a Jewish delicatessen owner adopts a young Irish girl who is both orphaned and crippled, pawning his shop to pay for an operation she needs. When the surgery fails to help her, she is sent to an orphanage. In the end her faith and her love for her benefactor literally put her back on her feet again.[6]

She returned to *The Cat* — scratched at it, she said. But before she could finish the manuscript, she set off on another tour, this one the most demanding of the lot. She went to Cannes and Bordeaux, then north to La Rochelle and Nantes, inland to Rennes, and finally to Blois; after a respite, she was off again, to Toulouse in the deep south and to Lyon and Grenoble in the east. She and her Maurice were "at the most difficult period of a business that we can't drop or allow to perish, because it is proving to be viable and even lively," she confided to Hélène Picard. If she had agreed to do thirty lectures during what was for her the worst season of the year (winter, of course), it was to guarantee their survival. "Maurice is as he should be," she told her friend. "He travels by subway, second class, and at the moment he's selling inexpensive washing machines and a charming device that cleans out water pipes and toilets."[7]

She made friends in Nantes. A young woman who attended her lecture there followed up with a letter, inaugurating a correspondence that was to span twenty years. A year after Colette's visit, Yvonne Brochard would team up with another woman to start a dairy farm, and their labors were to furnish a subject for many of these letters, while produce from their farm would often find its way to Colette's table, sometimes when it was sorely needed.[8]

Colette returned from such provincial triumphs to face Parisian realities. The beauty business was not allowing her the freedom from material concerns that she had hoped for, but she knew she could always make a little cash with limited, illustrated editions of her work. Now, for example, there was a new printing of *Break of Day,* for which Luc-Albert Moreau had provided lithographs of her Saint-Tropez paradise. But she was also counting on making some money on *The Cat.* The final weeks of work on the novel, brief though it was, were painful, and she felt ashamed of herself for finding them so. She shut herself up, working in bed. "Days (and nights) of eleven hours of work," she complained to Hélène Picard, adding that more than once she had still been at it as the sun rose.[9]

One thing now seemed certain: she would have to pursue her true vocation, for her beauty products would not put food on the table. The rouges and powders were good enough, and the ranks of satisfied customers were growing, but as Goudeket later summed up the problem, in order to develop their potential, they needed more capital and a commitment on Colette's part of several more years of her precious time. For the same effort, she could get a lot more out of writing, and they would soon recognize their error and turn the page. On the positive side, Goudeket thought that the beauty business enabled Colette to renew her contact with people, and thus also to renew her themes.[10]

It was now that a fortuitous movie job fell into her lap. She was asked to adapt Vicki Baum's novel *Ladies' Lake;* a young producer named Philippe de Rothschild had recruited an equally young film-maker, Marc Allégret, to direct. She was involved "in a stupid assignment," Colette let Hélène Picard know, and the hours were "capricious."[11] Indeed, during the final stretch Rothschild and Allégret booked a suite for themselves and their assistants on the fifth floor of the Claridge, just below Colette's rooms. They would go upstairs each afternoon at two, sprawling over every available chair as well as the carpet; they would be wearing bathrobes or pyjamas, or shorts and open shirts, and she would be stretched out on her sofa bed in a bathrobe. They took twenty minutes off for dinner and were back on the job. Then it would be midnight, or 1:30, or even later — and eventually she would chase them out. On the very last day she could not get rid of them before daybreak.

She did all this while trying not to forget the rest. One suffocating afternoon at the beginning of summer she signed 650 copies of *The Cat* in a department store, over a period of three and a half hours. While she was chatting with her fans, a display of Colette products was being set up in the perfume department of the same store.[12]

The day after her arrival in Saint-Tropez, the film's director, Marc Allégret, flew down for another four hours of work. Then there were some rehearsals with the young stars — Jean-Pierre Aumont and Simone Simon, who Colette decided had "hard eyes hidden behind a child's eyes."[13]

After much elation, she suffered a humiliation. There was a story in the press to the effect that she was being promoted within the ranks of the Legion of Honor; that would not have displeased her. But once more she was held back, on the grounds that she had not been at her present grade long enough. She was sure there were other reasons, however, and she was right. Although her old friend and partisan Anatole de Monzie was now minister of education, he felt he could not speak up on behalf of a vendor of face powder.[14] "I shared your disappointment," she was assured by no less than Edouard Herriot, twice the premier of France. "But believe me, you are above such puerilities."[15] She was to wait three more years for that promotion.

She took some consolation in the reviews for *The Cat,* even if reviews, like ribbons, often came from friends. Edmond Jaloux called the novel "a masterpiece of concision, of art, of classic perfection, with the maximum of truth, intelligence, and poetry." A female critic who went by a man's name, Gérard d'Houville, also praised the book, and Colette wrote from Saint-Tropez to thank her: "The Cat (the real one) is here with me, as she has been every summer for seven years. She is young for her age, and at dawn she dances like a demon."[16]

Early in August Goudeket returned to Paris, determined to take extreme measures to save their business. He fired their manager and put himself in charge.[17] It was just then that the phone rang with an offer from *Le Journal,* one of the leading Paris dailies: would she take over their theater criticism? "I do feel," she said to Hélène Picard, "that I've got to make a reentry, even if only a brief one, into journalism."[18]

THIRTY-ONE

Madame Goudeket

*F*OR YEARS to come — through the spring of 1938, when she was sixty-five — Colette was to remain the Sunday theater critic of one of the capital's dailies. As often as four or even five times a week, from autumn until summer, she would put on evening clothes, gather up her purse and her opera glasses — the famous black pair that provided the title for the successive collections of her theater articles — and set out to attend dress rehearsals of new plays. Some of these works were classics, others revivals of popular favorites; on occasion she would cover a circus or a recital by a Maurice Chevalier. Always she knew that her readers were expecting a Colette point of view, waiting for Colette to be Colette. When the first collection of these pieces came out in book form in August 1934, a reviewer reviewed Colette reviewing the theater. He compared her to a cat who knew how to wait, to watch for "that instant which reveals the quality or the defect, either of the play or of the performance" — for "Madame Colette goes about it like a cat cleaning a fish bone," he said.[1]

In the winter of 1934 she suffered from what she called neuritis, running up her right arm all the way to the shoulder and extending to that side of her back; writing was painful for her. She was treated with diathermy and X rays.[2] Late March in Saint-Tropez was her salvation; the weather was chilly and the heating of the villa inadequate, but the spectacle of early roses in the garden overwhelmed her. She and Maurice were also eating everything in sight: "You can't imagine what young onions are like," she exclaimed to Hélène Morhange, "with bread and butter!"[3] But no matter how pleasant it was down there, Paris called: the theater season, with its schedule of openings, was inexorable.

It was not long after this that a young man up from the provinces called on Colette, or tried to. One sunny day in June, he approached the Claridge hotel. "Bellboys in white gloves lie in wait for generous guests," he noted. "Porters look you up and down contemptuously, seeming to be judging the size of your wallet." He slipped past them and into an elevator, reached Colette's floor, and knocked at room 609. Pauline greeted him, along with "Monsieur Maurice," who he guessed was "the secretary or rather the chargé d'affaires." (Monsieur Maurice was still not a public figure.) The visitor remarked the scarlet roses on a small chest in the salon. He even got to see Colette's boudoir, which contained more roses, some peonies, and a small writing desk that he decided was quite inadequate for a professional writer. There were more flowers on the balcony, a small female bullterrier, and, of course, the Cat. But Colette herself was nowhere to be found; she had skipped school that day. The young man published an account of his visit all the same.[4]

As soon as the theater season was over, Ferenczi went to press with her collected reviews. After that she was off to Saint-Tropez again. She sat down at once to write a short novel, and once again opened with a moment of crisis. In *Duo,* Michel is a stage director who discovers that his wife has taken his assistant as her lover. He does not know how to deal with the discovery, so his wife, Alice, tries to help by being frank. Michel seems to be ready to accept her transgression as a crisis of sensuality; she, in turn, is upset to learn how little men understand about women. In the end, Michel resolves his quandary by drowning himself.

She worked on the book all summer and was still working on it when the cultural weekly *Marianne* published the first installment on September 12. Perhaps the reason she was taking so long to finish it was that she had something else on her desk, something representing ready cash: she was to create an original dialogue for a movie to be directed by Max Ophüls, the German-born filmmaker who was then living as a refugee in France. The story was in fact tailored for Colette's actress friend Simone Berriau. The publicity proclaimed it "the first scenario written directly for the screen by Colette," which, if we consider Musidora and the silent screen, was not quite true; and besides, the new movie was to be based partly on Colette's own *Music-Hall Sidelights,* portraying the evils of the city, the sordid realities of backstage life, and the contrasting innocence of the countryside. The film's failure was ultimately attributed to Ophüls's unfamiliarity with rural life, though François Truffaut was to call *Divine* a "healthy and spirited little masterpiece." Colette's daughter worked as an assistant to the director during the filming.[5]

Duo, Divine — it was a busy summer for Colette. But there was time for a daily swim all the same. Colette II came for a visit and stayed with friends at a nearby hotel. "When you think," her mother wrote to Misz Marchand, "that I could have made twelve of them, each just as pretty!"[6]

She gave her daughter a copy of *Duo,* inscribed "To my dear daughter, for whom I dream about a 'duo' without a false note . . . but her generation likes rough music, and free will. Let's forget what I just said. I happen to be a weak mother!" That was a lot of message for an autograph, but Colette de Jouvenel was now a marriageable twenty-one, and *Maman* could not let her forget it.[7]

A reader of the second volume of Colette's collected reviews may conclude that she approached variety acts with more gusto than she did conventional forms of theater. But whatever the medium, she always managed to be personal. Reviewing a play that starred a portly actress, she called attention to the undernourished — that is, to those women who dieted in order to appear in the movies, and who in consequence suffered a loss of energy. Sometimes extra pounds in breasts and backside enhanced beauty, she argued. Reporting on a display of nudity at a music hall, she expressed distaste for what she had heard about striptease acts in New York. The French preferred veils, she thought.[8]

It was time to move again. The Claridge was having financial problems and could no longer afford to subsidize Colette's rent, however prestigious a guest she might be. The move was a short one, just across the broad avenue to a new-old building, the Marignan office-apartment complex, on the corner of the street of that name and the Champs-Elysées. She was now to learn something about instant decrepitude — which is what happens when a building is put up in haste.

A draft that slammed a door on the second floor cracked her wall on the eighth. A neighbor informed her that the roof terrace above their heads was slowly sinking into his office. Nevertheless, she liked the ship's stairway that led up to the roof and would climb it with the Cat on her shoulder and the dog close behind, on a leash. From up there she could see much of the Paris roofline, including such landmarks as the Opera and the Sacré Coeur church atop Montmartre.[9]

She and Maurice had separate doors, separate doorbells, even separate telephones. It cost more that way, but they were not married. Later they were to decide that it would be simpler for them to wed. "Once the idea came up," Goudeket remembered, "it seemed to us both practical and attractive." He was now forty-five, she sixty-two.[10]

In a letter to Hélène Picard, telling her of a hasty departure for Easter in Saint-Tropez, the bride's announcement came as an afterthought: "By the way, we married, Maurice and I, some ten days ago. A ceremony in seventeen minutes, everything included, and two witnesses as our wedding procession. In over ten years we had never found a free morning to make things official!"[11] The first free morning happened to be on April 3, 1935; the ceremony took place at the town hall of Paris's eighth district. Goudeket later said that Colette never remembered anniversaries and would not remember this one, either, though she would recall the giant snowflakes that fell that day over the village where they took their witnesses, Luc-Albert Moreau and his Hélène, for the wedding lunch.[12]

Another version of the story, also told by Goudeket, has him suggesting marriage only because they were about to sail on the maiden voyage of the *Normandie,* and he thought it would be easier for them to get a double room in prudish America if they were man and wife.[13]

This was an assignment from *Le Journal,* one that Colette could not object to, for it offered a ten-day round trip on the world's most splendid passenger vessel, with six days in New York, dresses and coats furnished by the designer Lucien Lelong, pocket money, and a free crossing for her new husband as well. Despite the promise of lavish meals, Goudeket remembered, Colette carried a picnic basket aboard the special boat train to Le Havre, containing pâté, cold chicken, and hard-boiled eggs. The reporters on the train got their first story out of it, and also shared the contents.[14]

Colette's passport survives. It describes her as being just over 5'4" (one meter sixty-three), with light chestnut hair, eyebrows of the same color, a high forehead, and blue-gray eyes.[15]

They sailed on May 29. She kept a log in addition to writing articles for *Le Journal.* Even on board ship she worked in bed. She summed up her impressions for Hélène Morhange: "Calm sea, cool weather, bores at port and starboard. . . ." There were gossip columnists everywhere, even in the hold, but she had no complaints about the food.[16] She would have liked to have the whole ship to herself, she told her diary, and she even rose at dawn to try to capture something of that feeling, but a ship never sleeps.

They reached New York on June 3. While waiting to dock they were greeted by sirens and low-flying aircraft releasing confetti; strains of the "Marseillaise" floated over the wind. The first sight of the celebrated skyline produced the inevitable shock, an "almost religious seizure."[17] Goudeket noticed that the photographers who flocked aboard focused on Colette not because she was famous but because she was wearing sandals and had varnished toenails.[18] There was a mob at customs and a scramble to recover their luggage, and then they were away and up to a high floor of the Waldorf-Astoria. Colette tried to mark her very window on a postcard to Luc-Albert. "The city is much more beautiful than we thought it would be," she added in a postscript.[19]

The newlyweds did all of the expected things, going to see the Empire State Building, the Roxy movie theater, Central Park, and Harlem. When they discovered Woolworth's five-and-ten-cent stores, it almost put an end to the cultural side of the visit. They took an expensive taxi ride to the home of Parker pens, a pilgrimage for this writer who worshiped them. One night, returning from a Mae West movie at the Roxy, they came upon a cat. "At last, someone who speaks French!" Colette exclaimed to Maurice.[20] They boarded the *Normandie* for the return crossing on June 7 and were back on French soil six days later.

Then it was Colette II's turn to surprise them: she met and married a man whom nobody knew. A desire for emancipation? They all took it that way and worried that this shy and bearded husband, believed to be a virgin, would be no match for ebullient Colette de Jouvenel — and in any case, where was the love? All the same, there was a proper wedding, at Castel-Novel. Colette was not even told the date until it was over, but her ex-husband wrote her a "pretty" letter to thank her for allowing their daughter to be married there.[21] The honeymooners — Mr. and Mrs. Denis Adrien Camille Dausse — did go on to Saint-Tropez, where they booked into a hotel, appearing at ease with each other and with their new state. Within weeks, however, they were ready to divorce.

He could not be much of a husband to her daughter, suggested Colette. "Motive for which there is no ready answer: physical repulsion," was her explication to Hélène Picard. "Don't talk about it."[22] Colette II's first instinct was to run away. As she remembered it, after hearing her confused explanations, her mother reassured her, "I don't want you to be miserable at twenty-two. When you're forty-two, perhaps you won't be able to help it. . . . Talk to your father, and tell him that the oracle has spoken."

Henry proved to be equally understanding. He realized, he told his daughter, that "you are bored by this man, who also bored me when he droned on, though you and I had understood from the beginning what he had to say. Being bored with someone is what makes you think of murder. I left many women because of that." Leave him, her father urged her.[23]

THIRTY-TWO

My Apprenticeships

THAT EXTRAORDINARY and unfulfilled man Henry de Jouvenel died soon after. It happened on a Paris boulevard, on October 5, 1935. One story has it that when Colette was informed of his death, she asked what he had died of and was told, "The heart." Her reply was, "No kidding!" Another anecdote, which Colette II seems to have attributed to her mother, though it was widely repeated, held that Jouvenel, then fifty-nine years old, had been stricken while in the company of one of the young women whose regular beat was the garden behind the Champs-Elysées.[1]

Colette had not seen her second husband in a dozen years and did not think that she even would have recognized him had she met him on the street. Whatever she may have felt, she said all the appropriate things; she would not be petty. She knew that he had been of solace to their daughter and would have been more helpful still in the trying days that lay ahead for her. Better, then, to accept at face value the sentiment that Colette expressed some time after that: "God keep his soul! And let him set up a little Louis XIV section for himself in Paradise!"[2]

Colette II joined her half-brothers on the trip down to Castel-Novel for the funeral. They were faced with a problem: while he was grateful for all that Senator Jouvenel had done for his region, the village priest had to tell the family that the Church could not condone a religious service for this freethinking divorcé.[3] But no matter; a eulogy was delivered by an old friend of Sidi's, Anatole de Monzie. He paid tribute to the *dreyfusard* — "because to defend justice was noble in 1898" — and also to the senator and the twice-anointed minister. Henry had been discreet, he said, shunning effusive camaraderie; "in him the man was all but hidden behind the gentleman."[4]

Settling the estate was no simple matter. Jouvenel had never been wealthy, but there *was* property, meaning estate taxes to pay and mortgages to pay off. In the end the cash came from Renaud de Comminges — now Renaud de Jouvenel, for he had been recognized by Henry in March 1928 — who had married wealth and could keep the family estate in family hands. He sold Castel-Novel only in 1956, to a local businessman who transformed it into a first-class hotel with a fifteen-acre park.[5]

Colette, meanwhile, was digging deep into her memory, going back even earlier than the Jouvenel years, to reconstruct, very much on her own terms, her beginnings as a writer. *My Apprenticeships* often reads like a novel, and it was the opinion of some of Colette's old friends that it contained more than a little fiction. Willy, these people decided, was made out in Colette's books to be considerably worse than he had really been.

Her indictment of him was indeed severe. "Three or four women still tremble at his name," she wrote. He had been a jaded seducer despite his physical disadvantages. Too old for Colette, he had nonetheless prevented her from experiencing young men while she herself was still young. Money had been his chief interest: "To calculate, acquire, hold on to things — this was what took first place, even in his flood of correspondence."

She worked on the book, as had become her habit, even as it began to be published in installments. *Marianne* ran these from October 23 to December 18, 1935, and then the whole appeared as a book under the imprint of Ferenczi. André Gide remarked a "particularly feminine" genius in *My Apprenticeships* and praised the happy proportions underlying its seeming disorder. He discerned "perfect tact" and "courteous discretion" in the way Colette handled her contemporaries — even Willy![6]

And still she had to grub for money. "Panic work," she explained her current occupations to Hélène Picard. "A panic above all in book sales, you wouldn't believe it." The job at hand was a French adaptation of *The Royal Family,* a play by the American comedy writers George S. Kaufman and Moss Hart. First Goudeket did a rough translation from English, and then Colette rewrote the draft. Financial backing had not yet been found for the project, but the script had to be ready just in case. In the end, there was no production.[7]

But her coveted promotion to the rank of commander of the Legion of Honor came through at last. And while she could not be elected to the all-male French Academy — even if those proper gentlemen had desired her presence — there was room for her at the Belgian Royal Academy of French Language and Literature. Anna de Noailles had previously been elected to membership, and when she died, the academy deemed it appropriate to pass her seat on to France's other famous woman author.

She was to deliver her acceptance speech in Brussels on April 4, 1936. "Do I have to tell you," she wrote to Hélène Picard, "that I'm nothing but misanthropy, anguish, stomachache, stuttering, and general collapse?"[8] Goudeket added that she had forgotten that her passport had expired. The Belgian immigration officer wanted to take her off the train, but he was dissuaded by the Goudekets' friend Winnie — Princess Edmond de Polignac — who in forceful French, with an American accent, told him, "Madame is expected by your Academy to make a speech, and they cannot begin without her."[9]

So there was the spectacle (as recorded by the literary journalist Maurice Martin du Gard), in that "palace of the Prince of Orange, in that long hall decorated with pompous paintings of the history of Flanders," of an academician in sandals. (The reporter knew that her accident in Saint-Tropez was responsible for that.) The audience may not have noticed her feet, however, since the green velvet covering the speakers' table touched the floor, and in any case, her speech would have made them forget everything else.[10] She admitted to the assembly that she was very moved. She was still surprised to be taken seriously as a writer, having started out without even knowing that she *was* one. She also pointed out that this was a return trip to Belgium for her, in a sense, because of her Belgian relatives and her mother's nostalgia for her childhood home.[11]

She was a rousing success, of course. The members of the academy mobbed her after the speech, embraced her, complimented her; the next day she was received by the French ambassador, who had invited a salonful of distinguished guests to meet her. Colette whispered to Martin du Gard, "When I go to a place where I can't say 'Shit,' I feel sick." [12]

Always, between Colette's more ambitious books, there would be short articles, sketches, and privately published editions, produced in limited, sometimes numbered printings. This year she wrote an essay on butterflies that covered barely five pages in an album reproducing someone's collection. (The time was long past, she said, when she herself could kill a butterfly.)[13] An illustrated edition of her occasional writings was published in four large-format volumes whose purchasers were designated the Committee of Friends of Colette; each copy was signed. (The first of these volumes contained the Chéri stories, written years before the novel.)[14]

And then it was back to the work for which she was best known. "The job is dreadful," she complained to a new friend, Renée Hamon. "Every day, every day, despite the fine weather." She had gone to Saint-Tropez for the summer (one dares not add the word *vacation*). "I have to come back with a long story of over a hundred pages for *Gringoire*," she said; she had not been able to afford to bear a grudge against the weekly that had cut her novel, and her fee.[15]

This new long piece was a stunning tale, "Bella-Vista," published later as the title story of a collection. Colette painted herself into it: she has taken a room in a Riviera hotel while her house (recently acquired) is being gotten into shape. The hotel is run by two women, one of whom turns out to be a man. Colette is Colette, immobile but observant.

Renée Hamon, her new confidante, was thirty-nine. She had married at twenty and divorced at twenty-three, after the death of a baby. She had followed an American war veteran to Texas and taught in New York. Back in Paris, she modeled for painters and photographers, was introduced to the fashion designer Paul Poiret, and through him met and charmed Colette. Later she would marry again, pedal a bike around the world, and join a research team on its way to Tahiti, where she would become an authority on Gauguin. Colette called this wanderer her Little Corsair.[16]

The Little Corsair kept a diary and did not fail to record impressions of her famous friend: "A bourgeoise, an authentic woman of the honest middle class," she declared (to herself, at least). To explain this surprising judgment, she added, "Even in a hotel she has to 'decorate' her room." Colette was "feminine and virile: equilibrium," and had "strength. Health. Healthy: the sense of proportions. Very French." Renée was struck by her "professional honesty" and found her to be "in turn a cat, a panther, a ferret, a deer." And also "incredibly young."[17]

By then *Gringoire* had become a horror. Looking back, it is difficult to separate its cultural content from its political impact. The first installment of "Bella-Vista" appeared on September 18, 1936; on the front page of the same issue was an insidious exposé of the "non-French" origins of Léon Blum — for this Socialist prime minister was a Jew. A cartoon mocked France as Europe's garbage dump; the trash cans are seen to contain German Jews (refugees from Hitler's Germany) and other antifascists. There was a report on the annual Nazi rally in Nuremberg, praising Hitler as a true friend of France. Good Frenchmen, *Gringoire*'s reporter concluded, would refuse to take up arms against Germany.

That week's *Gringoire* also contained one in a series of attacks on Roger Salengro, Blum's minister of the interior. Salengro was said to have deserted during the 1914–1918 war (despite evidence that he had been captured by the enemy while carrying out an order to recover the body of a fallen comrade). Two months after this article appeared, on November 18, Salengro was found dead; he had killed himself by turning on the gas in his kitchen. Furious at *Gringoire* for its part in this, workers prevented the following issue from being published (by then, "Bella-Vista" had completed its run).

Henceforth Colette would limit herself almost exclusively to shorter fiction. Goudeket explained this as a desire on her part to return to essentials, not a drying-up of her talent or a lack of patience with the longer format. She turned away from the things that came easily to her, such as landscape description; once he saw her tear up some pages because, she said, she had caught herself "in the process of being Colette."[18] The book trade has always demanded longer works — readers as well as reviewers generally find themselves better able to come to terms with full-length novels — but some of Colette's best writing is in her short stories, many of them written after she turned sixty. "Gigi" is a product of her seventieth year.

To make a book, to be published by Ferenczi in 1937, Colette tied "Bella-Vista" to three other pieces. "Gribiche" was a return to a familiar venue: Colette meows and barks on stage and watches as a young dancer fades away after a clumsy abortion. In "The Rendez-vous," a group of inconsequential Europeans come to grips with the Arab underclass in Tangier. "The Patriarch" takes the author back to her childhood, when she accompanied her half-brother, Achille, on visits to his patients: while delivering a baby, Achille learns that the young mother's father fornicates with his daughters. Even the friendliest of literary critics, Edmond Jaloux, had to take note of the "troubling figures" offered by Colette. Yet he was able to praise her for her willingness to deal with "all forms of life."[19]

Not everyone would be so charitable: "You can see that she lives in this immoral atmosphere, not like a fish in water but like a worm in the mud" — that in a Catholic magazine. "But *I'm* a Catholic!" Colette exclaimed to Renée Hamon.[20]

THIRTY-THREE

Palais-Royal

No MEDIUM seemed inaccessible: in 1937 Colette began doing a weekly radio program directed at women and dealing with problems of daily existence, children, and pets.[1] "My little corsair," she advised Renée Hamon, "make sure you're paid for every article — nothing for nothing. If by chance you gave someone an article for free, everyone would know it at once, and you'd be finished!"[2] If Colette didn't earn money, she protested, how would she and Maurice live?

Not that Maurice wasn't trying: having given up after a round of hopeless business ventures, he was now an apprentice writer. In September 1937 he translated and adapted a play for the popular Georges Pitoëff acting company.[3] "Maurice showed himself inadequate in a touching way," Colette gently mocked him in reporting the results of a dress rehearsal to a friend. "Agitated, broken up, not eating, he appeared all of his fourteen and a half years of age."[4]

They spent the summer in Saint-Tropez, of course, but now there were campers — thousands of them, all with tents. Every bed on the coast was rented out. "The women are naked," Colette told Léopold Marchand. "Nudity is not athletic but frivolous." For her it was a hideous spectacle: "I find that men in briefs make women look bad," she complained.[5]

Men in briefs, or without them — Jean-Pierre Aumont, the young star of *Ladies' Lake,* now a mature twenty-six, came calling at La Treille Muscate that summer. "Heavy rather than fat," he sized up his hostess, "with muscles forged by work, by weeding, a flesh weighted with all the foods and all the loves, this stocky Burgundian who shakes up her world with the authority of a farmer's wife, who speaks to the dog, the cat, with the brusque impatience of the woman who knows, this sensuous peasant with a hoarse accent. . . ."

The evening was hot; Aumont asked if he could take a shower. Colette ordered him to strip right there in the garden. "My plants need watering," she said. So he stood naked in the midst of vines and bougainvilleas as she hosed him down, him and the plants.[6]

That summer she thought about Castel-Novel. The heirs were auctioning off the Jouvenel furniture and not getting much for it: there were lots of *school of*'s and *attributed to*'s among the paintings in that half-real castle. She had a moving exchange of letters with Renaud, who along with his wife was now in charge of the family estate. They issued the first invitation to visit there that Colette had had in a great many years; she thought she might take them up on it one day. She was hoping to forge a permanent link between Renaud and her daughter, "who still has a kind of passion for Castel-Novel." Of course she did; it had been her childhood.[7]

Now Colette was going to find her own true home. It began with an interview she gave to a popular daily, *Paris-Midi,* in which she let it be known that she was planning a move (to the Place Vendôme, she said, because of a novel she was writing that was to use that neighborhood as its setting). She went on to express her desire to live in the Palais-Royal apartment just above the low-ceilinged flat that had once been hers. Reading the interview, the present tenant of that very apartment informed her that he happened to be moving out; it was hers for the asking.[8] That was in November 1937; by the following January she was settled in her last and best home, the apartment that would become her trademark and in which she would receive the world, and its honors, in her final years. It almost became her museum.

The address, of course, was the same: 9 Rue de Beaujolais. And her return was like a homecoming. "It's a village," she proclaimed to Renée Hamon. "They all remembered me! They call me from their windows!" The neighboring snack bar delivered pancakes for her to taste, and even the concierge — the ubiquitous prying porter — was nice to her.[9]

On the garden side there was a large room with two windows, then a smaller room with one window. This smaller room had a bathroom with a tub, but Colette herself did not think such a thing was essential. Baths were unhealthy, she maintained: "You just connect a shower head to the faucet in the sink, you scrub yourself with a washcloth, and that's your shower."[10] The larger room and a connecting bedroom in the rear were Colette's domain; eventually her sofa bed would be moved up to the windows so that she could work on her bed or in it and still have both light and the view. Goudeket got the smaller garden room. It was a piece of history, this Palais-Royal, with a true palace completing the quadrangle to the south, and the Comédie Française visible from the window.[11]

As usual, Colette did the decorating, arranging and displaying all those things she collected, or accepted, such as crystal paperweights, religious trinkets, and mounted butterflies.[12] One day her Little Corsair looked on as Colette, her left hand bandaged because she had burned it on an electric socket, repaired a faucet with a wrench while water splashed around. Then she set about raising awnings. When her visitor offered to help, Colette exclaimed, "No, no, and no! I have to use my hands. When my hands aren't working, nothing goes right."[13]

Still, she had another, public face. When a neighbor, the film editor Denise Tual, paid a visit, Pauline had her wait while Colette made herself up. "From the dark entranceway I could make out her silhouette against the window, her gestures, the combing-out of the bangs on her forehead, and the cloud of powder being applied to her face," Tual remembered. Pauline tied a scarf of mauve tulle around Colette's neck, and she looked at herself in the mirror before having her guest shown in. Tual noted that Colette smelled good and had pink feet.[14]

The description is worth quoting because this Colette at home, Colette in an armchair or spread out on her sofa bed, was to become familiar to a growing number of visitors from the world over, from now until the end of her life; this was the only Colette they would know.

And this sitting room/bedroom was also her workroom. "Now get out!" she once commanded her Little Corsair. "When you see me in a bathrobe, it means I'm working!" Another day she announced, "I'm going to undress to work. I don't like to be dressed like a lady to write." She would dress again for the theater that evening, for she had a new play to review. "When I get an assignment," she confided, "I take the quantity of paper that I'll need to finish it, and then when I see the bundle I say to myself, 'I've got to fill up all those pages!'"[15]

In June 1938 her daughter had her appendix removed (the operation was performed by Colette's friend the literary surgeon Henri Mondor). Colette was told not to visit her at the hospital, but she ignored the doctor's orders.[16] The interdiction may not have been strictly a medical decision, for the latent crisis in mother-daughter relations persisted; Colette found her daughter exasperating, and we can assume that the reverse was also true. Her own energy had no echo in her offspring, Colette felt; Colette II was wasting her gifts. One friendly observer believed that the relationship between Colette and this beautiful and strange young woman was complicated by the constant presence of Maurice.[17]

Colette II herself would later reflect that far from being a faithful copy of her mother or father, she had instead inherited the incurable daydreaming of her grandfather Captain Jules Colette, as well as his inaptitude for managing earthly possessions and his feeling that he had twenty lives ahead of him in which to write his books. Then, too, she had a few drops of blood of "a half-wild brother" (meaning

Renaud) and the frivolity of her paternal grandmother (Mamita). She had so many ancestors, she said, and they all went round and round in circles, never advancing.[18]

Colette was back in Saint-Tropez early that July. She and Maurice went down to the harbor on the day of their arrival, just as the Duke and Duchess of Windsor sailed in from Antibes on their yacht to return a couple of vases to a local antiques dealer. The customs officer would not allow them to bring the objects ashore without a permit, as it turned out, and the superior who could issue the permit was having lunch. The onlookers enjoyed the scene; the duke swore he would never return to Saint-Tropez.[19]

Colette found the summer crowd more terrifying than ever. Like the Duke of Windsor, she was seeing her last of Saint-Tropez. Goudeket said that it was her own fame that made the house of her dreams uninhabitable; the eighteen hundred yards separating it from the overrun village were no longer sufficient. She herself had become a tourist attraction, drawing summer visitors who sailed by to watch her bathing in the sea. So the house she loved was put up for sale.[20]

She returned to Paris to find her friends caught up in an atmosphere of crisis. Chancellor Hitler was preparing to move against Czechoslovakia, the second step (after Austria) in his conquest of central Europe. The four leaders who were most directly concerned — Hitler, Mussolini, Edouard Daladier of France, and Neville Chamberlain of Britain — met in Munich at the end of September 1938. Hitler was satisfied, or so it seemed, with a slice of Czechoslovakia.

Colette asked Renée Hamon what she thought of the German dictator, and then she answered her own question: "A vegetarian gentleman who eats only porridge oats at lunchtime and maybe an egg at night . . . a gentleman who doesn't sleep with anybody, not even men. . . ."[21]

It was just as events were building toward Munich and appeasement that Colette signed on with *Paris-Soir,* which was rapidly becoming the most widely read daily in the capital and would have a circulation of nearly two million copies before the outbreak of World War II. "Everything would be perfect," she wrote to Hélène Morhange, "if we didn't have human folly hovering over our heads."[22]

THIRTY-FOUR

Every War in Paris

COLETTE WAS SUPPOSED to go to Brittany for Christmas, to a town and an inn found for her by her Little Corsair. But just when it was time to set off, an onslaught of winter spoiled the plan. It was not only the bad roads, she explained to Renée Hamon, but also the frigid temperature that she could not bear: "I want a lukewarm Brittany."[1]

In any case, there was plenty for her to do in Paris. Besides writing for *Paris-Soir,* she boasted (or complained), in the space of a fortnight she produced an advertising leaflet for tobacco, composed an essay to accompany a deluxe edition of flower paintings, and read through the proofs of another little book of hers, called *Le Toutounier,* to be published in January 1939 by Ferenczi.[2]

This novel is usually passed over by all but the most exhaustive of readers. She had tossed it off in Saint-Tropez the previous summer and barely mentioned it to her friends; even Goudeket, when he claimed that she was writing only novellas and short stories at this time, seems to have forgotten *Le Toutounier*. In it, the recently widowed Alice visits her sisters Colombe and Hermine, and they sit on an old divan that they call the *toutounier* as they bring each other up to date. The talk is of their men and their careers. Alice is going to obtain a considerable sum of money from an insurance policy and from the sale of some property (at this point we realize that she is also the heroine of *Duo,* and that her husband killed himself after learning of her infidelity). There is drama: Hermine shoots at the wife of her lover, whom they all call Monsieur Weekend. But it comes out mostly right in the end, when Monsieur Weekend asks Hermine to marry him. Colombe's man, though married to someone else, takes her away, too. Only Alice is left alone.

After a series of postponements, the Goudekets finally reached Brittany early in February, meeting up with Renée Hamon in Auray. Colette had offered to pay the hotel a supplement for extra heat and had asked her Little Corsair to buy her a good lamp so that she could work. They also had to have sand for "the crepuscular Cat," who made the journey along with "old Souci," the bullterrier; both of these pets needed fresh air as much as Colette and Maurice did. Renée showed the Goudekets through her little cottage, and Colette thought of returning to Brittany in some more permanent way, this time to this more clement southern coast rather than to another Rozven.

Almost as soon as they got back to Paris, on Sunday, February 19, the crepuscular Cat died. And then, on Sunday, March 19, after a long night of convulsions, the dog died, too. Both deaths were a great blow to Colette.

Around this time she undertook a particularly demanding assignment from *Paris-Soir:* she was to cover a gory murder trial. What the paper wanted, of course, was human interest, but even that angle could be terrifying in the case of a multiple murderer such as Eugène Weidmann, whose victims were all women (one of them an American tourist). Back at home, Colette was working on an equally delicate task: writing the preface to a friend's book. The problem, of course, was finding a way to do it without seeming to endorse the work with the full weight of her name. Her solution was to introduce Renée Hamon's account of her adventures in the South Pacific with a letter addressed to her friend, one supposedly written before

Renée's return, before she began writing the book. This was necessary, Colette explained privately, in order for her to remain true to
her "scruples" and her "obligations." In her draft, Colette offered
advice to a new writer: describe only what you see; be confident
about first impressions. Don't look for rare words; "a word is rare
only when it has the luck to meet another word that freshens it up."
Never write a book at the scene of the event; you can't write about
passion while making love.[3]

When spring called her to the country, she traveled with Maurice to
another substitute home, this one a "frightful" castle-hotel at Alizay,
not far from Rouen. Not only did she take along a writing project —
which would become the stunning tale "Chance Acquaintances" —
but Maurice, too, had an assignment: he was to do a series of articles
on French science for *Paris-Soir*. "Life is quite austere," she reported — not without pride, it seems — to Misz Marchand.

There were cats at Alizay. "All that is very nice," she wrote to
Hélène Morhange, "but one cat is missing, and everything is emptiness."[4]

She had sworn that after La Treille Muscate she would not own
another house — the responsibility was too much for her, she insisted — but she fell in love with one more, this at Méré, on the
outskirts of Montfort-l'Amaury; they passed it one Sunday evening
when they were returning from a visit with Luc-Albert and Hélène.
The house itself was insignificant, but the grounds were ample. What
attracted her most of all was the profusion of wisteria — that, and
the For Sale sign. She begged Maurice to look up the owner that
very evening and to pay whatever he was asking. Goudeket remembered the man's surprise; he must have thought that the house contained some buried treasure that he was unaware of.[5]

Renée Hamon visited Colette on the first of June and found her
thinner; her expression was touching, she thought. Colette said that
she was disgusted with herself; she had just discovered that she could
not walk.[6] It was an early sign of the incapacity to come, though it
would be quite a while yet before she ceased to be able to move at

all. Then and there she packed up to leave for the Riviera, for the actor Charles Vanel had made her an offer for La Treille Muscate; it was a modest sum, but she had to accept it for the sake of the new house near Paris. "People think I'm abandoning it gladly, or with indifference," she confided to her Little Corsair. "It's true that I'm doing what I can to make them think so."

There was much to do in the new house, in the little village of Méré; there was no hope of their moving in that summer. So a return to Brittany was called for. They wound up at the Grand Hotel de la Pointe des Pois, near Camaret. "That's a sea!" she exclaimed. "That's a Brittany!" Writing to the Marchands, they of northern Brittany, she told of feasting the way they had feasted as their guests: "They throw you lobsters as big as our thighs."[7] But Brittany was simply too far from Paris, where work awaited them. One solution, at least for what remained of this summer, was to find a seashore closer to the city. Dieppe, on the Channel coast, was only two hours away, and never mind that it was no longer very chic by that time; it had "so many humble summer people, so many old English ladies, so many 'varied attractions' in the awful Casino. . . ." It was a restful holiday for them, said Colette, "if it doesn't go on too long."[8]

Even in Dieppe one heard what was happening — even if one purposely removed oneself from the world's business, as she and Maurice did. "Calm, perfect calm," she was to assure Hélène Morhange from their Dieppe retreat at the beginning of the last week of August 1939, "the excitement due only to the Hitler-Mussolini-Stalin company, acrobatics, tightrope, knife throwing."[9] In fact, preparations for war were well under way by the time she wrote this; Goudeket was at the Dieppe station when a train pulled in, packed with English vacationers making their way home from the South of France in anticipation of what was to come.[10] Maurice himself was waiting to be called up for military service.

"We're returning to Paris tomorrow morning," Colette wrote to Renée Hamon on Sunday evening, August 27. "For how long? If war breaks out, Maurice won't let me live in Paris, as you can imagine."[11] On September 1, when German troops launched their invasion of Poland, she was snugly settled at the Palais-Royal, writing what she termed an appropriate piece for *Paris-Soir*.[12] It appeared in the September 2 issue, the front page of which headlined the call-up of able-bodied Frenchmen. Her contribution, a description of life in the capital on the eve of war, bore the delicate title "Blue Lights." On September 3, France and Britain responded to German aggression with a declaration of war.

And still Maurice, now fifty, was not called up, though many of their younger friends had been, and so had the workers who should have been getting the house in Méré ready for occupancy.[13]

"No question of my budging from here," Colette affirmed to Renée Hamon. "I don't have good eyes and can't see from far away — thus I remain in Paris."[14] "I'm bored everywhere else," she told the young women farmers in Nantes, who had invited her to take refuge with them.[15] On September 5 *Paris-Soir* announced: "Operations have begun on the French front." Colette's article on page 2 was spare, headed, "To Those Who Stay in Paris." "Every time there is a war, my dear," she explained to her neighbor Denise Tual, "I spend it in Paris. First you have to stock up on coal, and don't forget the potatoes. . . . You need a lot of wool sweaters to wear in the cellar during alerts. . . ."

Indeed, the alerts came nightly now. During the very first one, Tual found Colette installed in a shaky chair, covered with blankets and with a shawl on her head. Maurice was wearing pyjamas and had a blanket thrown over his shoulders; "he was quite dignified, as always, even a bit solemn."[16]

By the third alert, on September 5, Colette had decided that the crowd and the lack of air in the shelters were too upsetting, so she resolved not to go down there again. The next morning they heard antiaircraft guns but stayed put, opening the windows to keep them from being blown out by an explosion.

She took up weaving: "It's a vice I manage to satisfy only in wartime, like crocheting, but it's too soon for that."[17]

Goudeket discovered that his wife was a skilled hoarder; before the end of this first month of World War II, she had filled their cellar to the brim with coal. Everybody they knew in the provinces, not excluding the two women in Nantes, became their supplier.[18] They both picked up jobs as they could. He, for example, replaced younger men at the Prouvost periodical group (the owner of *Paris-Soir*) as they were called up; for a while he was even the editor of the women's magazine *Marie-Claire*.[19]

There was also radio. Colette and Maurice both worked for Paris-Mondial, whose programs were beamed abroad, most notably to the United States. Goudeket spoke in English to introduce classic French plays; she wrote her own talks, but after she spoke a few words in French, an English speaker would read a translation of the rest of the script. These were live broadcasts, which meant that she had to be in the studio long after midnight in order to reach Americans at home in the evening. "It seems to me that to speak to America today is not only an honor but a duty," she asserted to whoever was listening. "Neutral and friendly, bending over to hear these sounds coming from Europe, how can America not want to hear the voice of a Frenchwoman who has come to inform American women what we're like in October 1939, who we are, how we're fighting, even if we're not directly involved in combat. . . ."[20] Goudeket was to remember these dark nights when fog made the blackout blacker. They would drive blindly across the Seine to the radio station on the Left Bank; inside there would be movement and light and even a buffet where performers could mingle with technicians in an atmosphere that Colette liked.[21]

For the moment, they could not even use Méré as an escape. Twice in the first months of war soldiers were billeted in their house. Then, as Christmas approached, Colette began to suffer from arthritis; both hips were x-rayed. It was a turning point in her life, though she did not yet realize it. Later Goudeket could not remember when it was that she first began to limp, or when she first said, "My right hip hurts."[22]

New Year's was unusually quiet, celebrated in the company of Luc-Albert and his Hélène, with fresh oysters sent from Brittany by the Little Corsair.[23] Later in January Colette wrote to Hélène to cancel a weekend visit, saying, "My leg hurt so much yesterday and again tonight that it's better not to budge." One consolation was that her daughter was coming to see her regularly.[24] On a sad note, her brother, Léo, now seventy-three and residing in the Yonne, not far from Saint-Sauveur, was living the last of his days. "A strange and efficacious chasm has always stood between him and reality," she told a friend. But there were the childhood memories, and complicities; now there would be no one to help her to relive them.[25]

"What ties me to Maurice, what attaches him to me?" she repeated Renée Hamon's question. "It's my male virility," Colette replied. "Sometimes I shock him, and yet I'm the only one he can live with. When he wants to sleep with someone, he chooses a very womanly woman; he likes to surround himself with that kind of woman, but he couldn't live with them."[26]

But when Renée came to see her on February 12, 1940, she discovered a very tired Colette. She was going to Nice, she said, and was looking forward to sun, to sea bass cooked with fennel, to hotel service. She would also be seeing her daughter, accompanied by a charming young man then on leave from the army. "A pity they're not sleeping," Colette added. "Then everything would be perfect."[27]

There would be good days and then some very bad ones when her hip and leg hurt. By the end of the month, however, she felt herself to be on an upward curve and was working hard on a story called "The Rainy Moon." It was in the second week of March, when she was in Nice, that she got word that her brother, Léo, had died.[28] Getting home at all was a problem in wartime, and she had to use her influence to obtain a sleeper for Paris.

On her return, she learned that soldiers were still billeted in Méré. "The impossibility of setting up the house gives a bitter taste to everything," she confessed to Renée Hamon. She went all the way to Anatole de Monzie, then the minister of public works, to get her house back. When at last the soldiers had left, Colette posed for a crew of photographers from *Marie-Claire,* which was planning to devote an entire issue to her, its circulation at that time being nearly a million copies. "I still have the longest piece to write for *Marie-Claire,*" she told Renée Hamon early in May. "Tonight, Radio-Mondial — I had simply forgotten to prepare a script [for translation in advance], and the cyclist had to wait an hour. . . . This afternoon Radio PTT to finish [for another weekly broadcast, this one beamed to Frenchwomen], and X rays at four o'clock. Aside from that, nothing to do."[29] In one of her domestic broadcasts — the manuscript is dated May 12 — Colette advised lonely women (whose men were at the front) to shake up their lives, even if only by moving their household furniture around. For this was not the time to move *out*.[30]

Just two days before that, the Germans had begun the blitzkrieg against the Netherlands and Belgium. On May 13 they began moving against France's northeastern frontiers, and from then on they were not to be stopped. Some of Hitler's troops drove west and northwest to the Channel, separating the French and British allies, while another army advanced on Paris. The French government moved south on June 9, the day Rouen fell. Colette thought that she would join her daughter, who was already in the Corrèze, if circumstances made it really necessary; meanwhile, Méré would be her first line of retreat. She spent her last days in Paris getting X-ray treatments for her arthritis. Jobs were disappearing, including her radio work.[31]

The transfer to Méré took place on May 30. When they got there, they had to evict a Moroccan detachment with no fewer than fifteen horses; the deputy mayor was brought in for that. But after all, as she told Misz, there were plenty of unoccupied villas for the soldiers to commandeer. Maurice spent long weekdays in Paris and then drove out to Méré to sleep and for weekends. A summery sun replaced Colette's X-ray treatments.[32] And of course there was much more to do in and around the house. She plowed through dust and dirt, reporting to Renée Hamon, "I don't leave the grounds, I'm learning them by heart. Legs still painful at certain times, but they seem less weak."[33]

Then came the first faint echoes of real war. A friend named

THIRTY-FIVE

Occupied Paris

PARIS WAS DECLARED an open city and overrun by the Germans on June 14. On Maurice's last day there — June 11 — he found a city in disarray: automobiles loading up, trunks roped to their roofs. Smoke rose from government offices where official documents were being burned. There was little to do at *Paris-Soir* except to say good-bye. When he arrived in Méré, he argued the case for departure with Colette, but she continued to say that she was not going anywhere — how could their calm village become a battlefield? He took her out for a drive and let her see the procession of refugees. He also told her that the newspapers were moving south, and that if they were to earn a living they would have to follow them. So on June 12 they rose in the middle of the night and overloaded their automobile, not forgetting extra jerricans of gasoline. With Maurice at the wheel, and Pauline in the backseat, they were off by four A.M.[1]

Writing about this departure that was a defeat of her desires (and writing about it immediately afterward), Colette conceded that every writer had to find a way that conformed to "his faculties, chance, the decline or the vigor of his age." Her shelter was with people who worked the land. She added that her brother, Léo, had been fortunate to die before having to face the challenge that circumstances had now brought upon them — that is, "the knowledge and awareness of the modern age."[2]

They drove, and drove, and somehow got to Curemonte, a medieval hilltop village protected by not one but two feudal castle-forts. Colette de Jouvenel lived there, surrounded by high stone walls; her domain included a house that had been built over an ancient stable. It was habitable, while the neighboring castles were not.

Robert de Jouvenel, Henry's brother, had acquired Curemonte in 1912. On his death, in 1924, it had passed to Henry, and after Henry's death Renaud's wife, Arlette, had bought it. (In November 1940 she would sign it over to Colette's daughter.)[3] The house had three bedrooms, a living room, and ample land for growing vegetables; it must have seemed like the promised land to the twenty-seven-year-old Colette, who was still looking for herself. Henceforth it was to give her the opportunity to befriend and to protect refugees, even to take in stray cats and dogs, and then to build and repair her own haven.[4]

Exasperated by her isolation and her growing helplessness, Colette mère called the place a green tomb. For she and Maurice and Pauline were to spend the first weeks at Curemonte without a radio or a newspaper, without telegrams or a telephone. They were low on gasoline as well.[5] During this period, the French government, then installed in Bordeaux, surrendered to the Germans; a new regime was set up in Vichy and proceeded to transform France into a neo-fascist state. The country was divided into German-occupied and Vichy-controlled zones, with Paris on one side of the line and Curemonte on the other.

In retrospect, Goudeket marveled at the life they had led there. The weather was good, and the grounds were covered with flowers. It was as if they were stranded on a far-off island, but one with a pleasant village tavern (seemingly unaffected by war shortages).[6] "We exploit a stockpile of fallen beams, we boil the laundry (as at Rozven) with the debris from a Louis XV alcove," Colette wrote to Germaine Beaumont on a postcard, when postcards could be sent again. "From time to time the ruin stretches itself and lets go of a stone block, as thick as the obelisk but shorter."[7]

When Renée Hamon was able to send Colette a letter, she reported the joint suicide of Erna Redtenbacher and her companion, Christiane. Erna had been released from internment by the French, but then the arrival of the Germans had threatened her freedom, and her life. The two women could see no other way out.

Colette wanted to get back to Paris all the same.[8] "I'm in the habit of spending my wars in Paris," she explained once more.[9]

She got along well enough with her daughter, but Colette II and Maurice found cohabitation difficult.[10] One day the Goudekets drove as far as Clermont-Ferrand in search of news; they learned nothing useful there and returned home horrified by the spectacle of that overpopulated town. They even began thinking about going to Saint-Tropez to wait out this time of uncertainty, at least until the *Paris-Soir* group of periodicals began to appear again. In fact, the *Paris-Soir* editors were to do considerable wandering of their own after the fall of France, settling at last in Lyon in October 1940. When the Goudekets realized that they did not have enough gasoline to get to the Riviera (and with Paris still out of bounds), they too would choose the largest city possible, a place where things could happen. The trip to Lyon was itself rugged, for somehow water had gotten into their jerricans of gas. Once there, they settled into a decrepit hotel whose chief amenity was a view of the Rhône River. They soon found their newspaper friends and began to plan a return to Paris, stocking up on gas first of all.

Early in August, armed with official travel papers from the prefecture, they were ready to cross the demarcation line that now separated the zones. At the crossing point, Goudeket was asked by a French soldier whether he was Jewish, and he admitted that he was. "Alas, I married an honest man," Colette wrote to a friend from Lyon, for of course they were quickly ordered to return there.[11] For his part, Goudeket remembered the story a bit differently. A German soldier, he said, first accused Colette of being Jewish and then turned to Pauline, with her dark hair and skin, and added in broken French, "You surely Jewish." It was then that Goudeket stepped up to say that he was the only Jew among them — and *that* was what got them sent back to Lyon.[12]

Money was now more of a worry than ever. Colette's savings were in Paris (she hoped), and so were her publishers (perhaps). In the meantime, she could sell extracts of her war diary to *Candide,* a periodical in the Vichy zone that seemed less tainted by propaganda than most.[13]

The naïveté of the Goudekets — Colette and Maurice both — seems, in retrospect, to have been unbounded. Thus, when Mary Marquet, a famous actress of the time, left Lyon for Paris, where she intended to see the German ambassador, Otto Abetz, they could give her a note for him, requesting permission to travel to the German-occupied capital. But in the end it was the Swedish consulate that was to provide a document convincing enough to get them past both French and German checkpoints. Goudeket recalled that Colette had a loaded revolver in the car, hidden in a glove; she wanted to be ready for anything. It was late in the evening of September 11 when they reached Paris; distracted, Goudeket drove through a red light. A Paris policeman whistled them down, then let them go, warning, "Walk on tiptoe."[14]

They found the Palais-Royal apartment intact, but life was going to be different, and at once. They could have no automobile in Paris, for one thing, and Colette's arthritis made it difficult for her to use the subway, which was still operating. As soon as she had put things in order, she began to think about money-making projects. She quickly finished the second story for a collection that Fayard was to publish (this was "The Rainy Moon," the title referring to the haloed moon that signals the arrival of bad weather).[15]

Slowly, life returned to the city. At least two of their favorite neighborhood restaurants reopened. In a letter announcing this to Hélène Morhange (and asking her to stop at Méré on her return from her country house, to pick up some things that Colette needed in Paris), Colette also sent news of mutual friends. Julien Cain, who was Jewish, had been removed as director of the National Library, losing his official residence; he was now freezing in a borrowed flat. The Léopold Marchands, meanwhile, were off to Algiers, where he was to be propaganda chief for press and cinema. Colette thought that this would be good for Léo's Jewish wife, Misz, who was thin, nervous, and deeply affected by recent events.[16]

In Paris the Germans soon had a say in every aspect of life that might concern an enemy occupation. Newspapers could be published only under their supervision, usually with their financial support; books were to be censored before publication, and of course publishers had to respect Nazi criteria.

The owners of Ferenczi, which had published so many of Colette's books, were Jewish. They managed to get out of the city before the arrival of the Germans and were hoping to insure the survival of their firm by selling it to another publisher, Hachette, which had agreed to turn it over to them again after the war. The Germans refused to allow that arrangement. Instead, the company was placed in the hands of an administrator who had been handpicked by the Germans; this happened to be Jean de La Hire, one of Willy's hagiographers. La Hire removed the Ferenczi sign; henceforth the imprint was to be known as Editions du Livre Moderne.[17]

There was no escaping the new order. "Having returned here for bread-and-butter reasons, we discover that the problems are not minor, especially for one of us," Colette cryptically explained to Renaud de Jouvenel. "Fortunately Fayard wants to publish again, and will do one of my books. For who knows how long Ferenczi will have to stay far from Paris?"[18]

The Fayard book was called *Chance Acquaintances;* the title story marks a return to the author's music-hall years. At a mountain resort she meets a couple who seem very average, though something about the man arouses her curiosity. Clearly distraught, he confesses that he is without news of his mistress. Since she must make a quick round trip to Paris anyway, she promises to look up the woman, even though she feels a lack of esteem for this manipulative man.

She discovers that his mistress has moved without leaving a forwarding address, and she is inwardly delighted. When she reports her findings to her neighbor at the hotel, he swallows poison, but he takes too much and throws it all up. Soon he has another girlfriend.

In the accompanying story, "The Rainy Moon," two sisters love the same man; one of them is married to him. The wife seeks to kill her husband through witchcraft, and one day Colette finds her wearing mourning.

"A cold wave has put Paris to torture, without coal or wood," Colette told Renée Hamon (her Little Corsair was safe, but ill, in Brittany). "If I hadn't bought more coal than I needed for one winter. . . ." Colette mailed her friend a five-hundred-franc check, in exchange for which Renée was to ship her a sack of potatoes, garlic, and onions. If we are to trust the dates that have been subsequently affixed to undated letters, it took just under a month from order to delivery, and what a delivery: red-skinned potatoes, unfindable garlic. "And those golden onions!" Colette began to receive equally gratifying food parcels from her pen friends on their Breton farm, and she insisted on paying in advance for them. Later she would send them a "new customer," whose shipments she was also to pay for, "for he is at once an amputee, Jewish, and unemployed." This was Maurice Goudeket's brother.[19]

For her Little Breton Corsair — her "food-supply Little Corsair," as she now called her — Colette described the first Christmas in German Paris, "in silence and retreat, while thinking of so many far-off friends." She had been kept indoors by flu and bronchitis, and when at last she might have gone out, on Christmas Eve, the cold had proved too much for her. "No more wool, no oranges for the past week," she reported; apples were dear. The Germans (she referred to them as "our guests") had taken everything for their own holidays. Snow fell in Paris on New Year's Day 1941; the view was superb from her Palais-Royal garden windows, but she pitied the birds. The frost persisted; in mid-January she took a temperature reading of nine below zero, centigrade, at her window.

Colette and "Missy" (the Marchioness de Belbeuf), 1910

"Claudine" at her writing table

Colette

"Sido" à soixante ans

Colette's mother at sixty

Bertrand de Jouvenel with his mother
(née Claire Boas)

Henry de Jouvenel

Colette's daughter (also Colette) at Castel-Novel

Colette circa 1930

Colette II as a young
woman

Colette with Maurice Goudeket, on top of the Empire State Building, 1935

Maurice Goudeket with Colette

Colette on her "raft" (her sofa bed equipped with writing table) at the
Palais-Royal, 1947

Her enforced isolation was productive. She began what she called a "seeming-novel" and surprised herself with the speed at which she wrote it; she did not stop even to arrange flowers in their vases.[20] The seeming-novel would rapidly take shape as *Julie de Carneilhan.*

She was working, to ensure her bread and butter, for a daily, *Le Petit Parisien* — and no matter that this was not the *Petit Parisien* of prewar days. Its owners had sold not the plant but their souls to the Germans, and whatever they had lost in readership was now being made up by enemy funds; but life in Paris in war, at least for those who scanned the newsstands, was meant to resemble life before the war. Colette soon had a press card stamped with the swastika of the German Propaganda-Staffel.[21]

The articles she wrote for *P. P.* (as she nicknamed it) were apolitical and in no way echoed that paper's servile collaborationism. She took as her subject such concerns as cold apartments, household pets, and child-raising; she turned out vignettes of life under the occupation, scenes that are never bitter but that nonetheless make it clear that some degree of adaptation was necessary.

In a letter to Hélène Morhange, so near and yet now so far away at Montfort-l'Amaury, she mentioned people she was seeing, among them Germaine Patat (who was trying to make her way to the Riviera) and Pata de Polignac (Countess Jeanne de Polignac). She added, "Often see our neighbor Cocteau, worried, charming, tormented by money problems." [22] Cocteau lived in the Palais-Royal as well, in the same kind of "tunnel" she had occupied in the 1920s. He would say that he had moved there in part to be close to friends, notably Emmanuel Berl of *Marianne* and Pierre Lazareff of *Paris-Soir,* both of whom had since evacuated their flats because they were Jews. Cocteau was not Jewish, but he was a homosexual, as well as an avant-garde artist of a kind that the Nazis despised. "I lived there for six years, a victim of insults," he was to remember of the occupation years, "attacked in my work and my person." Perhaps it was "six years" in his recollection because his occasional complaisance with the collaboration and its press was criticized after the war.

They were neighbors, in any case. He could lean out his window to chat with Colette as she crossed the garden "with her cane, her scarf tied around her neck, her flat felt hat, her fine eye, her bare feet in sandals."[23]

Maurice Goudeket survived, though he was a Jew whose presence was known to all, including Hitler's ambassador Abetz. If the new rules — the Germans' and Pétain's — banned him from journalism, the career he had chosen late in life, he could try something that was still permitted: selling secondhand books. "He applies flair and passion to it," Colette assured a friend. Books, even damaged copies, had become precious in that time.

She, on the other hand, was slowing down. After writing seventy-five pages of *Julie de Carneilhan,* she suddenly found herself "before a wall." Would she tear it down, or steer around it? she wondered. She told her food-supply Little Corsair of the persistent shortages, the soaring prices. Still, she rarely felt jealous of friends in the South. As always, Paris, "however melancholic," was where she wished to be.[24]

She described life in melancholic Paris to the Moreaus in February 1941. She was getting food packages from her "little ones of Nantes," which meant eggs, sausages, greens, and a roast beef. Goudeket's mother had received a questionnaire asking for details about her two sons. The staff of *Le Petit Parisien* had resigned en masse, and as a consequence she expected to be without work (in fact, the paper carried on). Julien Cain of the National Library had been arrested. She and Maurice had been to the theater, to see *Britannicus.* Nero had been played by Jean Cocteau's companion, Jean Marais, and Colette had not appreciated his interpretation of the role.[25]

A severe frost that winter made it easy for her to focus on her work, and her activity was curtailed in any case by her increasing incapacity (she found walking painful even with a cane).[26] "Life is narrow," she commented to Renée Hamon. "Those who venture out of isolation find something at once that hurts. So we're stay-at-homes, and modest."[27]

When Hélène Morhange asked her to sign a petition on behalf of the Julien Cains, Colette begged to be excused. Her signature would only serve to draw attention to Maurice, she feared, and those to whom the petition was addressed would attribute selfish motives to her. It was her feeling that any French initiative of this kind would lead to a result contrary to that desired.

She wished her reply to remain confidential and hoped that her friend would tell people that she had not even raised the matter with Colette, given her "marital situation."[28]

THIRTY-SIX

Julie

JULIE DE CARNEILHAN is a countess. She has been married and divorced twice. Her first husband was a wealthy Dutch baron, and her second a prominent politician and member of parliament, Herbert d'Espivant; we learn that *his* claim to a title is not very old, and that he has had not only wives but mistresses. After divorcing Julie, he married a woman who has a son from a previous marriage.

As the story opens, Herbert suffers a heart attack and collapses on the street. He asks to see Julie, and during their encounter he reminds her that she once sold her jewelry in order to obtain a million francs in cash for him. She even holds a receipt for that loan. Now he wants her to demand payment, for his wealthy wife detests debts and will surely give her the money. Herbert will then share the million with Julie; his half of the payment will allow him to divorce his wife.

After some hesitation, she agrees to Herbert's plan. When his wife calls it blackmail, Julie does not protest, but when Herbert gets the money, he gives her only a hundred thousand francs. "That's ten percent," she thinks with bitterness, "which is what a rental agent gets."

There are subplots, too, in this short novel. One of them involves the son of Herbert and his rich wife; when this son attempts suicide, it is discovered that he secretly loves Julie. . . .

Finishing the book, she told friends, had been painful (as usual).[1] "It had to be done," was her explanation — meaning that she needed the cash. The book was to appear "in the occupied zone," but it would also be dispatched "through a hole in the hedge" to the so-called free zone controlled by Vichy.[2] In that way it could be published in installments in none other than *Gringoire*. The June 4, 1941, issue of that paper announced the forthcoming serialization of Colette's novel; just below the announcement there was a cartoon showing the Statue of Liberty holding not a torch but a Jewish menorah. *Gringoire* had gotten even worse.

It was an occupied country, on both sides of the demarcation line. When Fayard published the book version of *Julie de Carneilhan,* the back cover carried an advertisement for a book by Hitler. Postwar movies suggest that there was a Gestapo agent on every corner in wartime France, with a member of the Resistance lurking somewhere nearby; but occupied France was most remarkable for its ambiguities.

Renée Hamon came to town in the spring of 1941. She found Colette thinner, weary-looking; her voice was less lively, and she seemed cautious. "We've never lived further from the future," she told her Corsair. For the moment, she felt that Goudeket was safe; he had, after all, been a volunteer under French colors in World War I, winning the Military Cross and a citation. Maurice had turned gray, Renée noted, but he appeared not to have lost his imperturbability. Clearly Colette was proud of him.

Upon paying another call at the Palais-Royal, the visitor from Brittany decided that lunch at Colette's reconciled one to wartime shortages. The menu consisted of cauliflower in a white cream sauce, a Nantes roast chicken, a salad of lettuce and hard-boiled eggs, cake, and real coffee. This time Colette seemed in better form; when Renée arrived, she was downstairs in the garden, leaning on Maurice's arm while using a cane. Renée told her that she wished to get away — to Morocco, for example — and Colette suggested that she wait for the return of the Marchands from Algiers. Léo had been doing well in his government job there, but both he and his wife wanted to be back in Paris; they could feel happy only among friends.[3]

A diary survives (written for publication or not, it could not have been published just then) covering a bit of that summer of 1941. One vignette takes us into a black-market restaurant where Colette is particularly admired; the owner slips a Camembert cheese into her bag as she leaves.[4] Even with France split in two, her daughter got food through to her from the South, and the young farmers of Nantes never tired of sending her parcels. And at least once, Colette's neighbor Denise Tual witnessed Pauline's furtive return from the central markets, her arms laden with rare foodstuffs. When Tual offered to help her carry the food upstairs, the servant accepted only reluctantly. Colette watched them from her window. A cut of beef was hidden under the fresh vegetables at the bottom of the basket; would they broil it? Colette wondered. "Madame is joking!" responded Pauline. "It will go a lot further in a stew."[5]

One day in June, the Goudekets joined the writer Georges Duhamel, his wife, and Henri Mondor for lunch at the elegant Café de Paris, where they were the guests of Léon Barthou. "The clandestine dietary resources of Paris are indeed curious," Colette subsequently reported to Hélène Morhange. "We opened our eyes (and our mouths) as wide as possible, Maurice and I, before these boiled lobsters, these steaks. But this can't be done if you don't hide yourself in one of those sinister compartments that are called private rooms."[6]

There were more dangers, for Colette was now going to publish her first book with a new-old house called Aux Armes de France. With the enthusiastic approval of the Germans, an avowed anti-Semite had been placed in charge at Calmann-Lévy, a publishing company that had been founded over a century earlier by a Jewish family and had until now remained in the family's control. The man endorsed by the Germans, Louis Thomas, changed the name of the house and stamped the covers of its books with the royal coat of arms, with its fleur-de-lis. (As he was maneuvering, unsuccessfully, to buy the firm outright, he managed to publish several books that he himself had written.)[7]

Colette's book, *Mes Cahiers* (My Notebooks), was published by Armes de France on fine paper; it holds up better physically today than most of her other books, published either before or after World War II. The edition was limited to 3,800 copies, with an etching of Colette by Luc-Albert Moreau as a frontispiece. An unsigned preface declares the writer's pleasure at having been able to persuade Colette to let her notes and drafts be read. In truth, these notebooks had first been published some years earlier (by those Friends of Colette already mentioned). In another paradox typical of occupied Paris, Goudeket served as his wife's go-between with her new publisher, Louis Thomas.

Thomas (who fled to Germany as the Allies liberated France but was sentenced to life at hard labor all the same) was to pursue his professional courtship of Colette. In November 1941 his Armes de France published *The Pure and the Impure,* which was promoted as the definitive edition of *Ces Plaisirs.* . . . In the anonymous preface, surely written by Thomas himself, Colette is quoted as saying that this is her best book.[8]

Of course, these were not new books, but henceforth there would be many new editions, and new collections, of previously published works. Not that Colette, at sixty-eight, had any less drive; in fact, she was doing something new that very summer, "a strange assignment," she said: writing sketches for a variety show.[9] "You could say that I'm never too old to learn," she declared to her Little Corsair with obvious glee.[10] Not only did she write the material, but once again she had a say in directing the cast, spending two weeks in September at rehearsals, from two in the afternoon until seven, and then again from 8:30 to 10:45 at night.[11]

Her reward was a percentage of the box-office receipts, but for her efforts she also received, and passed on to friends, an attack on her "perverse mind," first from an occupation daily called *Aujourd'hui* and then from a reader of the same paper. "We've had enough of your decadent literature," wrote a Parisian woman. No more "pederastic stories by André Gide," no more erotic drawings by Pascin or Dignimont. "All that," explained the letter-writer, "is Jewish art. Thank God the National Revolution is changing this!" She closed with a resounding "Long Live Pétain!"[12]

Paris emptied out that summer, occupation or no. Somehow its best citizens got away to beaches or country places; Colette sat in the Tuileries gardens "with no more of a crowd than I used to have in the Bois de Boulogne," as she informed Marguerite Moreno (herself far to the south, in the Vichy zone).[13] She no longer had the heart, or the health, to go to Méré on weekends; as soon as a buyer could be found, the Goudekets sold it and stored the furniture. One day she was able to listen to a concert of Mozart performed by Germans at the other end of her own Palais-Royal garden. In August, on doctor's orders, she mounted a bicycle for a first ride in the Bois, where she discovered that pedaling was painless even for her bad leg (the left one).

Then came chest pains — a "false heart attack," she called it. The spasms continued for five days and nights, forcing her to postpone a reporting job that had been assigned by *Le Petit Parisien*. Her weight may have been a contributing factor; describing a mutual friend, Colette commented, "She has lost forty pounds, like everybody except me. . . ."[14]

She was sent a letter that she would hold on to. It began, "I am the woman whose hand you shake so kindly in the Palais-Royal arcades." The writer was one of the local prostitutes whose terrain was the covered walkway around the garden. "I am in need of your advice at the present time," she went on to explain. She also said she wished to read Colette's work, and Colette saw to it that she could. She and the woman became friends; much later she would autograph a copy of her *Blue Lantern* to "a neighbor whose blue lantern is switched off so late."[15]

In late November 1941, *Julie de Carneilhan* was ready, looking very much like any book published by Fayard in a happier time. She signed copies for the press, as she had done for every new book of hers since she won the right to sign her own name to them.

It took a while for the novel to reach Anatole de Monzie and more time for him to read it and then talk about it with friends. Even then, he hesitated. But finally he had to speak out: he did not like the book. And though he had been told that the character named Herbert d'Espivant — the politician who cheats Julie out of most of her money — resembled Henry de Jouvenel, he disagreed.

He begged Colette not to make light of his concern; he took his loyalty to his dead friend most seriously. *Was* Jouvenel the model for the awful Espivant? he asked. "If you didn't recognize him in Espivant," Colette assured him, "it's because he isn't there, and my little character is imaginary. . . . No, Espivant is not Jouvenel."[16]

THIRTY-SEVEN

Maurice and Misz

MAURICE GOUDEKET had lived as public an existence as was possible for a Jew — and a naturalized Frenchman, at that — in German Paris. This charmed life could not continue forever, however. The German embassy knew him to be a Jew, as did the professional anti-Semites; the occupation authorities had a roster of all the Jewish residents of their zone. Jews in Paris were caught in the crossfire between Hitler's anti-Jewish restrictions and Vichy's. Not only could a Jew not work in certain jobs, for instance; he could not even possess a radio.

On December 12, 1941, in retaliation for Resistance attacks, the Germans arrested a thousand of France's best-known Jewish citizens. Shortly after seven that morning, Pauline walked into Goudeket's bedroom, followed by a German police officer, who asked him, politely, to pack. Pauline then woke Colette, who came in to help Maurice get ready.[1] "He left calmly for I don't know where," Colette informed Hélène Picard, "accused of the crime of being Jewish, of having fought in the last war as a volunteer, and winning a medal. I am waiting." In the same note to her housebound friend, she managed to say that she had gone to see a bird-lover who was prepared to take some of Hélène's parakeets off her hands.[2]

The Nazis were not going to kill their hostages, though Goudeket heard that the detainees would have been packed off to Germany if all of the trains had not been crowded with German soldiers on Christmas leave.[3] It took nearly a week for Colette to learn where her husband had been taken; she finally found out thanks to a phone call from a prisoner who had been released. Goudeket, he told her, was in a detention center in Compiègne, sleeping on straw and keeping up his morale. After giving Renée Hamon this news, Colette went on to reproach her for trying to toilet-train a kitten by putting its nose in the mess. That would drive it to despair, she said, and teach it to be dirty; it would literally poison the animal.[4]

The first message from the Compiègne prisoner was a small scrap of notepaper containing a list of nutritional foods he wanted.[5] As he later remembered it, their torture was hunger; for those in good health, the conditions were "merely rough and depressing." He felt that all he could do for Colette was to survive, so he taught himself how to do that. Still, in every message he could slip out to her, he asked for bread.

He would speak, later, of a certain French writer who had been a war prisoner but was released by the Germans after promising to collaborate with them. This man called on Colette to offer an arrangement: the Germans would give Goudeket a permanent job at the camp, where he would be well treated and well fed. All he would have to do in return was furnish occasional information on his fellow prisoners. "I refuse," Colette told this intermediary. He insisted; it was that or death for Maurice. "Then I choose death," she said. "Not without consulting your husband, I imagine?" he asked. "*We* choose death," she repeated.[6] The description of this unidentified caller fits Robert Brasillach, an admirer of Colette's from his student years.[7]

Although Colette emphatically refused this offer, she was nonetheless now seeking the help of collaborators. Her neighbor Denise Tual remembered that the first person whom writers turned to was their fellow writer Pierre Drieu La Rochelle, an avowed fascist who had been put in charge of the prestigious *Nouvelle Revue Française*.

When Colette told Tual, "They're looking into Maurice's case," her neighbor preferred to ask no questions.[8]

Sacha Guitry, an actor to the tips of his fingers, later boasted that by threatening to kill himself in front of a German officer, he had obtained Goudeket's immediate release. It is true that Guitry had access to high-ranking Germans, including Ambassador Abetz and Minister Rudolf Schleier, who specialized in Jewish affairs (the actor claimed that he saw such people only so that he could help friends in need).[9] Guitry knew, for example, that Schleier could easily be moved by the actress Arletty, and in one version of these events he appealed to her on behalf of the people he wished to help — Goudeket among them — and she won their freedom from her friend the minister.[10]

It has also been suggested that Goudeket's savior was the artist José Maria Sert, who was then Generalissimo Franco's ambassador to the Vatican, though he was living in Paris.[11]

In a sense, Colette needed no intermediaries, for she could reach Ambassador Abetz — the highest-ranking civilian representative of the Nazi regime in Paris — directly; he was a friend of Bertrand de Jouvenel's from prewar days, and Jouvenel maintained contact with him now, if only in order to keep French intelligence officials informed.[12]

Letters survive from Abetz's wife, Suzanne (who was French by birth), to Colette, one of them dated February 17, 1942, shortly after Goudeket's release from Compiègne. Here the wife of the German ambassador thanks Colette for some flowers she sent during her convalescence, adding, "and I'm pleased at your happiness." In May, Suzanne Abetz sent her chauffeur to the Palais-Royal with copies of books by Colette to be autographed for a friend. In her note she invites Colette to tea at the embassy and expresses the hope that Goudeket, "always ready to fly somewhere, will be in Paris all the same. Affectionately. . . ." (Imagine it: tea at the German embassy for Maurice Goudeket, only sixty days before the historic roundup of Jews that signaled the commencement of the death-camp deportations.) At the end of the same year, Suzanne Abetz wrote to " 'My'

Colette" — the quotation marks are hers — to thank her for some flowers and to wish Christmas cheer for "my dear protégée" (referring to Colette herself).[13]

She had gone everywhere, Colette had — to the worst of the collaborators and the cruelest of the Nazis — and then there had been Suzanne.[14]

Arrested on December 12, 1941, Goudeket spent the rest of that month and all of January in detention. Colette received pathetic scraps of paper on which he spelled out his needs, his and his fellows': bread, gingerbread, biscuits, butter, cheese, jam or honey. But he also begged his wife to think of herself, and he hoped that their friends were helping her. He did ask whether she was intervening on his behalf, and he put in a request for books and neckties — but old ones. After getting her third food parcel, he commented, "Bread perfect, butter priceless, gingerbread is the best thing the intestines can have. . . ." He had lectured to the other prisoners on Pascal, he said, adding that his fellow detainee René Blum (who had staged *Chéri* at the Théâtre de Monte-Carlo) wished to read her work; could she send an anthology?[15]

The ban on letters was the worst privation, and then food parcels were forbidden. But at last, on February 1, Colette was informed that Goudeket was to be released on the following day. In fact, he was not let out until February 6. He remembered returning to the Palais-Royal with an empty valise, for he had given his clothing and other personal effects to prisoners who were left behind. After climbing the stairs to the apartment, he rang at the kitchen door so as to talk first to Pauline. She told him that Colette was at the hairdresser's. He was disappointed but "vaguely relieved." Pauline reached her by telephone and he got on the line to confirm his return. It took her some time to come home, and she beseeched a friend whom she met on the street to keep her company; she was afraid to confront the released prisoner. Goudeket, meanwhile, stripped to the skin in the entrance hall to keep bugs out of the apartment, and then soaked and soaked in the tub.[16]

"Besides the weight loss," Colette later remembered, "I had never before seen such extrahuman colors on a man, a complexion white and green, reddened eyelids, gray lips. . . ."[17] "If I haven't written to you," she explained to Marguerite Moreno — on one of the somber little postcards required for all correspondence between the Nazi and Vichy zones — "it's because I have carried something too heavy to bear for the past eight weeks. . . . I kept a stubborn hope at bottom. At present I am allowing myself the luxury of being exhausted." "As for me," Goudeket told Renée Hamon, "I'm gaining back the lost eighteen pounds and find every hour of the day wonderful."[18]

Colette could not now do more for the collaboration than she had done before, but nor could she do less. In March, Sacha Guitry undertook to put together "a veritable monument to the glory of France" in book form, and he traveled down to Vichy to discuss it with Marshal Pétain himself. The volume was to be called *From Joan of Arc to Philippe Pétain;* in it leading French writers were to pay homage to their predecessors. Colette was assigned Balzac.[19]

Of course, there was also plenty one could do without committing oneself. The fashion magazine *L'Officiel de la Couture* continued to be published, its glossy pages filled with temptations for women who were still able to care about such things; it contained only the barest hint of material concerns, and none at all of political or moral ones. The January 1942 issue featured an article by Colette celebrating the pleasures that were still available. "Do you have any champagne?" she asked. "No? Don't turn your eyes away, I know that you are lying. I also lie."

In April she began a somewhat more strenuous attack on her arthritis, receiving X-ray treatments and intravenous injections of sulfur and iodine. "I must know whether my condition can be better," she declared to a confidante. The immediate result was exhaustion and more pain. Misia Sert would call for her in a Spanish embassy automobile and take her to the same doctor who had treated her husband; on the days when Misia could not make it, Colette would hire a bicycle taxi, one of the most reliable forms of transportation in occupied Paris. In June she ordered an electric-powered wheelchair.

The treatments had one useful side effect: they took away her appetite. "I am capable of losing weight," she told Renée Hamon, "as incredible as that may seem." Her Little Corsair, for her part, was living her final months. She had cancer; Colette's gynecologist was treating her with radium.[20]

In May, Louis Thomas published in book form the articles that Colette had written for the occupation press. The title was *De ma fenêtre* (From My Window), appropriate for an author who was becoming increasingly housebound. This collection actually showed a unity that many other Colette anthologies lacked, for all of the sketches concerned a "ravaged" France.

She could indeed see much from her window, and could exchange complaints with neighbors about unheated apartments and the lack of food. She could provide tips on coming to terms with German Paris, sharing recipes, giving advice on substitute foods and materials. Young women were dressing too provocatively, she found, considering the situation; but perhaps they were simply paying their respects to the peace to come?

After his release from Compiègne, Goudeket stayed close to home. There was always the possibility of another ring at the door at dawn. A neighbor who lived in a maid's room under the eaves offered to take him into her bed at the first sign of danger; they would never look for him there! The bookseller downstairs arranged a cache behind the shelves and invited him to lower himself down by rope should the police come to the door. Another shopkeeper, an upholsterer, gave him a key to the back of his shop.[21]

It was to make *Colette's* life easier, Goudeket said later, that he packed his valise again. He returned to Saint-Tropez, not to La Treille Muscate but to a house across the road, inhabited by loyal friends. He did their gardening and fished for them. And when he wrote to Colette, using unsealed interzone cards, he signed his host's name.[22]

Some things did not go smoothly. Misz (Miche) Marchand, who of course was born Hertz, a Polish Jew, knew something about the Nazi death camps, for members of her family were already among their victims. In July 1942, Jews of non-French origin were rounded up in a massive raid in Paris, the first step on the way to the camps; apparently it was in an effort to protect Léo that Misz swallowed a handful of barbiturates. She did not die right away; a doctor fought to keep her alive over a period of four days. "So pure a human being, so removed from everything that is ugly," Colette described her for her dying Little Corsair.[23]

THIRTY-EIGHT

Waiting for the Communiqué

SHE WROTE HER tribute to Honoré de Balzac, telling how much the supreme storyteller had meant to her — this for the elegant volume that Sacha Guitry was producing for France, for Pétain, and for himself. She also composed a lighthearted account of her successive homes in Paris, *Places,* first published as a series of sketches in the daily *Petit Parisien.* She even did an advertisement for perfume. "I have always thought that this kind of work demands a maximum of attention and care," she explained herself to her "little farmers" of Brittany, "and I put my pride into it."[1]

Maurice, meanwhile, was spending lazy months in Saint-Tropez. He was able to report, from his observation post just across the road, that the actor Charles Vanel had sold their old house. And her flowers had gone to war and been resuscitated as vegetables. His hope had been that his self-exile to the comparative safety of southern France would put Colette at ease; instead, her letters betrayed impatience. She would have liked to join him in that summer of 1942.[2]

While waiting, she worked. She was writing a little story that was to make her even more famous than she already was, and richer. For "Gigi" she returned to a world that she had observed from the middle distance: the society of the demimondaines of the turn of the century. Goudeket remembered that the theme — an innocent but not stupid young woman being initiated into the arts of seduction by a worldly aunt — had been suggested to Colette by a couple who had operated a hotel in Saint-Raphaël in 1926. It was the story of their own niece.[3]

She finished "Gigi" at the beginning of September. It appeared the same month in *Présent,* a magazine published in the Vichy zone, which she had never seen and did not mind not having seen (so she told a confidante).[4] She was hardly unwilling to publish in Paris, however, and that autumn she also sold an article to *La Gerbe,* a paper that favored military cooperation between France and Hitler's Germany. Many of *La Gerbe*'s writers went to jail after the liberation, and at least one was executed.

Her contribution, published in the issue of November 26, 1942, was called "My Poor Burgundy"; in it she painted her childhood province one more time.[5] Her article was featured on a special page devoted to Burgundy, along with an essay by a Nazi propagandist who pointed out that the region had originally been colonized by Germans.

This time her collaboration with collaborationists was not to pass unnoticed. In its mimeographed issue for December 1942, a Resistance monthly ran an article entitled "Colette, Burgundy, and Mr. Goebbels," which argued that Nazi propaganda knew how to make use of prestigious French names. This was why *La Gerbe* had asked Colette for an article, even if it was a totally nonpolitical one. "And it is significant to see how much political meaning her little article, essentially descriptive, was to take on on that special page" — for of course it had been deliberately placed just above the German's propaganda article. The Resistance editors wondered whether Colette understood exactly what sort of maneuver it was that she had so imprudently lent herself to. It was a maneuver, they said, that proved "that in giving to the press controlled by the occupiers the slightest scrap of an article, even without a political touch, a writer plays his part in the concert of enemy propaganda orchestrated by Goebbels.

And it is painful to see the name of Colette, respected until now, serving such a task."[6]

The month of November had begun badly. Colette kept away from friends and kept them away — like an animal, she said. "Right now I am paying, with a hidden weakness, for my three consecutive years of Paris. I'm losing oxygen physically and morally," she confided to Renée Hamon. "Maurice writes to me every day, I write to him every day. But so many days pass, and I feel so old. . . ."[7]

This letter was dated Friday, November 6. The next night, American and British forces launched an invasion of that part of the North African coast controlled by Vichy. In order to protect southern France from a similar assault, Hitler sent troops into the Vichy zone.

The South of France was now a dangerous place for Maurice Goudeket, and in any case he had planned to leave Saint-Tropez before the end of the year. After finding a temporary refuge with some Parisian friends who were themselves obliged to remain far from the capital, he was ready to brave the demarcation line. As he told it, his forged identity papers did not fool the French gendarme who inspected them; finally Goudeket told him that he wanted to see his wife in Paris but lacked permission to cross the line. "Go on," the gendarme said, waving him over. "I didn't see you."[8] "A tramp has tramped for forty-eight hours and more to come back to me," Colette soon announced to Lucie Delarue-Mardrus, a writer friend.[9]

He was not hiding, Colette hastened to explain to Renée Hamon: "We live prudently, that's all. We wait."[10] It was his idea, Goudeket remembered, to sleep in a maid's room on the attic floor; for the next eighteen months he would leave the apartment each night when the clock struck twelve, to come down again at nine. No one was ever arrested that late in the morning.[11]

"You did hear me on the radio, didn't you?" Colette asked Renée Hamon — for the famous writer had offered a holiday greeting to the French nation on Christmas Eve.[12]

*   *   *

"We lead a narrow little life," she told Renaud de Jouvenel, who was spending the grim occupation years at Castel-Novel. "I continue to tremble for a companion who himself shows much steadfastness. And this arthritis of the hip hasn't made a wanderer of me. . . ." In another letter she thanked Jouvenel for a sack of flour; that very morning Pauline was whipping up some pancakes for them. And she was holding on to the precious sack itself, for future use.[13]

There was money to be earned, even now, from deluxe editions and limited printings. She complained of "an intolerable little job" that turned out to be an essay for a book of sketches called *Nudité,* published in a city that was even more heavily occupied than Paris: Brussels.[14] In 1943 she wrote a text, *Flora and Pomona,* to accompany a set of watercolors published by an art gallery. This came easier, for she could return for the colors of flowers and the taste of fruit to her childhood in Saint-Sauveur, to the house she had shared with Willy in Franche-Comté, to the South of France, and even to North Africa. She wrote of flowers, she said with a sigh, because she no longer had a garden of her own.

There was also some fiction. *The Kepi,* published by Fayard, contains a story of that name and three more to fill out the volume. In the title story, a woman of forty-six, who is separated from her husband, has an affair with a twenty-five-year-old lieutenant, until she tries on his cap after lovemaking and breaks the spell. "The Tender Shoot" is the confession of a roué, whose story explains why he now avoids young girls. "Green Sealing-Wax" is at once a tender reminiscence about her nonwriting father's writing materials and the tale of how a neighbor is caught stealing the wax needed to forge a will. In "Armande," finally, a village doctor discovers that a rich young woman cares for him. All are light stories, far removed from war and occupation.

In June 1943 she began to be treated with acupuncture, and there were times when her pain seemed to disappear. Her doctor advised that the lesion was an old one and that the cure would not be rapid. She was unable to leave home to say farewell to Renée Hamon, who was operated on for cancer of the uterus and died on October 26, at the age of forty-four.[15]

Duo, in an adaptation by Paul Géraldy, went on stage in German Paris, with Valentine Tessier starring; it had a good run. Still Colette stayed home, kept there not only by her arthritis but by an intestinal ailment that lasted for months. So at last the war came to her: at the beginning of autumn a plane crashed just outside the Palais-Royal quadrangle, causing a fire and a commotion.[16]

Goudeket did not go out much either, for his own reasons. "He never says that Paris seems tiny and unsafe," Colette wrote to Marguerite Moreno. "He never loses his good humor, or his steadiness, and when I explode in barks and meows and impatient insults, he says to me, 'Tomorrow, I promise, you'll have a pretty little communiqué.' "[17]

If by that he meant the Allied landing in Normandy, they would have another seven months to wait; if he meant the liberation of Paris, another ten months.

In any event, friends were now returning to Paris from southern safety, and many had no place to stay. Colette's daughter arrived, as did Renaud, whose Castel-Novel had been requisitioned by the Vichy militia (which raided the countryside from such bases, returning with human prey). In Paris, meanwhile, Colette knew that her dear Maurice would never be safe as long as the Germans held the city.[18] Still, she admitted, "I don't tell Maurice when I say to myself, 'It's all too long and I'm too worn out, I'll be finished before it [the war] is.' That would make him too unhappy. He himself is marvelously true to himself, and firm."[19]

Sacha Guitry came calling at the end of March. At last his *From Joan of Arc to Philippe Pétain* was ready for printing. He went over the proofs of Colette's essay on Balzac with her. She had something on her mind — the arrest of a protégé of Marguerite Moreno. In the end she decided not to mention it, fearing that it might be a mistake. She didn't know Sacha that well, she told Marguerite.[20]

THIRTY-NINE

Liberation

WHEN ASKED TO autograph a photo of herself for the omnipresent dealer-collector Richard Anacréon early that spring, Colette wrote, "God, but I don't like that old lady!"[1] She was now seventy-one years old. At the beginning of April 1944 she complained that she had been ill all week and had seen no one; she was suffering from a pain in a spot that had once been diagnosed as "pleuritic," not to mention the continuing misery of her arthritis. In May, for the first time in two years, she took a ride in a horse-drawn carriage to the Bois de Boulogne, which was deserted but "too beautiful to bear." No longer cared for, the lakes had dried up; wildflowers sprouted in the middle of one of them.

It was the longest spring, and then it would be the longest summer, of the war. Everyone thought that he knew the precise moment when it would end — that is, when the American and British troops would first step onto French soil. "It will be the sixteenth," someone would say — the sixteenth of May. "Not at all, you'll see, it'll be the twenty-third." "No, it'll be June fifteenth." Colette repeated these wild guesses to Marguerite, far off in her southwestern retreat. When the Allies did land, on June 6, Colette took note of the "excitement" but stayed at her desk, finishing a book for a Swiss publisher. The collection of stories called *Gigi* was to be published in Switzerland that year, as was *Paris from My Window,* a new edition of *From My Window*.

During the night of June 5 and early morning of June 6, she counted seven or eight alerts; the commotion robbed her of energy for her daytime tasks. Meanwhile, food was becoming scarcer, and prices were rising. Colette told Marguerite about the latest fashions: short skirts that showed the thigh, hair worn high. Since coiffeurs had no electricity, she noted, they did a lot of back-combing.[2]

Ten weeks separated the Normandy landings from the liberation of Paris. To the housebound couple the wait seemed interminable.[3] Once, in July, she tried to describe the scene to Marguerite: "It's the third alert since this morning, if I'm not mistaken. But who pays the slightest attention? Children play with their little cars in the garden alongside their mothers."[4] They began to pay more attention as the Allies drew nearer, listening to rumors and to radio news, which was not always reliable. "They're at Antony! . . . They're on the heights of Châtillon. . . . No, they're still fighting. . . . They're repairing the road so the tanks can pass. . . . They're arriving. . . . They've arrived. . . ."[5] On August 24, American and British forces gallantly made way to allow the Free French, represented by the Second Armored Division of General Philippe Leclerc, to be the first to enter their capital.

That night was the worst of the war. While the air battle raged over Paris, Colette sheltered three of her less fortunate neighbors in her entrance hall. Homemade flags appeared on buildings. She heard guns but also carillons; she took part in the liberation as she had partaken in the occupation: from her window.

Then, tragicomedy. The beloved Maurice, desiring a closer view, was caught in the Tuileries garden. He had ducked into one of the shelters dug below the garden level to avoid a German patrol, for he did not want to have to show his papers, which were stamped "Jew." Then, when he tried to leave, he was caught in the crossfire between some insurrectionists and the departing Germans. For three days and two nights he was pinned down, unable to contact his wife.

She tried to consult the lists of casualties; he kept trying to get home. "I confess, Marguerite, that I greeted him with a broadside of curses," she said when it was over.[6]

For the victory parade on August 26, Ambassador Sert sent his chauffeured limousine to pick her up, and she and Maurice watched from a balcony on the corner of Rue de Rivoli, not far from the spot where Goudeket had been trapped a few days earlier. Then shots were fired from somewhere below; Sert's guests retreated to the rear of the apartment as ornate mirrors and windows were shattered. After that Misia Sert brought out a feast of Spanish cold cuts and French champagne.

"At present," Colette admitted to the far-off Marguerite, "I want to eat. It's all going so slowly! I want beef stew, and marinated herring." But it was not to be, for the autumn that followed the liberation, and the winter after that, seemed to be the worst of the war for the people of Paris. Trains and trucks that might have brought food and fuel were instead mobilized for the front. Even the weather that winter was more arduous than before, thought Colette.[7]

There was good news and bad. Down in the Corrèze, her daughter's services to the cause were rewarded: she was appointed mayor of Curemonte. But for Colette, there were also all of those compromised friends, some of whom were arrested and humiliated (Sacha was one of these). She listened to their stories without comment. Clearly she was proud of her daughter: "Let me tell you, I'm the only one who really knows that charming girl. . . ."[8]

The purge trials began. Among the first to be brought to justice were writers — writers for the press, that is — since evidence was ready to hand in the form of print on paper. Robert Brasillach was one of this lot. A staff member of the pro-Nazi *Je Suis Partout* even before the war, he had given propaganda speeches for the Germans and traveled with other collaborationists to Germany on behalf of the Nazi war effort. When an attempt was made to spare Jewish children from deportation, Brasillach had written, "We must rid ourselves of all the Jews and not keep the little ones!"

Brasillach was tried for collusion with the enemy on January 19, 1945, and pronounced guilty before that day ended. The verdict bore the mandatory sentence of death by firing squad. His attorney, Jacques Isorni, organized a campaign on his behalf, enlisting the aid of fellow authors who had not been compromised by the occupation (or who had managed to slip by unnoticed). The result was an impressive petition, with fifty-nine familiar signatures, asking General de Gaulle to pardon Brasillach.[9]

Convinced that Colette had good reason to respond favorably, "unless she lacked dignity — that is to say, courage," Isorni asked her for a testimonial. She replied bluntly, "I don't know the Robert Brasillach of *Je Suis Partout*. I knew the young writer, the novelist who began his career so brilliantly. I cannot and shall not speak of any other." She added that she had received the young man only once during the occupation, at which time they had limited themselves to literary talk.

When Isorni showed Colette's reply to Brasillach, the prisoner insisted that she was not telling the truth. In the meeting she referred to, he said, she had expressed her gratitude toward Suzanne Abetz for having obtained Goudeket's release — this after Colette's imploring calls to himself and another collaborationist writer had failed to produce the desired result. Brasillach followed up with a note to Isorni: "When I think that Colette signed her letters 'your old friend' and that she wrote, 'I am happy that I watched you grow up. . . .' That was during the occupation; she knew quite well what I was doing; I haven't changed since then. . . . Better just to shrug our shoulders!"

Cocteau asked Isorni if he had Colette's signature and was told that she had declined to give it (so Isorni remembered later). Cocteau promised to win his neighbor's consent, and the lawyer had her endorsement in hand the following day.[10] In addition to Colette, the final list of petitioners included Paul Valéry and François Mauriac, Paul Claudel and Cocteau, and even the Resistance journalist Albert Camus — another reluctant signer. In the end, de Gaulle refused to stay the execution or commute the sentence to a prison term;

Brasillach was shot at Fort Montrouge on February 6. Colette, for her part, was to decide that the purge trials were "disgusting."[11]

In that first January of liberated Paris, she celebrated her seventy-second birthday, "having resigned myself to many reasonable things," as she confessed to another old-timer (Charles Saglio's wife, Lucie). Still, she gave up as little ground as she could: "For as long as my general condition remains honorable, I consent to official help-lessness, on my well-organized bed. When you see my small and regular handwriting, just tell yourself that it camouflages long, stub-born debates with myself, in silence."

She shared the material concerns of her friends, feeling the short-age of coal first and foremost. "I burn what I have left and live under blankets, with a hot-water bottle," she declared.[12] By the first week of February, she was able to reassure her farm-women friends: her fuel had lasted until the thaw. They were still sending food pack-ages — notably butter and beans — but she had no coffee. Maurice, meanwhile, had gone off to the countryside looking for old books to sell and had returned with a dozen eggs and a hare.[13]

Hélène Picard died, alone. She would allow no one to see her in her infirmity. Afflicted with a bone disease, in her last days an "un-recognizable dwarf," she could get around only on her hands and knees. Colette had always felt close to this woman poet, but Picard herself had never quite accepted Goudeket. It had made it more difficult for the two friends to meet.[14]

Colette could not have gone to the hospital even if, in her final moments, Hélène had wanted her there. A mutual friend who did go came to see Colette at the end of January and found her "bound to her bed by arthritis." The food shortage was now at its worst, but Colette picked up a bar of chocolate, bit it in two, and asked the visitor to give half to Hélène. But by the next day Hélène was dead.[15]

One had to go to the Palais-Royal to see Colette now, and many people did. Some went for interviews, some to consult her as one would an oracle. The visitor would sit on a chair decorated by Co-lette herself, while she lay on the magical object on which she worked and then slept, the daybed that she called her divan-raft.[16] One of her first postwar visitors from abroad was *Vogue*'s intrepid reporter-photographer Lee Miller (an old Paris hand and former disciple of Man Ray), who found Colette on the telephone, her fuzzy hair a halo against the light from the window. The room was warm, the fur coverings of the divan "tawny rich." When she had completed her telephone conversation, Colette gruffly asked what the visitor wanted, "but her hand was warm and her kohl-rimmed eyes matched in sparkle and clarity the myriads of crystal balls and glass bibelots which strewed the room." So they talked, and Lee Miller snapped pictures, and then Colette brought out older photographs, some going as far back as Willy's time. She also showed her surviving manuscripts of the Claudine books.[17]

Colette's daughter was now back in Paris, this time apparently for good; as she had in Curemonte, she made her presence felt. Her militancy took the form of articles in the antifascist press, notably in a weekly called *Fraternité,* founded during the Resistance. Unlike her mother, Colette II insisted that those who had collaborated with the Nazis should be punished; she deplored the indulgence that was being shown to enemy sympathizers.[18] Bel-Gazou herself was to remember that she put an end to her newspaper career on the day when her mother said to her, "I like this article less than the others."[19]

Whether or not she complained in public, the complaint became public knowledge. In a frank profile published in *Vogue* in 1945, Bel-Gazou was seen to be living a rural existence on Paris's Left Bank. Although she could write for the press, indolence and an inferiority complex kept her from more creative writing.[20] Her mother was also to deliver herself of what might be considered her private feelings about her daughter, in that rich memoir written even as it was being lived, *The Evening Star*. She told of this daughter who might at that moment be traveling in defeated Germany, making notes for an article, or sitting in "a somber Parisian shelter," writing a poem that she would refuse to let her mother read.[21]

In a will drafted in July 1945, Colette left half her royalties to her

FORTY

Cures

THE WAR was not yet quite over. For Marguerite Moreno, in her self-exile, Colette described the atmosphere of Paris in the third week of April 1945. They all remained on edge; the radio, with its hints of important news to come, did not help to calm nerves. One of those who had come back to the city was her publisher Ferenczi, who was anxious to do a book by her. She was still writing stories for the little volume that would open with the magical "Gigi"; she let Marguerite know that if that story ever reached the screen, there would be a role in it for her (the worldly-wise aunt). But by the time the first movie was made of this tale that is so much like a scenario, her actress friend was dead.[1]

On May 2, this woman who enjoyed honors received a singular recognition: election to the Goncourt Academy, an unofficial panel of writers that had been created by the will of the nineteenth-century novelist and diarist Edmond de Goncourt. The academy was supposed to be made up of ten men; Colette was the second exception (after Théophile Gautier's daughter, Judith). They were all novelists and were often less stodgy and less sullied by institutional connections than the members of the French Academy.

At that moment, however, the Goncourts seemed as war-scarred as their seniors in that latter body. Proportionately *more* of the Goncourts, in fact, had been accused of Nazi collaboration. Eight votes were required to expel a member, but three of the ten were too compromised even to be allowed to meet with the others. Colette occupied the chair of a fourth compromised member, who had resigned before his fellows had a chance to throw him out.[2]

But she was going to be joining friends, or at the very least friendly reviewers of her books, such as Francis Carco and André Billy. On their side, the Goncourts were delighted to co-opt a strong personality who could show up at meetings wearing sandals with no socks.[3] She took her new responsibilities seriously, chief among them being the obligation to come to lunch in a cushioned restaurant not far from the Palais-Royal. She also had to read stacks of new fiction in order to help select a novel worthy of the coveted annual prize given by the Goncourt Academy.[4]

At Easter she and Maurice had a change of scenery, accepting the hospitality of Simone Berriau, whose estate at Les Salins d'Hyères was not far from Saint-Tropez. The house was large and situated smack in the middle of a vineyard, with the sea only a hundred yards away. But Maurice remembered it as being like a "railway station," and not even their hostess knew in advance who was coming for lunch and who would be spending the night.[5] The transition from Palais-Royal tranquillity seemed too sudden to Colette, yet even tumult was change, she decided. They swore that they would go back again and stay longer next time. Sleeping-car berths were not easy to book in those early postwar months, so when reservations became available in late July, they seized the opportunity, giving themselves a full month in the South this time. It would not be a month's holiday, Colette made it clear to friends; she had another book to write. If the Berriau house was too crowded, she would leave.

It *was* crowded, but in compensation their hostess kept them well supplied with food, one day even coming home with a live sheep.[6] "I won't bother telling you the names of drop-in visitors," Colette wrote to Hélène Morhange, "for we don't really know them, and they change — except when they implant themselves with their wives, their mistresses, and their hunting dogs."[7] One of the guests was her friend and benefactor Al-Glâwi, who had been Simone Berriau's friend first.[8]

She had a terrace of her own, where she worked on the very personal memoir that she would call *The Evening Star,* which followed her life through the war. She returned to Paris with a manuscript, as did Goudeket, who had composed a comedy that would actually go on stage the next winter.[9] By now the many-faceted Goudeket had elected still another career: he would be the editor and publisher of the complete works of his wife. She spent part of that autumn filling out *The Evening Star,* which her regular publisher had found too slight; she herself was also unsatisfied with her summer's work.[10]

In the book as we know it — and it is still a slender volume — Colette speaks of her physical condition and her pain (which is occasional, not constant). She tells her admirers how she and Maurice sleep with a closed door between them so that she can get up when she wishes to move about or to read. Once, when she did accidentally disturb his sleep, he woke with a start, "and I could see by his face . . . that an unexpected awakening would always bear the date of December 12, 1941."

She thinks about old age, her handicap. A window is her only distraction; what can she write about besides the changing of the seasons and her memories? After what happened to Maurice that December, nothing more could happen to her. She returns to the sights and sounds of German occupation, recalling the roundup of Jewish families in July 1942.

Even before the war, she writes, the Palais-Royal was a village, and occupation only reinforced the camaraderie. Inside their quadrangle, Jews, Englishmen, parachutists, and young Frenchmen refusing to be drafted as German laborers all found a place to hide, but so did black marketeers.

Even cats and dogs of years past enter her book; now she calls each of her pets the "last" one. She also tells us that this is the first book she has written without counting pages or worrying about a deadline. For fifty-three years she has been writing to be published. There will be no more novels, she says, for what can she see from her room? Can she learn not to write anymore?

She would not, in any case, give up trying cures. Maurice accompanied her to Uriage, a famous and traditional watering place whose sulfurous and ferruginous springs were believed to cure a variety of ailments. She could not be cured, but improvement was possible, and that was what she needed if she was to get a better grip on herself.

The regimen, beginning in the early summer of 1946, was in itself exhausting. There were injections of thermal water and baths in the same. Her hotel was connected to the spa's treatment center and to a casino as well — but the program allowed little time for leisure.

It was all, seemingly, to no avail. The pain got worse and even reached new parts of her body. The local doctor called it saturation and suspended the treatment. She felt better just lying in bed, and then she learned that she would have to wait another six weeks before the Uriage cure could begin to change her life. So it was time for them to pack and leave. They drove south to Provence, picking up the real summer there as guests of Charles and Jeanne de Polignac in a house on the outskirts of Grasse. "How tired I am, and how little I can take this southern aridity anymore," Colette lamented. "The South is over for me."[11]

Back home in Paris, she began to organize her life around the pain that would not fade. She switched rooms with Maurice because his snug, smaller room would be easier to heat. (She would still have a window on the garden.)[12] In January 1947 she met a Swiss doctor who seemed to be the miracle man she was looking for (he was so thorough that he came to Paris to follow his patients' progress); it was agreed that she would visit him for treatment that spring. Meanwhile, she developed rheumatism in her right shoulder; for a fortnight it kept her from writing. When at last she was ready to start off for Geneva, she confessed to a confidante that she did not really think that the treatment would help.[13]

They were booked into the elegant Hotel Richemond, overlooking the lake. Once again, the new treatment made her feel worse at the beginning. She received electric charges as well as injections, coming out of it dizzy and momentarily deaf. "I make the best of it I can," she explained to Hélène Morhange, "for Maurice's sake; he's being noble." There was no improvement. Oh yes, she said, the doctor was a fine man; she felt like lying to him and telling him that she was better.[14] But it was good to be in Geneva, if only because it was not postwar Paris; problems of food supply, and of political uncertainty, did not exist here.[15] When she left Switzerland, she took a prescription home with her, and proceeded to follow it to the letter. "Don't overestimate the benefits of my treatment," she advised Hélène Morhange. "I'll never walk again. But to gain some optimism, a general good feeling (which doesn't exclude sudden sharp pains and howls), will go halfway toward satisfying my modest hopes."[16]

And she did feel better, a mite better. "That's enough for me," she assured Marguerite Moreno in June. "It makes Maurice so happy!"[17] One sunny day that same month, a young American writer came calling, and so we have a portrait of Colette by Truman Capote, whose only published book then was *Other Voices, Other Rooms*. He found her with "reddish, frizzly, rather African-looking hair; slanting, alley-cat eyes rimmed with kohl; a finely made face flexible as water . . . rouged cheeks . . . lips thin and tense as wire but painted a really brazen hussy scarlet."[18]

Natalie Barney was back in France, but not without problems. Incredibly, she had preferred America's enemies during the war and had moved to Mussolini's Italy, where her fascist friend Ezra Pound lived. Under the influence of the politically confused poet, she had accepted some of the worst aspects of fascism, including anti-Semitism.[19] Now she was having difficulty getting a new residence permit in France, and Colette offered her assistance.[20] Her intervention, or someone else's, worked; Flossie was able to stay in France until she died, many years later.

In 1946 the doctor who rented the Colettes' old house in Saint-Sauveur retired and transferred his clientele to a young general practitioner, Pierre Muesser. Colette asked the new tenant for a realistic rent and a limited lease; she did this, she said, to protect the rights of the real owner, who had given her lifetime use of the property.[21]

Eventually the owner — her benefactor — decided that he was tired of paying taxes and insurance on a house that he had so little to do with. With Colette's agreement, it was sold, in December 1950, to Dr. Muesser. The deed stipulated that the purchaser had to leave in place the marble plaque identifying the house as Colette's birthplace; nor was he allowed to alter the facade or the double flight of steps on the street side.

Inside and out, of course, changes had to be made. The toilets were moved indoors at last, and Sido's lower garden was replaced by a pool for the doctor's children. Colette's room, meanwhile, was transformed into the setting for a model railroad with all the accessories.[22]

FORTY-ONE

Colette at Seventy-five

THAT AUTUMN Colette sold the film rights to *The Ripening Seed,* a transaction that required a considerable number of business meetings in her little Palais-Royal room. After several false starts, the movie finally went into production in 1953, for release the following January, and it is remembered now mainly for Edwige Feuillère's performance as the Lady in White.[1]

"Yes indeed, I'm suffering," Colette wrote to Marguerite Moreno, answering her caring friend's question. She was also busy reading novels that had been submitted for the end-of-year Goncourt Prize. And she really read the books, even though the books themselves were getting longer: seven- and eight-hundred-page sagas printed in small type were then the fashion. Some of these sagas, she said, were even worthy of consideration.[2] She attended the Goncourt lunches thanks to a little elevator that took her up to the dining room that had been set aside for the jurors. She was to describe "the still very feminine delight" she took in being the only woman at these gatherings.[3] In later years, her fellow academicians would climb her stairs to hold their meetings clustered around her divan-raft.[4]

Of course, her seventy-fifth birthday, in January 1948, had to be an event. It was "our Colette" here, "our Colette" there. The press published appropriate tributes; her peers dispatched telegrams. Then there were the readers, who sent humble or elaborate greetings from everywhere. Rainier III, the sovereign prince of Monaco, sent a basket of fruit and flowers. In a thank-you note, she recalled stays in Monte Carlo when she was dancing on the stage. After a performance she would always look for a bar "where hot drinks served as my defense against the dangerous cold of sun-land." [5]

Someone found a dusty bottle of Bordeaux wine from the harvest of 1873, Colette's birth year; the Goudekets kept it cradled respectfully until it was time for dinner on January 28, when they found that it had retained some of its savor. In her reminiscences she reminded readers that she too remained inclined and managed to retain some of *her* savor.

She had begun writing *The Blue Lantern* in 1946 and was still at it as she celebrated her seventy-fifth birthday; she would finish it only the following year. Goudeket made the point that this was actually the last book she wrote, since the next work she published after that consisted of essays that she had written earlier. [6] She had thought that *The Evening Star* would be her final work, she would tell readers of this next one. Her radius of movement was shorter now, her physical torment more constant. When she traveled (to Geneva, say), she told her readers about it, but most of the new book concerned other people's visits to *her* apartment. She would go on writing, she thought; when did one stop? "What is the warning?"

Close friends of hers were dying. One was Luc-Albert Moreau, early that spring. Then, in July 1948, while Colette was visiting Les Salins d'Hyères again, it was the turn of the oldest member of her group, Marguerite Moreno. Mutual friends sent letters of sympathy to Colette, as if she were part of the family. [7]

Some of her own most moving letters were written to friends who had lost a household pet. In one such, to the divorced wife of Francis Carco, she seriously recommended work as a way for her to forget the death of her Pekingese. Selfish people might say that she should get another dog at once, warned Colette, "but you and I don't like that kind of remedy." [8]

During this landmark year, she embarked on another ambitious literary project. This one required not writing but rereading, editing, and occasionally revising, all for a "complete works" to be packaged by Maurice Goudeket for his new venture, a publishing house called Le Fleuron. "Idiotic work," she had denigrated it in one of the last letters she wrote to Marguerite Moreno.[9] Much of her output might have been considered ephemeral — reviews of forgotten plays, for example — but it was nevertheless to be preserved here, together with her own forgotten works, her plays and adaptations, and even some of the advertisements she had written on assignment. Goudeket reminds us that much of Colette's publishing life up to that point had been a function of necessity. She would rush to put together a miscellany of newspaper stories for publication, and occasionally the same sketch would appear (by error) in two different books. Now she scribbled a brief preface for each of the works collected in this finely printed fifteen-volume edition.

Sometimes she would say to him, "Did I really write all that? Maurice, is it possible that I wrote all that?" Or, better, "It's not a bad job, you know!"[10]

Her lofty position had not gone to her head, however. She was still ready to write an advertisement, if the fee was satisfactory,[11] or even the dialogue for the film version of "Gigi," first brought to the screen as a French production with Danièle Delorme as the ingenuous young lady who rejects her education as a courtesan.[12]

She wrote the latter in July, while at Simone Berriau's estate in the South. As usual, there was a regiment of guests. "But my room is sacred," she assured a friend, "and Maurice is vigilant." She was in pain and had decided once and for all that warm weather was not necessarily the answer. Simone Berriau and her husband drove the Goudekets to Grasse, dropping them off at the Polignacs', where they were houseguests once again. Colette arrived there "exhausted, old, lazy," she told Hélène Morhange; when the crowd, Maurice included, drove down to Cannes, she stayed behind.

They flew back to Paris. The flight from Nice took two hours and fifty minutes then; for her it was now the best way to travel.

She returned to a cartload of galley proofs of her complete works, which were being printed a volume at a time.[13]

It was at around this time that Goudeket's company, Le Fleuron, the capital for which had been put up by his friends and himself, acquired the Palais-Royal apartment in which they had until now been living as tenants.[14] Meanwhile, Le Fleuron also began publishing, in addition to Colette's complete works, limited editions of previously published books of hers. Thanks to Goudeket's resourcefulness, she was getting the most out of what she had done and what she could do now.

They returned to Provence in the summer of 1949, for another holiday up in the hills at Grasse, with the Polignacs. Once again Colette arrived exhausted and hurting, and the climate failed to alleviate her pain.[15] It was even suggested that she go to Lourdes to pray for a cure. "Maybe I'll accept that one day," she said. "The day comes when you abandon yourself. . . ."[16] But she never did try Lourdes.

They were back in Paris by the end of August, "and the sweet little face of my daughter was waiting for us on the stairs," she reported to Hélène Morhange. Colette de Jouvenel had begun a new career, as an antiques dealer on Rue Bonaparte.[17] And her mother was as active as ever. This time there was a play to bring to the stage, a revival of *Chéri* in which the much-admired Valentine Tessier was Léa to a Chéri played by Jean Marais. Once more Colette had a hand in designing the stage set and directing the cast. "You'd laugh," she told a friend, "if you saw the actors rehearsing around my bed — even on my bed!"[18]

The new *Chéri* opened at the Théâtre de la Madeleine at the end of October. After the final curtain on the first night, Jean Cocteau took the stage to pay tribute to the author. "She joined no literary school," he declared to an obviously receptive audience, "and she charmed them all." One of France's toughest critics, *Le Figaro*'s Jean-Jacques Gautier, was admirative. The work was "true," he said, and the cast outdid itself.[19]

When the president of the Goncourt Academy died, Colette was elected to replace him. She was now part of the establishment. She was asked, for example, to intervene on behalf of Henri Béraud, a once-prominent author and winner of a Goncourt Prize in his day, who was currently serving a life sentence at hard labor for collaborating with the Nazis. Colette did intervene, and whether or not because of her help, Béraud's sentence was reduced to ten years.[20]

Then it was the turn of the Communists. Louis Aragon, that party's best-known intellectual, had been convicted of libeling police who put down a miners' strike; his sentence included the loss of his civil rights. A rally was organized in defense of Aragon at the end of October 1949, and Colette was invited to participate. She could not, of course: "Aragon, who so recently paid me an affectionate visit, knows how arthritis has confined me to bed. But I join my voice to the chorus demanding the abolition of a measure that I find as incomprehensible as it is inadmissible. Removed from politics all my life long, I simply insist on having Aragon whole — that is to say, the poet, the novelist, and the voter." The combative Aragon could have wished for no better testimonial.[21]

FORTY-TWO

Monte Carlo

ONE MORNING IN November 1949 Colette wrote to a friend, the writer Claude Farrère, "The sun has reached my raft and will stay there for as long as the season allows." Her friend had indicated that he would like to pay her a visit. Telephone first, she told him. She would certainly be home, for she went out only to the Goncourt lunches or to an opening (every twenty-five years or so). She suggested that he come on a nice day so he could have a look at the garden.[1]

An American correspondent based in Paris, Joseph Barry, climbed the flight and a half of stairs to find an "aging, ailing, arthritic Danaë . . . condemned to her bed-divan in the orchid-warmth of her room." People — Americans included — were always giving her things, even offering her kittens. "Why should I have another kitten?" she wondered. "They always die before we do." She had what she needed: "a few friends and all this." "This" was the view out over the garden, her writing table with its bouquet of fountain pens, a log fire, and Maurice seated nearby.

She was asked for all sorts of things, Barry discovered — letters of introduction, for instance, to the actor Louis Jouvet, say, or to Jean Cocteau. She had to deal with "the daughters of daughters of friends." In the United States, at that time, she was either unknown or considered to be a writer only for women, while in France her popularity extended even to the youngest generation.[2]

"I never go out . . . but I'm not bored," she assured Natalie Barney in January 1950, just before her seventy-seventh birthday. "Suffering, even when violent, doesn't exclude distractions of the mind." Her American friend was off on a holiday; Colette wished she could join Natalie on one of those trips. "I am, in daily life, so silent and immobile that you would not be aware of my presence. As for Maurice, I think that he is the pearl, the diamond of houseguests. Present and absent just as one desires. He's the man I should have adopted twenty years earlier . . . but then we'd probably have created a scandal."[3]

Henceforth, all the evidence comes from bedside visitors. Colette's world had not been particularly expansive during the war and occupation; now the divan-raft was her universe. Nevertheless, her room was no monk's cell. Goudeket pointed out that Colette always made sure that ceilings as well as walls were papered; a ceiling was also a wall, she insisted, for man was created not to sit but to stand or to lie down, and was as often horizontal as vertical. Her sofa bed was drawn up to the room's single window. The writing desk was a clever construction: a table with an adjustable stand, wide enough to fit over her divan. She would use her canes as hooks to pull the desk up to her bed or even to draw a book or other desired object within reach. (She called this fishing from her raft.) In her last years she had another means of broadening her horizons: a television set.[4]

Goudeket also tells us about the bric-a-brac, her collection of collections. The inventory of objects in her room alone required four single-spaced typed pages. In addition to the divan and the desk, there was a proper bureau in the Directoire style, a smaller table, a dressing table, still another table, this one in the English style, and a seven-drawer chest, plus two armchairs, one of them covered by Colette, and two Louis-Philippe chairs, also done by her. On her writing desk there was a blue jar with five pens, eyeglasses and a magnifying glass, a paper cutter — still needed then to open the pages of new books — and a fly swatter. The blotter holder contained her father's military record. Most of the books in and around her bed, at least at the end of her life, had to do with animals and insects.

The mantel had room for a porcelain lamp, a paperweight made of four crystal balls, and then more than fifty smaller crystal paperweights and similar objects. Elsewhere in the room there were vases, small statues, paintings, sketches, engravings, photographs, a barometer, and a thermometer. And this was just to cite the essential items — though perhaps the wheelchair, the canes, and the blue lantern were the real essentials.[5]

The day came when Colette could no longer manage the stairs even with assistance. So Goudeket and Pauline attached poles to the wheelchair, creating a kind of modern sedan chair that two strong men could carry. Her best chance to enjoy a semblance of freedom came when she went on a journey, and in May 1950 the Goudekets made the first of their trips to Monte Carlo, where luxury was able to compensate for the constricted life of an invalid. In Monte Carlo there was also the added attraction of an English doctor who thought that he could cure her with injections.[6]

After another pleasant flight, they were greeted at the Nice airport by a veritable delegation from that municipality, a delegation bearing flowers. In Monte Carlo, the Hotel de Paris, across the street from the casino, was *the* place (as it still is today). The Goudekets were given a ground-floor room on a garden, with a key to a private gate that opened onto the street. "My pain is at its worst," she reported to Hélène Morhange. But she did have a view of a palm tree, a magnolia, some poppies, the sea, and a piece of the rocky hill on which the palace sat. Prince Rainier sent candy and flowers to her room.

In her wheelchair she could go directly to the ground-floor restaurant. One day they had lunch outdoors with Léopold Marchand, who, along with Goudeket, was soon busy adapting *The Other One* for the stage. Her publisher Ferenczi sent her two hundred copies of *En pays connu* (Familiar Country), a new collection of old writings, so that she could autograph them in the sun.

She pursued the treatment, wanting to believe that her pain had diminished. In truth, she felt worse than ever on her return to Paris in the middle of July. The best her own doctor could say was that the treatment itself was not to blame. The month of August was passed at a luxe hostelry close to Paris, the Trianon Palace in Versailles. Goudeket was able to commute, and Léo Marchand could visit and work on *The Other One*.[7] When it was time for rehearsals that autumn, Goudeket took charge, though the cast occasionally made its way to the Palais-Royal to perform before the raft.[8]

On January 1, 1951, Colette assured Pierre Blanchar and his wife that she had not been outside for one hundred days. "Obviously I'd prefer not to suffer, or to suffer less," she told Claude Farrère. "But my window looks south, over the garden, facing the sun; do I have the right to complain? And then, I married a saint. So. . . ." It was an uneventful winter, spent largely in waiting for Monte Carlo. "It's on May 10 that they will put me on a plane," she informed Francis Carco. She hoped they could have lunch together before that at the Grand Véfour.[9] It is clear that she did not consider lunching at the Véfour going out; that elegant restaurant — once a café whose customers included Napoleon, now listed as a historical landmark — was just steps away, beneath the arcade. She could be carried there.

Shortly before her departure for the South, she sat up in bed to write one of the most moving letters of hers that has survived. "Do you have a pretty house?" she asked Bertrand de Jouvenel. "Children of whom you are proud? Show all of this to me — am I not partly responsible for all of this? — if only on a little postcard." So many years had gone by since their last encounter or exchange of messages. "In five days Maurice takes me to Monte Carlo. . . . On my return the mirror will tell me if I can call you. But will you still be young enough?"[10]

He remembered a final visit. He brought flowers, and she gave him an illustrated edition of one of her books, seeming to look longingly at the nature photographs therein. That was her ordeal, he thought: to have her horizon confined to what she could see from the window.[11]

The trip was short and sweet again. There were photographers at the airport, and titled friends. They were given that glorious garden suite at the Hotel de Paris once again; they found the hotel staff too nice, the food too good. Everything would have been perfect if she could have walked, if she had not been suffering so.[12]

A movie was being made in the hotel. Goudeket remembered that as he maneuvered her wheelchair into the dining room between the cameras and their cables, Colette caught a glimpse of a pretty young actress standing in front of the lens, and she at once declared: "That's our Gigi for America." Goudeket looked up the young woman that very day and learned that she was Audrey Hepburn, a dancer who had not acted before.[13] That autumn Hepburn was a sensational Gigi on the New York stage. "My love and gratitude to you always," she wrote to Colette after the Broadway opening.[14]

In June, still in Monte Carlo, Colette confessed to her oldest friend, Hélène Morhange (who had long since become Madame Luc-Albert Moreau and was now widowed), that she was not working anymore. "It's that I have nothing, nothing more to say, surely," she admitted. And, too, there was the pain.[15] But she did try to write: on her arrival in Monte Carlo she started keeping a diary. "In six months I shall confront my seventy-ninth birthday," she began. At that age, her father had told her, one was not yet ready to give up loving: just a thought. She proceeded to describe a meeting of the Goncourts at her apartment the previous March. They had left her to go on to their traditional lunch — but one could not have everything, she sighed. From the Goncourt meeting she turned back to her child-hood again — Saint-Sauveur, Sido — seemingly prepared now to employ a more earthy approach than she had presented in her books. "We knew how to use the necessary village vulgarity with tact," she recalled.

At times the handwriting and the prose itself are choppy:

The ponds of my countryside slept within me long years
The ponds of my countryside have slept within me long
The ponds of my countryside have caressed my shores
    for long years
The ponds of my countryside have caressed an
    abundance of fish known to the generation of my
    father [16]

Her life pursued the pattern: after Monte Carlo, Versailles with its venerable Trianon Palace, where she was not the only famous or well-to-do old-timer; for many of her generation, this castle-hotel close to Paris was all the adventure they wished for now. But for her it was not only a holiday. In the middle of August a troop of Americans arrived from Hollywood to talk about a movie version of "Gigi," and perhaps a *Chéri* too.[17]

The next trip to Monte Carlo began earlier, right after the first of the year (the year being 1952). The Goudekets left a dark, rainy Paris to find splendid Mediterranean weather, and this time it seemed to help. "Isn't my writing better already?" she asked Hélène Moreau. She was received by Prince Rainier's father, her old friend Pierre de Monaco; another day she was invited to lunch by Pierre and Rainier both. (She admired the father more: "the job of prince suits him better than it does his son," she thought.)[18]

Cocteau dined with the Goudekets on February 21. "I find her in bad shape," he told his diary, "separated from the world by her ears and her exhaustion." It is useful to have such a witness, since neither Colette nor her closest friends talked about her hearing deficiency. Cocteau described the scene as Goudeket wheeled his wife into "the astonishing dining room of velvet and gold, with its ornamental ceiling, drapes, caryatids, immense frescoes representing nude women, peacocks, tigers." A gypsy violinist played the theme of "Gigi" in her honor, and the gypsy with his instrument and Colette seemed a "phantom group, invisible to the other tables."

Her hearing was so bad that Cocteau had to communicate with his old friend through Goudeket, who would relay only the essential to her ear. "Sometimes she hears me," noted Cocteau, "sometimes she tries and doesn't succeed." He summed up: "Great sadness. Age. Thus I shall be. Thus begins the end."

He gave credit to Goudeket for the way he managed his wife's affairs. *Her* way had been to throw bank notes into a drawer after she was paid for a piece of writing, he remembered, and then to dig into the drawer to pay Pauline. From what Goudeket said about their income tax, Cocteau gathered that she earned a lot of money. "She is a peasant and a child," concluded this lively if shallow man. "She lets herself live. She is almost happy with this cloud in which she dwells and which protects her against a cruel world that has passed her by and no longer resembles the one containing her flowers and pets."

Cocteau saw her again the next morning and remarked, "She is another person. . . . She hears us. . . . I see her bright eyes again."[19]

A year after Colette's death, in the speech he gave in accepting the seat she had occupied in the Belgian Academy, Cocteau offered a final assessment of the couple: "Foreign to the intellectualism of our era, if Madame Colette was not a monster, she was nothing, and if this monster frightened no one, it is because Maurice Goudeket was in charge of her."[20] Goudeket himself later remembered how grateful Colette had been for his constant ministrations; she told him that she only regretted that he had such an old wife. *He* felt, on the other hand, that the difference in their ages helped them to get along with one another.[21]

FORTY-THREE

Last Writings

UNDER THE DATE of July 16, 1952, Cocteau recorded in his diary, "Maurice tells me of Colette, who is in pain night and day and who accepts this pain because it creates a wave of life in which Maurice never leaves her alone."[1] Goudeket did stay close by, and even those who did not admire him would remember that.

That summer they decided to avoid the South; heat was not such a good thing for her. Their choice instead was a northern Monte Carlo, Deauville, another casino town on the sea that never seemed to go out of fashion. "I suffer a great deal, and I tell you this without reserve," she confided to Francis Carco on the eve of her trip, though she asked him not to give her condition too much publicity. "From me to you, note that I don't believe that this pain is totally without a purpose. But I haven't yet learned what it is. It's hard."[2]

It was her very first visit to Deauville, that convenient Channel resort where so many of her friends had spent so much time. (The wit Tristan Bernard loved the place, he said, because it was "so close to Paris and so far from the sea.") They found the weather colder than they had bargained for; one had to sit in the sun to warm up, and Colette needed a hot-water bottle in bed. "Many strangers ask for autographs," she reported, "but Maurice keeps them politely at a distance. . . ."[3] Goudeket tells us that he wheeled her to movies, to evening entertainments, to promenades along the hundred yards or so of fashionable beachfront.[4]

One of the things she did that autumn was to wait for another promotion in the Legion of Honor. Once more there were premature reports and unmerited congratulations, for the next rank, if she got it, would be the highest that any woman had attained. On December 10, Cocteau was invited to lunch at the presidential palace, where he found himself seated beside Vincent Auriol, the president of the Republic and an easy man to talk to. Auriol told the artist of the "struggle in which he is engaged to obtain Colette's cross." The president was himself surprised that after allowing her to rise to the rank of commander, the guardians of the nation's dignity would not let her go further; but after all, Auriol helplessly explained, "She showed herself entirely naked on the music-hall stage."[5]

Before the end of the year Colette took up her pen again, this time for "a little job," as she informed an admirer. If it turned out to be publishable, she would call it simply "Memories."[6]

We have these pages — or lines, rather — which were preserved and then published posthumously by her husband. "In a month I shall reach my eightieth birthday," the text begins. "Today, December 17, I decide to write a few pages on love. . . ." (These pages, if they existed, have not come down to us.) "Around me," she begins again, "it is December and Paris and the warm red of my pleasant prison and the quadrangular geometry of the Palais-Royal, and the almost rhythmic waves that strike my thighs, my hips, my knees." Does she have a "skill for suffering?" she wonders. Perhaps, but she also knows how to laugh. She tells her notebook that she has just asked Pauline to bring her a perfume to which she has been faithful for fifty-three years.[7]

"I can't walk," she wrote to Henri Mondor. "But I fly. First into your arms. Then every day above my garden. Don't worry about me at all. I'm in pain and gradually learning what it is that can diminish pain."[8] This gem of a letter was posted just a week before she turned eighty.

An unexpected consecration came now in the *Nouvelle Revue Française,* in the form of an essay by Dominique Aury whose title translates as "Colette or the Gynaeceum," a reference to the women's quarters in houses in ancient Greece. Colette had built her own, this critic claimed, and "no one has ever built so well in the imaginary." These dwelling places of hers were well defined and very much alive; the heroines who lived in them were "made to be possessed." Each of them was a libertine but also a woman, "a rival of but also joined to the others." They waited for their men, men who would rule over "slaves who scorn them." The submission of Colette's women was not that of good Christian spouses, explained the writer; men were enemies, perhaps, and elements of disorder, but they were necessary for women's fulfillment.[9]

Later a scholar would say that Colette had taken readers over the barrier, to the other side, to show them how women really felt about men. There had been strong women before — George Sand, for example — but their vision of relations between the sexes had remained conventional. Colette was the first to be the subject "in the face of a man become object" — object, that is, as well as sexual object.[10]

Soon after that landmark of a birthday, she and Maurice were in Monte Carlo again, in the comfort and security of that palace for hire. Celebrities of times past, with familiar names and faces, would tell her that when one could afford it, one ought "to settle oneself in a place that was a bit anonymous, like this one, and make the best of things." There were fewer excursions now; it was just too hard for her to get in and out of an automobile. But there were plenty of old friends right there in this princedom where she was treated as a queen.[11]

On February 17, Cocteau joined them for lunch, noting in his diary afterward, "Colette has placed herself in a sort of naive mist

in which she hears only what she wants to, and she uses it to keep
her distance from our world." The contrast between this "mist" of
Cocteau's and the sharpness of her letters from this time, however,
makes us wonder whether she may not simply have felt that com-
munication with this man was not worth the effort.

Some days after that he returned to his notebook with a medita-
tion: "Life of Colette. Scandal upon scandal. Then everything tips
over and she joins the ranks of the idols. She concludes her life of
pantomimes, beauty parlors, and old lesbians in an apotheosis of re-
spectability." The reflection had been inspired by newspaper accounts
of her promotion within the ranks of the Legion of Honor. "This
kind of award is given in extremis. How right she is to counter that
with the half-sleep of a mole, the deep and lucid irony that one
perceives, as during a lightning flash, in her eye." [12]

Goudeket, meanwhile, was keeping busy, working on an adaptation of "Gigi" for the Paris stage. And as for Colette — "As for me,
nothing yet," she told Hélène Moreau. [13] She was still attempting to
work; her husband saved some of the jottings she did now, such as
this one:

> March again! Between a painful state and a still more painful
> one, while my invader settles itself inside me, I allow myself a
> smile. As long as the dream of a cure persists in us, we can
> easily put a good face on things.

She tried another idea, then rewrote it. This is the improved version:

> March — or April — If I had, in what the Fleuron edition
> calls my "Complete Works," omitted the account of an amorous
> adventure, what to do with this commodity now, however uti-
> lizable it might be? Where to lie henceforth? Or to confess?

She was talking, of course, about the close of a writing life; as for
the end of life itself, however, she was having not a bit of it. A
moving passage in these notes touches on Maurice. They were old
bachelors now, the two of them, whose relations were friendly but
ever new.

I should indeed like . . .
   1) to begin again . . .
   2) to begin again . . .
   3) to begin again. . . .
Thinking about it, it seems to me that they weren't always easy, those seventy-nine years. But how short they were![14]

They were back in Paris by mid-April. A play whose French adaptation she had put her name to, Jan de Hartog's *The Four-Poster,* went on stage with Pierre Fresnay and François Périer in the leading roles. And then came the long-awaited ceremony, at which she was to be given the symbols of her new rank in the Legion of Honor — her new dignity, as it was called. One of those who climbed her stairs this time, along with Pierre Brisson of *Le Figaro,* Jean Cocteau, and François Poulenc, was an official who was also a literary man, André-Louis Dubois (the following year he would become the prefect of police). He described the occasion in his diary: "We find her very tired and apparently absentminded, not knowing exactly what is happening. Cocteau explains it to her; Brisson shows her the medal. He presents it to her. I believe that she simply thought it was a gift that 'this good Monsieur Auriol' was giving to her, as she said. Nothing more."[15]

Did they really think she did not know what was going on? A scrap of paper survives, with considerable crossing-out and substitution of words, on which she tells her side of the story.

"Softly, softly," she begins.

> At present I'm all too moved by these gentlemen who come to see me, to kiss me, offer me drink, pin a star on my breast. . . . And the handsome male eyes that flashed at me while I gave them in return my most tender look of a Grand Officer![16]

The very next month the National Institute of Arts and Letters in New York elected her to membership, "in recognition of distinguished work in the arts," so the certificate read.[17] This time it was the American ambassador, Douglas Dillon, who came to the

Palais-Royal to present the citation, in the company of Pierre de Monaco, Henri Mondor, and other accomplished friends.[18]

By the year's end Cocteau appears to have revised his diagnosis. "This morning," he wrote in his diary on December 5, 1953, "Colette seemed to have come out of her cocoon, of her torpor. She wasn't even deaf anymore. She sparkled. Everything that had gone soft in her face became sharpened. She told stories, she listened, she laughed."[19]

FORTY-FOUR

Reckonings

SOMETIMES SHE TALKED about dying. She might say, "Do you think that I'm going to die soon?" And he would reply, "Not until I give you permission." That would bring a smile.[1] Once, when the antiquarian Richard Anacréon bound a batch of illustrations into his copy of *My Mother's House* and asked Colette to autograph it, she annotated each of the prints. Under a reproduction of a drawing of the house in which she had been born, she scrawled, "I'd like also to die there."[2] Of course the house in Saint-Sauveur had long since been sold.

Her handwriting began to betray her age, and Goudeket noticed that her memory seemed to focus on events long past. Two months before her death, she held up a photograph of thirty Saint-Sauveur classmates and identified every one of them.

Their trip to Monte Carlo, planned for early in 1954, was postponed for the opening of the French stage adaptation of "Gigi," though Goudeket refused to allow Colette to go to the theater; the enthusiasm of the audience, he felt, and the crowd on the sidewalk, would be too much for her. For the press preview, the French television network set up a dialogue between Colette (at home) and her Goncourt Academy colleagues (at the theater). The very next day the Goudekets were off to their suite at the Hotel de Paris.[3]

She wrote to no one from Monte Carlo, not even to her daughter. Finally, to her beloved Hélène Moreau, she explained the reason for her silence. "I find my excuse in my rheumatism of both feet and forearms. A few days ago I shouldn't have been able and wouldn't have dared to write to you. . . ."

Three weeks later she was still finding writing difficult; paper, she feared, had become "another thing I must deprive myself of." Her hands as well as her arms hurt: she was "A writer who can't write. . . ." Nevertheless, she could still receive tributes. "Am I not a queen?" she asked with cheerful irony. "Pierre de Monaco, Rainier de Monaco, the pashas, etc., etc., what a mob. . . ."[4] By May, the Goudekets were home again, at the Palais-Royal.

There were periods of total silence now. Goudeket remembered two more automobile rides, during which she would do her best to look out the windows, holding out her hands in an expression of wonder. On both occasions she returned to the apartment in a state of exhaustion. In June he remarked a definite decline in her vitality. She did not touch the newspapers that were brought to her and barely opened her mail. Her naps grew longer. Her only distraction was a picture book. In the third week of July, she stopped getting up altogether. Her husband, her daughter, and the omnipresent Pauline took turns watching over her.[5] Pauline was to remember that Colette gave her strict instructions about what she wished to wear on the day of her death, adding, "But I don't want anyone to see me afterward." Pauline fed her bouillon, eggs, and milk laced with port wine. A glass of milk that they forgot to dilute with water made her a bit sick.

On Monday night, August 2, she revived unexpectedly. Her face lit up, and she even had a bit of champagne. Then she slept through her death. (This was how Pauline told it.)[6]

Goudeket offered more details: she leafed through a new illustrated book about birds and butterflies; she had that, and the real birds outside the window, and the boxes of butterflies on the shelves near her bed. "Look," she said to Goudeket, her arm raised as if to encompass all of these. "Look!" she never pronounced another word. On August 3, Goudeket went out for an evening stroll and then (he remembered) hastened his steps on the way back. He joined Pauline at the bedside of their invalid. Her breathing grew harsh, but after a quarter of an hour there was silence; her head dropped to one side. He found the movement supremely graceful.[7]

Colette is Dead in Paris at 81; Novelist Wrote "Gigi" and "Cheri"

So read the headline in the New York Times. Her "fifty-odd novels and scores of short stories were as popular with housewives, shop girls and laborers," the anonymous obituary writer said, "as they were with intellectuals."[8]

She was buried not in Saint-Sauveur-en-Puisaye but in Paris, at Père Lachaise, that cemetery as big as a town, the final resting place of her hero Balzac, of Molière and Oscar Wilde. (Her grave is listed first in a Guide Michelin map of the site.) The real question, though, was not where she would be buried, but how. Goudeket, who would one day convert to Catholicism, later revealed that he had asked the Church to grant his wife a religious funeral, feeling that she would have approved. She had not been anticlerical, he insisted; she had wanted him to become a Catholic during the occupation, as a shield against persecution. (He had agreed to the idea but had been turned down.) Occasionally she had even lit a candle at Notre Dame des Victoires, virtually the village church of the Palais-Royal.[9]

The Church said no. There is no evidence that Colette wished to have a religious burial, even if her husband and some of their friends wanted it for her, but the refusal became a cause célèbre. The Catholic novelist Graham Greene published an open letter to the cardinal archbishop of Paris, Maurice Feltin. He dated it August 7, the day of the funeral — a ceremony that for Catholics seemed curiously truncated, wrote Greene, for in that faith the dead are never abandoned. Every baptized Catholic had the right to be accompanied to the grave by a priest, he went on; it was a right that could not be lost. But because of Cardinal Feltin's ruling, no priest officiated at this funeral. Everyone knew the churchman's reasons, said Greene, but would they have been applied to someone less well known than Colette? He asked the cardinal to forget the writer and to remember the old woman who, even before Feltin joined the clergy, had suffered an unhappy marriage through no fault of her own, unless innocence could be considered a fault. Was the fact of her two civil marriages so unpardonable? The lives of some of the saints offered worse examples.

Without wishing to, said Greene, His Eminence had given the impression that the Church pursued error beyond the deathbed. Was he not running the risk of shocking enlightened souls? Would it not suggest to non-Catholics that the Church lacked charity? Many Catholics in Britain and the United States as well as in France were hurt by the cardinal's strict interpretation, Greene said in closing. It seemed to deny the hope of grace, which everyone, including the cardinal, would need at that last hour.[10]

The eminent churchman replied: Graham Greene needed to be reminded that the Church did have its laws, he said. A baptized person could have a religious funeral only if he had not given up the Church. If others had received a Catholic funeral despite this, it was because they had shown signs of repenting. People who were shocked by his ruling could not really be enlightened souls.

He concluded softly, saying that the exclusion of public prayer did not prevent private prayer. So Greene could certainly pray for God's pardon of Colette.[11]

Le Figaro Littéraire, which published this exchange, also carried a selection of letters from its readers. The great majority disapproved of Greene's protest, the editor, Pierre Brisson — Colette's friend — had to admit.[12]

It happened that Colette had a splendid nonreligious site for her funeral in the court of honor of the Palais-Royal, where her coffin was draped with a flag. In August one could do without the shelter of a church roof.

"If you would know her, think of a garden in Brittany, by the sea," so Bertrand de Jouvenel paid her final tribute. "The earthly paradise is here; it is not lost for her; others merely fail to see it." [13] The press in France during the week following her death was all Colette.

Here and there a false note was sounded, but not for publication. Explaining how he would deal with Colette in his speech to the Belgian Academy, Cocteau wrote to a young poet: "I'm trying to show her alive and not in that wax museum of articles by intellectuals. Colette is the very type of anti-intellectual. Stupidity become genius." [14]

A draft declaration of inheritance survives, indicating that at the moment of her death, Colette had cash in the bank, some stock, and royalties paid by or due from several publishers (including her husband's own Le Fleuron).[15] As Colette had wished, her husband, Maurice, and her daughter, Colette, shared the estate equally, with Maurice as executor. The Palais-Royal apartment, owned by Le Fleuron, was part of his succession.

He lived there for a time, receiving visitors (including the present writer) while seated at a desk alongside the garden window; after remarrying, he died in 1977. In 1961, as manager of Le Fleuron, he leased the apartment to Colette's daughter. A plaque was put up on the facade, and for a time Colette's window was identified by a gold-plated shield bearing the initial C. The latter disappeared when Colette II did. The contents of the apartment — including furniture as well as lamps and desks and collections — were stored for the museum-to-be in Saint-Sauveur.[16]

In his eulogy before the Belgian Academy, Cocteau did not forget Colette's only child, whom "the material monster intimidated to the point of preventing her from writing to her mother," he declared.

"Since the nature of this shyness escaped the mother, I could see mother and daughter calling to each other from a distance, groping toward one another as in an amorous game of blind-man's buff or hide-and-seek." [17]

Friends found this daughter something of a tragic figure, still overwhelmed by her mother even after her mother's death.[18] The mother-daughter drama was so well known that when Colette de Jouvenel visited the United States in 1970, the reporter who interviewed her for the *New York Times* could tell the world that she had "always lived in the shadow of her world-famous mother" and that she continued to dismiss questions about herself, for "she does not believe that anyone could be interested in just her." When asked if she herself had ever thought of writing, Colette replied that she had not — "And wouldn't I have been a fool if I had?"[19]

She may have been passive just then, but she was to become a pasionaria in her mother's cause. And not only in her mother's: someone who met her for the first time in the decade following Colette's death was impressed by her ardent efforts to rehabilitate the memory of Henry de Jouvenel, who she felt had been damaged by her mother's constant criticism.[20] On the centennial of Colette's birth, when a newspaper stressed Willy's contribution to the Claudine books, she defended her mother's role. The journalist countered by raising doubts about the daughter's competence in this area, since she had not seemed to be terribly interested in her mother during the latter's lifetime.[21]

Whatever negligence she may have shown before, Bel-Gazou was to make up for it now. She became the best promoter of Colette's work, both in France and abroad, and even sought to read in advance any books being published about her mother.[22] She contested the right of Goudeket's second wife (then his widow) to sell the Palais-Royal apartment or the Colette manuscripts and books in her possession, and she went to the press with her case.[23] When she lobbied to have a street named after her mother, Minister of Culture André

Malraux, whose offices were in the Palais-Royal, noticed that Rue Saint-Honoré widened alongside the Comédie Française. In 1966 that became Place Colette.[24]

If she did not publish much, this daughter of Colette, she did write, at least for herself, and some of her manuscripts have seen the light of day thanks to loyal friends. There were thoughts on her mother — "What delights us, what causes us to marvel, is that she never belonged to the mainstream of the human condition," began one of them. "[She] understood that life is allowing oneself to become attached, to flee, to be humiliated at times, then to recover. . . . It's to accept being, after all, only a woman, and not being able to prevent oneself from feeling superior to a great many men."

And then:

> It is undeniable that there was connivance and sympathy between Colette and women. That doesn't make her a feminist; it was men that she thought about, it was to men that she returned.[25]

The daughter's campaign has now been taken up by others. Colette de Jouvenel was survived by her brothers, Renaud and Bertrand, and since their deaths, their heirs have accepted both the management of the material estate and the moral legacy. Nothing, of course, is better for a writer's survival than fresh editions of her work, in French and other languages, and they keep coming.

Acknowledgments

AMONG THOSE WHO offered advice, encouragement, and access to materials, the author owes a particular debt to Anne de Jouvenel (Madame de Tugny), Foulques de Jouvenel, and Marguerite Boivin (of the Société des Amis de Colette in Saint-Sauveur-en-Puisaye), as well as to Sanda Goudeket, Jeannie Malige, Richard Anacréon, and Michel Rémy-Bieth.

Also to Jean-Louis Aujol, Pierre Belfond, Denise Cabanis, Madame André Cantegreil (Curemonte), François Caradec, Elisabeth Charleux-Leroux, Robert Fouques Duparc, Gilles Le Beguec, Jean-Luc Mercié, Dr. Pierre Muesser (now deceased), Jean-Claude Saladin (Arcade Colette), Esa di Simone, Nicole Stéphane, Roger W. Straus, Jr., Denise Tual, and Simone Wertheim.

The author has received the kind cooperation of the Harry Ransom Humanities Research Center at the University of Texas (Austin), and of its research librarian Cathy Henderson; the Société des Manuscrits et Autographes Français; the Bibliothèque Littéraire Jacques Doucet and its curator François Chapon; the Bibliothèque Nationale, under the direction of the attentive Emmanuel Le Roy Ladurie; and the Morgan Library (New York), the Archives de la

Corrèze, the Association des Amis de Curemonte (Jean Lalé), and the Archives de France.

Quotations from Colette's writings are used with the kind authorization of the Colette Estate.

Notes

References to work by Colette published in her lifetime contain no bibliographical details or page numbers, since the reader has a choice of editions and formats. All translations are my own.

Abbreviations used in these notes:

BN   Bibliothèque Nationale, Catalogue de l'exposition *Colette,* Paris, 1973.

LHP   Colette, *Lettres à Hélène Picard* (Paris: Flammarion, 1958).

LMM   Colette, *Lettres à Marguerite Moreno* (Paris: Flammarion, 1959).

LMT   Colette, *Lettres à Moune et au Toutounet* (Paris: Des Femmes, 1985).

LPC   Colette, *Lettres au petit corsaire* (Paris: Flammarion, 1963).

LSP   Colette, *Lettres à ses pairs* (Paris: Flammarion, 1973).

LV   Colette, *Lettres de la vagabonde* (Paris: Flammarion, 1961).

PC   Maurice Goudeket, *Près de Colette* (Paris: Flammarion, 1956).

Prologue

1. Colette, *Claudine à l'école* (1900).
2. Colette, *Claudine à Paris* (1901).
3. Colette, *Claudine en ménage* (1902).
4. Colette, *Claudine s'en va* (1903).
5. Colette, *La Retraite sentimentale* (1907).
6. Colette, "Le Miroir," *La Vie Parisienne,* February 15, 1908. (Reprinted in Colette, *Les Vrilles de la vigne.*)

CHAPTER 1: The Real Village

1. *Guide pittoresque portatif et complet du voyageur en France* (Paris: Firmin Didot, 1846), 64.
2. Quoted in Elisabeth Charleux-Leroux, "Le départ de Saint-Sauveur," *Cahiers Colette* (Saint-Sauveur-en-Puisaye) 5 (1983):35.
3. Colette, "Le Rire," in *La Maison de Claudine* (published in English as *My Mother's House*).

4. Colette, "La 'Fille de mon père,'" in *La Maison de Claudine.*

5. René Robinet, "L'ascendance champenoise et ardennaise de Colette," *Etudes Ardennaises* (Mezières), April 1957, 9–12.

6. BN 113. Letter from Sido to Colette, June 21, 1909.

7. Colette, *Discours de réception à l'Académie royale belge de langue et de littérature françaises* (Paris: Grasset, 1936), 15.

8. From original documents copied by Marguerite Boivin, Saint-Sauveur; Elisabeth Charleux-Leroux and Marguerite Boivin, "Personnages de Montigny et Habitants de Saint-Sauveur," *Cahiers Colette* 8 (1986): 71–72.

9. Sido, *Lettres à sa fille* (Paris: Des Femmes, 1984), 259.

10. Records in the Archives Départementales de l'Yonne, courtesy of Marguerite Boivin.

11. Emile Amblard, in *Bulletin de la Société des Sciences Historiques et Naturelles de l'Yonne* (Auxerre) 96 (1953–1956): 287–298; Raymond Escholier, "Du nouveau sur l'adolescence de Colette," *Le Figaro Littéraire,* November 17, 1956.

12. From the original documents, courtesy of Marguerite Boivin.

13. Archives Départementales de l'Yonne.

14. Courtesy of Michel Rémy-Bieth.

15. Colette, "Les Mamans," *La Baïonnette,* April 6, 1916.

16. Emile Amblard, "Les Elections au Conseil Général de Saint-Sauveur en 1880," *Bulletin de la Société des Sciences Historiques et Naturelles de l'Yonne* 97 (1959): 201–202, 209–210.

17. Colette, "Le Capitaine," in *Sido.*

18. Colette, "La Cire Verte," in *Le Képi.*

CHAPTER 2: *Growing Up*

1. Colette, *Le Fanal bleu.*

2. Colette, *Sido.*

3. Colette, "Les Sauvages," in *Sido.*

4. Colette, *Flore et Pomone.*

5. Colette, "Ma soeur aux longs cheveux," in *La Maison de Claudine;* Elisabeth Charleux-Leroux, "Sur une page de *Journal à rebours,*" *Cahiers Colette* 10 (1988): 35–40.

6. Claude Chauvière, *Colette* (Paris: Firmin-Didot, 1931), 29.

7. Colette, "Les Sauvages."

8. Colette, "Le sieur Binard," in *Bella-Vista.*

9. Colette, *De ma fenêtre.*

10. Colette, "Ma mère et les livres," in *La Maison de Claudine.*

11. Colette, "Lectures," in *Oeuvres complètes,* vol. 15 (Paris: Le Fleuron, 1950), 343–347.

12. Nicole Houssa, "Balzac et Colette," *Revue d'Histoire Littéraire de la France,* January–March 1960, 18–46.

13. Colette, "Les Sabots," in *Contes de 1000 matins* (Paris: Flammarion, 1970), 193–196.

14. Colette, "Ma mère et le curé," in *La Maison de Claudine; LPC* 41.

15. Colette, *Sido.*

16. Sido, *Lettres à sa fille* (Paris: Des Femmes, 1984), 468, 471.

17. Elisabeth Charleux-Leroux, "Gabrielle Colette à l'Ecole élémentaire," *Bulletin de la Société des Sciences Historiques et Naturelles de l'Yonne* 114 (1982): 87–89; Colette, "La Chaufferette," in *Journal à rebours.*

18. Colette, "Ibanez est mort," in *La Maison de Claudine.*

19. Elisabeth Charleux-Leroux and Marguerite Boivin, "Personnages de Montigny et Habitants de Saint-Sauveur," *Cahiers Colette* 8 (1986): 75.

20. Olympe Terrain to Jean Larnac,

March 15, 1925. Courtesy of Harry Ransom Humanities Research Center, the University of Texas at Austin.

21. Quoted in Chauvière, *Colette*, 190–191.

22. Olympe Terrain to Jean Larnac, March 19, 1925. Courtesy of Harry Ransom Humanities Research Center.

23. Léon Dubreuil, "Le Brevet de Colette," *Le Cerf-Volant*, July 1957, 16–17.

CHAPTER 3: *The Village Lost*

1. Colette, *De ma fenêtre*.

2. BN 119.

3. From Marguerite Boivin, Saint-Sauveur; Raymond Escholier, "Ce que Colette n'a pas dit," *Le Figaro Littéraire*, November 24, 1956.

4. *PC* 133–134.

5. Courtesy of Marguerite Boivin; Sido, *Lettres à sa fille* (Paris: Des Femmes, 1984), 210; Partage, Colette Papers, Saint-Sauveur.

6. Colette, "Le Capitaine," in *Sido*.

7. Sido, *Lettres à sa fille* 247.

8. Colette, "Maternité," in *La Maison de Claudine*.

9. Elisabeth Charleux-Leroux, "Le Départ de Saint-Sauveur," *Cahiers Colette* 5 (1983): 21–33. In "Le Képi" Colette says that the furniture was sold by court order.

10. François Caradec, *Feu Willy* (Paris: Carrère, 1984), 22–51; Willy, *Souvenirs littéraires . . . et autres* (Paris: Montaigne, 1925), 30, 68, 101.

11. Caradec, *Feu Willy*, 39; Lucie Delarue-Mardrus, *Mes Mémoires* (Paris: Gallimard, 1938), 141.

12. *Art et Critique*, December 7, 1889, reprinted in *Lettres de l'Ouvreuse* (Paris: Vanier, 1890), 37–38; *Lettres de l'Ouvreuse*, 152.

13. Colette, *Mes Apprentissages*.

14. Colette, "Noces," in *Oeuvres complètes*, vol. 7 (Paris: Le Fleuron, 1949); Caradec, *Feu Willy*, 60–61.

15. *LMM* 256–257.

16. Caradec, *Feu Willy*, 61–62.

17. Colette, "Graphismes," *Cahiers Colette* 2 (1979): 7–8.

18. Colette, "Noces."

19. Willy, *Indiscrétions et commentaires sur les Claudine* (Paris: Pro Amicus, 1962), 22–23.

20. Meg Villars, *Les Imprudences de Peggy* (Paris: Société d'Editions et de Publications parisiennes [1910]), 176.

21. Colette, *Mes Apprentissages*.

22. Colette, "Mon amie Valentine," in *Paysages et portraits* (Paris: Flammarion, 1958), 41–42.

23. To Renée Hamon. Bibliothèque Nationale MS NAF 18711.

24. Caradec, *Feu Willy*, 64.

25. Willy, *Indiscrétions*, 23.

26. *Gil Blas*, May 4, 1893.

27. Caradec, *Feu Willy*, 65.

28. Letter to Marcel Schwob, reprinted in Pierre Champion, *Marcel Schwob et son temps* (Paris: Grasset, 1927), 272.

29. Courtesy of the Town Hall, Saint-Sauveur-en-Puisaye.

30. In the Richard Anacréon Collection, Granville, France. The photograph is included in the insert following page 122.

CHAPTER 4: *The Literary Life*

1. Colette, *Mes Apprentissages* and *Trois . . . Six . . . Neuf. . . .*

2. Marguerite Moreno, "Colette," in Claude Chauvière, *Colette* (Paris: Firmin-Didot, 1931), 55.

3. Jacques-Emile Blanche, *La Pêche aux souvenirs* (Paris: Flammarion, 1949), 288.

4. Colette, *Mes Apprentissages*.

5. Colette, *La Vagabonde*.

6. Fernand Gregh, *L'Age d'or* (Paris: Grasset, 1947), 117.

7. Colette, *Les Vrilles de la vigne*.

8. Franqis Caradec, *Feu Willy* (Paris: Carrère, 1984), 88–98.

9. Colette, *Mes Apprentissages*.

10. Georges Lecomte, in *Les Hommes d'aujourd'hui* 412 (ca. 1893).

11. Colette, *Mes Apprentissages*.

12. Pierre Champion, *Marcel Schwob et son temps* (Paris: Grasset, 1927), 59–61, 272.

13. Colette, *Mes Apprentissages*.

14. *LSP* 11, 13–15, 20, 24.

CHAPTER 5: Inventing Claudine

1. Colette, *Mes Apprentissages*.

2. X. M. Boulestin, *A Londres naguère* (Paris: Fayard, 1946), 42–43.

3. Adrien Faucher-Magnan, *C'était hier: Souvenirs d'un demi-siècle* (Paris: Scorpion, 1960), 73.

4. Colette, "Marcel Proust," in *Marcel Proust* (Paris: Editions de la revue Le Capitole, 1926), 13–14.

5. *LSP* 34–35.

6. Colette, "Claude Debussy," in *Trait pour trait*.

7. Arthur Gold and Robert Fizdale, *Misia: The Life of Misia Sert* (New York: Knopf, 1980), 52.

8. Colette, "Marguerite Moreno," in *LMM* 9–10.

9. Pierre Champion, *Marcel Schwob et son temps* (Paris: Grasset, 1927), 108–109.

10. Curnonsky [Maurice-Edmond Sailland], *Souvenirs littéraires et gastronomiques* (Paris: Albin Michel, 1958), 164.

11. *LMM* 27.

12. *LSP* 32.

13. Alfred Diard, "Au temps de Claudine," *Les Nouvelles Littéraires*, June 1, 1950.

14. Colette, *Mes Apprentissages*.

15. Ibid.

16. François Caradec, *Feu Willy* (Paris: Carrère, 1984), 88.

17. Colette, *Mes Apprentissages*.

18. Willy, *Indiscrétions et commentaires sur les Claudine* (Paris: Pro Amicus, 1962), 14–15.

19. Olympe Terrain to Jean Larnac, March 1925, courtesy of Harry Ransom Humanities Research Center, the University of Texas at Austin.

20. Willy, *Indiscrétions*, 14.

21. Colette, *Mes Apprentissages*.

22. Albert Lavignac, *Le Voyage artistique à Bayreuth* (Paris: Delagrave, 1897) 573.

23. Quoted in Jean Larnac, *Colette: Sa vie, son oeuvre* (Paris: Simon Kra, 1927), 56.

24. *Le Critique*, December 5, 1986.

CHAPTER 6: Ascension of the Willys

1. Colette, *Trois . . . Six . . . Neuf . . .* and *Mes Apprentissages*.

2. Jacques Gauthier-Villars, "Willy et Colette," *Les Oeuvres Libres*, October 1959, 178–179.

3. Colette, "Le Képi," in *Le Képi*.

4. Colette, *Mes Apprentissages*.

5. Willy, *Un Vilain monsieur!* (Paris: Simon Empis, 1898), 94.

6. Colette and Willy, *Claudine en ménage*, ed. Paul d'Hollander (Paris: Klincksieck, 1975), 146–147.

7. François Caradec, *Feu Willy* (Paris: Carrère, 1984), 107.

8. Jules Renard, *Journal (1887–1910)* (Paris: Gallimard, 1960), 469, 765, 951.

9. Caradec, *Feu Willy*, 107.

10. Sido, *Lettres à sa fille* (Paris: Des Femmes, 1984), 241.

11. Caradec, *Feu Willy*, 106.

12. *BN* 3–4.

13. Claude Chauvière, *Colette* (Paris: Firmin-Didot, 1931), 56–57.

14. Colette, *Mes Apprentissages*.

15. Ibid.
16. Ibid.
17. Ibid.
18. Armory [C. R. Dauriac], *50 ans de vie parisienne* (Paris: Renard, 1943), 36–37.
19. Willy, "Quelques détails sur la collaboration Colette-Willy," *Les Nouvelles Littéraires,* April 3, 1926. It is clear from Willy, *Indiscrétions et commentaires sur les Claudine* (Paris: Pro Amicus, 1962), 22, that the reference is to *Claudine à Paris.*
20. Colette, *Mes Apprentissages.*
21. Willy, *Indiscrétions,* 15.
22. *Revue Encyclopédique,* May 5, 1900.
23. *Mercure de France,* May 1900, 472–475.
24. BN 5.
25. Colette, *Mes Apprentissages.*
26. Elisabeth Charleux-Leroux, "De Saint-Sauveur à Montigny," *Cahiers Colette* 9 (1987): 13–21; Elisabeth Charleux-Leroux and Marguerite Boivin, "Personnages de Montigny et Habitants de Saint-Sauveur," *Cahiers Colette* 6, 7, 8, and 9 (1984–1987).
27. Elisabeth Charleux-Leroux, "Réalité et fiction dans *Claudine à l'école,"* *Bulletin de la Société des Sciences Historiques et Naturelles de l'Yonne* 113 (1981): 122–155.
28. Willy, "Quelques détails."
29. Willy, *Indiscrétions.*
30. Charleux-Leroux and Boivin, "Personnages de Montigny," *Cahiers Colette* 7 (1985): 53–54; Charleux-Leroux, "Réalité et fiction," 134–135.
31. Marise Querlin, "Centenaire de la naissance de Colette," *Revue des Lettres,* October–December 1973, 11.
32. Olympe Terrain to Jean Larnac, March 19, 1925, courtesy of Harry Ransom Humanities Research Center, the University of Texas at Austin.
33. Charleux-Leroux and Boivin, "Personnages de Montigny," *Cahiers Colette* 6 (1984): 40–41.
34. Archives Nationales, 409 AP 32. The postcard is reproduced in the insert following page 122.
35. Colette, *Mes Apprentissages.*
36. Willy, *Indiscrétions,* 16.

CHAPTER 7: *The Claudine Factory*

1. Colette, *Mes Apprentissages.*
2. Ibid.
3. Ibid.
4. Lucie Delarue-Mardrus, *Mes Mémoires* (Paris: Gallimard, 1938), 141.
5. Ibid.
6. Natalie Clifford Barney, *Souvenirs indiscrets* (Paris: Flammarion, 1960), 188–189.
7. François Chapon, "Nommons Miss Barney . . . ," *Autour de Natalie Clifford Barney* (Paris: Bibliothèque Littéraire Jacques Doucet, 1976), 7–9.
8. George Wickes, *The Amazon of Letters: The Life and Loves of Natalie Barney* (New York: Putnam, 1976), 222, 226.
9. Natalie Clifford Barney, *Aventures de l'esprit* (Paris: Emile Paul, 1929), 202.
10. Natalie Clifford Barney, *Selected Writings* (London: Adam Books, 1963), 8–11, 152–160.
11. Liane de Pougy, *Idylle saphique* (Paris: La Plume, 1901), 38–39, 93.
12. Barney, *Selected Writings,* 161.
13. Barney, *Souvenirs indiscrets,* 191–192.
14. Colette, *Mes Apprentissages.*
15. Meg Villars, *Les Imprudences de Peggy* (Paris: Société d'Editions et de Publications parisiennes [1910]), 176.
16. Willy, *Indiscrétions et commentaires sur les Claudine* (Paris: Pro Amicus, 1962), 29–30.
17. Albert Lavignac, *Le Voyage artistique à Bayreuth,* 3rd ed. (Paris: Delagrave, 1903).
18. Text in Colette and Willy, *Claudine*

en ménage, ed. Paul D'Hollander (Paris: Klincksieck, 1975), 367.

19. Ibid.

20. *LSP* 51.

21. Colette and Willy, *Claudine en ménage,* 368–369.

22. Charles-Henry Hirsch, "De Mlle de Maupin à Claudine," *Mercure de France,* June 1902, 577–588.

23. Marcel Boulenger, "Les Livres," *La Renaissance Latine,* June 15, 1902, 254–255.

24. Polaire [Emilie-Marie Bouchard], *Polaire par elle-même* (Paris: Figuière, 1933), 116–119.

25. Colette, *Mes Apprentissages.*

26. *LPC* 80.

27. X. M. Boulestin, *A Londres naguère* (Paris: Fayard, 1946), 39–40.

28. Denise Tual, *Au coeur du temps* (Paris: Carrère, 1987), 164.

29. Colette, *Mes Apprentissages.*

CHAPTER 8: Squirrel in a Cage

1. Féli Gautier, *Revue Illustrée,* July 15, 1902.

2. *Le Cri de Paris,* August 31, 1902.

3. Colette, *Trois . . . Six . . . Neuf. . . .*

4. Colette, *Mes Apprentissages* and *Le Pur et l'impur.*

5. Jacques Gauthier-Villars, "Willy et Colette," *Les Oeuvres Libres,* October 1959, 185–186.

6. Colette, *Mes Apprentissages.*

7. *LSP* 54–55.

8. Willy, *Indiscrétions et commentaires sur les Claudine* (Paris: Pro Amicus, 1962), 33–35.

9. Colette, *Mes Apprentissages.*

10. Willy, *La Maîtresse du Prince Jean* (Paris: Albin Michel, 1903), viii–xxxi; François Caradec, *Feu Willy* (Paris: Carrère, 1984), 154–155.

11. *La Vie Heureuse,* May 1904.

12. *LSP* 106; BN 43–46.

13. Quoted in Colette, *Sept Dialogues de bêtes.*

14. *LSP* 109.

15. Colette Willy, "Elle est malade," *La Vie Parisienne,* November 26, 1904.

16. *Gil Blas,* June 4, 1904.

17. Jean Ernest Charles, "Le Cas Willy," *Revue Politique et Littéraire* (Revue Bleue), October 7, 1905, reprinted in Ernest Charles, *Les Samedis littéraires, 5e série* (Paris: Sansot, 1907), 114–128.

CHAPTER 9: Claudine Walks Out

1. François Caradec, *Feu Willy* (Paris: Carrère, 1984), 173–174.

2. *Colette en tournée: Cartes postales à Sido,* ed. Michel Rémy-Bieth (Paris: Persona, 1984), 14.

3. Colette Willy, "Lettre de Claudine," *Le Damier,* April 1905, 26–30.

4. Willy, *Maugis amoureux* (Paris: Albin Michel [1905]), 67.

5. Michel del Castillo, "De Colette Willy à Colette," in *Colette en tournée,* 8. See also Armory [C. R. Dauriac], *50 ans de vie parisienne* (Paris: Renard, 1943), 154–157.

6. Caradec, *Feu Willy,* 120. Marguerite Maniez was born on June 16, 1885: see her death certificate, Noirmoutier town hall.

7. Colette, "Le Rire," in *La Maison de Claudine.*

8. Sido, *Lettres à sa fille* (Paris: Des Femmes, 1984), 35–39.

9. BN 119.

10. Sido, *Lettres,* 38–39.

11. Caradec, *Feu Willy,* 178.

12. Sido, *Lettres,* 44.

13. Colette, *Mes Apprentissages.*

14. Tristan Rémy, *Georges Wague: Le Mime de la Belle Epoque* (Paris: Girard, 1964), 18–19, 65, 191–192.

15. André Rouveyre, *Mercure de France,* June 1, 1926, 428.

16. Sylvain Bonmariage, *Willy, Colette et moi* (Paris: Fremanger, 1954), 18–21.

17. Coeltte, "Printemps de la Riviera," *La Vie Parisienne,* March 21, 1908.

18. Colette, *L'Etoile vesper.*

19. *Le Gaulois,* April 1, 1906, quoted in *LSP* 114.

20. Caradec, *Feu Willy,* 180–181.

21. BN 157–158.

22. Paul d'Hollander, *Colette: ses apprentissages* (Montreal: Presses de l'Université de Montréal, 1978), 135–137.

23. Colette, *Oeuvres,* vol. 1 (Paris: Gallimard, 1984), 1528–1529.

24. Morgan Library, New York: Heineman Collection, 780.

25. Caradec, *Feu Willy,* 187–188.

26. *Paris Qui Chante,* October 14, 1906.

27. Colette, *La Vagabonde.*

28. Notes for *Mémoires d'une Européenne* by Louise Weiss, Bibliothèque Nationale, MS NAF 17794 f. 17–18.

29. Meg Villars, *Les Imprudences de Peggy* (Paris: Société d'Editions et de Publications parisiennes [1910]), 177.

30. Colette papers, Saint-Sauveur-en-Puisaye.

31. Bibliothèque Littéraire Jacques Doucet, Paris.

32. Sido, *Lettres,* 56–57.

33. Franc-Nohain, *Fantasio,* November 1, 1906; Sido, *Lettres,* 57.

34. *LV* 13.

35. Fernand Hauser *Le Journal,* November 17, 1906.

36. *Le Cri de Paris,* November 18, 1906.

37. Ibid., November 25, 1906.

38. Ibid., December 2, 1906.

CHAPTER 10: Missy

1. *LV* 14–15; François Caradec, *Feu Willy* (Paris: Carrère, 1984), 189–190.

2. *Le Rire,* December 15, 1906; reprinted in Caradec, *Feu Willy,* 189–190.

3. *Fantasio,* December 15, 1906, 416–417.

4. Ibid., April 15, 1907, 215.

5. Sido, *Lettres à sa fille* (Paris: Des Femmes, 1984), 58–62.

6. Colette, *Trois . . . Six . . . Neuf . . .* and *Le Pur et l'impur.*

7. Colette, *Le Pur et l'impur.*

8. Sylvain Bonmariage, *Willy, Colette et moi* (Paris: Fremanger, 1954), 86, 211–212.

9. Cited in Caradec, *Feu Willy,* 194–195.

10. *Le Figaro,* January 3, 1907.

11. *Le Matin,* January 5, 1907.

12. *LV* 15.

13. Caradec, *Feu Willy* 196–200.

14. Bonmariage, *Willy,* 14–15, 23–24, 71–74, 85–89, 97–99.

15. Sido, *Lettres,* 65–69.

16. *Frou-Frou,* March 9, 1907.

17. Catalogue, Delaverne-Lafarge sale, Paris: Colette Papers, Saint-Sauveur-en-Puisaye.

18. January 9 and 15, 1907. Courtesy of Michel Rémy-Bieth and of the Colette Estate.

19. Colette Papers, Saint-Sauveur-en-Puisaye, with the authorization of the Colette Estate.

20. Richard Anacréon Collection, Granville.

21. Sido, *Lettres,* 80.

22. Quoted in Caradec, *Feu Willy,* 190–191.

23. Armory [C. R. Dauriac], *50 ans de vie parisienne* (Paris: Renard, 1943), 40.

24. Bonmariage, *Willy,* 81, 88, 212.

25. Courtesy of Michel Rémy-Bieth, with the authorization of the Colette Estate.

26. Quoted in Colette, *Oeuvres,* vol. 1 (Paris: Gallimard, 1984), xciii–xciv.

27. Sido, *Lettres,* 73.

28. *Colette en tournée: Cartes postales à Sido,* ed. Michel Rémy-Bieth (Paris: Persona, 1984), 15.

29. Sido, *Lettres,* 82, 85, 93–94.

30. *La Vie Parisienne,* April 27, 1907,

306–307. The dedication appeared in
the first edition of *Les Vrilles de la
vigne.*

CHAPTER *11: Making It Alone*

1. Sido, *Lettres à sa fille* (Paris: Des
   Femmes, 1984), 94.
2. Archives Nationales, SGDL papers,
   454 AP 172; François Caradec, *Feu
   Willy* (Paris: Carrère, 1984), 208.
3. Sido, *Lettres,* 125, 129.
4. BN 61.
5. Sido, *Lettres,* 25.
6. Colette, *Mes Apprentissages.*
7. *Comoedia,* January 3, 1908.
8. Sido, *Lettres,* 148.
9. *La Vie Parisienne,* January 4 and 25,
   February 15, March 21, May 23, June
   20, and September 5, 1908.
10. Sido, *Lettres,* 186.
11. Bibliothèque Nationale, MS MIC
    3322 f.296.
12. Sido, *Lettres,* 189.
13. *Colette en tournée: Cartes postales à
    Sido,* ed. Michel Rémy-Bieth (Paris:
    Persona, 1984), 18–19.
14. *Akademos,* January 15, 1909.
15. Claude Chauvière, *Colette* (Paris: Fir-
    min-Didot, 1931), 127.
16. Sido, *Lettres,* 167, 169, 172–173, 175–
    178.
17. BN 59–60.
18. *Comoedia,* May 9, 1908.
19. Sido, *Lettres,* 196.
20. *Colette en tournée,* 21.
21. Ibid., 22–23; *LV* 21–22; Caradec,
    Feu Willy, 216.
22. Bibliothèque Nationale, MS MIC
    3320 f.54, with the authorization of
    the Colette Estate.
23. Sido, *Lettres,* 220–221.
24. Ibid., 204–208, 211, 213–214.
25. *Comoedia,* October 17, 1908.
26. Sido, *Lettres,* 222.
27. Louise Lalanne [Guillaume Apolli-
    naire], "Littérature féminine," *Les
    Marges,* March 1909, 127.

28. Caradec, *Feu Willy,* 217–218.
29. Alain Brunet, "Editions originales,"
    Cahiers Colette 9 (1987): 37–38.

CHAPTER *12: The Vagabond*

1. Sido, *Lettres à sa fille* (Paris: Des
   Femmes, 1984), 234, 236.
2. *LV* 27.
3. *LSP* 120.
4. Bibliothèque Nationale, MS MIC
   3320 f.55, with the authorization of
   the Colette Estate.
5. *Comoedia,* January 23, 1909.
6. Gaston de Pawlowski, quoted in Jean
   Larnac, *Colette: Sa vie, son oeuvre*
   (Paris: Simon Kra, 1957), 173.
7. Adolphe Brisson, *Le Temps,* February
   15, 1909.
8. Sido, *Lettres,* 256.
9. *LV* 30.
10. François Caradec, *Feu Willy* (Paris:
    Carrère, 1984), 225.
11. Sido, *Lettres,* 249–250.
12. *LV* 30.
13. Ibid.
14. Colette, "Mon amie Valentine," in
    Paysages et portraits (Paris: Flamma-
    rion, 1958), 47–51.
15. Caradec, *Feu Willy,* 218.
16. BN 60.
17. Sido, *Lettres,* 263–264.
18. *Comoedia,* April 18, 1909.
19. *Colette en tournée: Cartes postales à
    Sido,* ed. Michel Rémy-Bieth (Paris:
    Persona, 1984), 28.
20. Ibid., 30–43.
21. Colette, "Notes de tournées," in *Mes
    Cahiers* (Paris: Aux Armes de France,
    1941), 43–44.
22. *LV* 34–35.
23. *Colette en tournée,* 53–55; *LV* 36.
24. *LV* 38.
25. *Colette en tournée,* 56–57.
26. Maurice Chevalier, *Ma route et les
    chansons* (Paris: Julliard, 1946),
    178–180.

27. Colette, "Maurice Chevalier," *Cahiers Colette* 2 (1979): 42–45.
28. Sido, *Lettres,* 306–309.
29. *Paris-Théâtre,* October 23 and November 6, 1909.
30. BN 35.
31. Sido, *Lettres,* 312–314.

CHAPTER 13: *The Vagabond Domesticated*

1. *Le Messager de Bruxelles,* February 6, 1910, quoted in *Colette en tournée: Cartes postales à Sido,* ed. Michel Rémy-Bieth (Paris: Persona, 1984), 59.
2. Sido, *Lettres à sa fille* (Paris: Des Femmes, 1984), 338.
3. Ibid., 329.
4. *LV* 39.
5. Sido, *Lettres,* 351.
6. *Colette en tournée,* 86.
7. *LSP* 151.
8. Ibid., 152.
9. Sido, *Lettres,* 364.
10. *Colette en tournée,* 86.
11. Bibliothèque Nationale, MS MIC 3322 f. 225–229, 233.
12. Colette, *Sido; Sido, Lettres,* 323.
13. Colette, "Ma mère et le fruit défendu," in *La Maison de Claudine.*
14. *LV* 41–42.
15. *LV* 42–44.
16. *Colette en tournée,* 89.
17. *LV* 45.
18. *Album Masques: Colette* (Paris: Masques, 1984), 96.
19. Sido, *Lettres,* 398.
20. BN 67.
21. To Judith Cladel of *Paris-Journal,* December 1, 1910. Catalogue, Les Autographes, Paris, June 1988, 35.
22. Bibliothèque Nationale, MS MIC 3322 f. 235–245; François Caradec, *Feu Willy* (Paris: Carrère, 1984), 237–240.
23. Frédéric Lefèvre, "Une heure avec Henry de Jouvenel," *Les Nouvelles Littéraires,* March 24, 1928; *Dictionnaire des Parlementaires français* 4 (Paris: Presses Universitaires de France, 1970): 2039–2040; interviews with Anne de Jouvenel and Gilles de Le Beguec.
24. Louis Gitard, *La Petite Histoire de la IIIᵉ République: Souvenirs de Maurice Colrat* (Paris: Les Sept Couleurs, 1959), 50.
25. Bertrand de Jouvenel, *Un Voyageur dans le siècle* (Paris: Laffont, 1979), 22–25.
26. Lefèvre, "Une heure avec Henry de Jouvenel."
27. Quoted in *Dictionnaire des Parlementaires* 4:2040.
28. Jules Sauerwein, *Tente ans à la une* (Paris: Plon, 1962), 33–34.
29. Jouvenel, *Un Voyageur,* 35.
30. Renaud de Jouvenel, "Lettres de Colette à Renaud de Jouvenel," *La Revue de Paris,* December 1966, 6–7.
31. From Jean-Louis Aujol.
32. Colette, *L'Etoile vesper.*
33. *Le Matin,* January 27, 1911; Maurice Martin du Gard, "Colette au 'Matin,' " *La Parisienne,* November 1954, 1220.

CHAPTER 14: *The Shackle*

1. Sido, *Lettres à sa fille* (Paris: Des Femmes, 1984), 408.
2. Ibid., 411.
3. *LV* 45–46.
4. Sido, *Lettres,* 414.
5. *Colette en tournée: Cartes postales à Sido,* ed. Michel Rémy-Bieth (Paris: Persona, 1984), 92.
6. Colette, *L'Entrave.*
7. *Colette en tournée,* 90–94.
8. Colette, "En visite," in *Contes des 1001 matins* (Paris: Flammarion, 1970), 117–123.
9. *LV* 48.
10. *Colette en tournée,* 94.
11. *LV* 49.
12. Ibid., 47–48; Sido, *Lettres,* 431.

13. *LV* 52.
14. Ibid., 53–54.
15. Sido, *Lettres,* 434–435, 437.
16. Ibid., 434–441.
17. *Colette en tournée,* 96.
18. *LV* 54–55.
19. Louis Guitard, *La Petite Histoire de la IIIᵉ République: Souvenirs de Maurice Colrat* (Paris: Le Sept Couleurs, 1959), 63.
20. Ibid.
21. *LV* 55–57.
22. Sido, *Lettres,* 443–446, 448.
23. "Historique de Castel-Novel," courtesy of the present owner, Albert Parveaux.
24. *LV* 58–59.
25. Ibid., 59–60.
26. Quoted in Henri Martineau, "Paul-Jean Toulet, 'Collaborateur' de Willy," *Mercure de France,* October 1956, 235.
27. Willy, *Lélie, fumeuse d'opium* (Paris: Albin Michel [1911]), 61–64.
28. François Caradec, *Feu Willy* (Paris: Carrère, 1984), 244–247.
29. Colette, *Trois . . . Six . . . Neuf . . . ; LV* 61.
30. Germaine Beaumont and André Parinaud, *Colette* (Paris: Seuil, 1951), 8–14.

CHAPTER 15: Sido and Sidi

1. BN 80, 82.
2. Colette, *Contes des 1001 matins* (Paris: Flammarion, 1970), 15–23, 26–33, 35–41, 43–48.
3. Colette, *L'Etoile vesper.*
4. Sido, *Lettres à sa fille* (Paris: Des Femmes, 1984), 454–457.
5. Compare *Le Figaro Littéraire,* January 24, 1953, with Sido, *Lettres,* ix. See BN 78.
6. Sido, *Lettres,* 465, 467–468, 471, 478–482.
7. BN 114.
8. Sido, *Lettres,* 485–487.

9. *Fantasio,* May 1, 1912, 673, reprinted in *Contes des 1001 matins,* 85–87.
10. Sido, *Lettres,* 462.
11. *LV* 68–73.
12. Ibid., 73–75.
13. Ibid., 75–78.
14. Ibid., 80–82; Colette, *L'Etoile vesper.*
15. *LV* 83–84.
16. Ibid., 84–86.

CHAPTER 16: Baby Colette

1. Colette, *L'Etoile vesper.*
2. *LV* 87–90.
3. Ibid., 90.
4. René Gillouin, *Essais de Critique littéraire et philosophique* (Paris: Grasset, 1913), 89–91, 93–95.
5. *LV* 91–93.
6. *L'Officiel des Concerts,* June 19, 1913, quoted in *LV* 290–291.
7. Colette, "Maternité," in *Paysages et portraits* (Paris: Flammarion, 1958), 17–30.
8. *LV* 94.
9. Sido, *Lettres à sa fille* (Paris: Des Femmes, 1984), 13.
10. Ibid., 13–14.
11. Colette, *L'Etoile vesper.*
12. Colette, "Anglais que j'ai connus," in *Paysages et portraits,* 141.
13. *Journal de l'Abbé Mugnier (1879–1939)* (Paris: Mercure de France, 1985), 559.
14. *LV* 95.
15. Ibid., 96–97.
16. *Mercure de France,* December 1, 1913, quoted in BN 73.
17. *LV* 99–100.
18. *LMM* 36–38.
19. Natalie Clifford Barney, *Souvenirs indiscrets* (Paris: Flammarion, 1960), 198–199.
20. *LMM* 44–45.
21. *LV* 101–102.
22. Ibid., 104–106.

23. Colette, "La Nouvelle," in *Les Heures longues.*
24. *LV* 107–108.

CHAPTER 17: Verdun

1. BN 79.
2. Marguerite Moreno, *Souvenirs de ma vie* (Paris: Flore, 1948), 226, 231–232, 236.
3. Colette, "La Lune de pluie," in *Chambre d'hôtel,* and "Marguerite Moreno," in *LMM* 13–14.
4. *LV* 108–111.
5. Ibid., 112–115.
6. Ibid., 114–117.
7. BN 79–80.
8. Colette, "Anglais que j'ai connus," in *Paysages et portraits* (Paris: Flammarion, 1958), 141.
9. Colette, *Les Heures longues.*
10. *Journal de l'Abbé Mugnier (1879–1939)* (Paris: Mercure de France, 1985), 503.
11. Claude Chauvière, *Colette* (Paris: Firmin-Didot, 1931), 23.
12. Jean-Luc Barré, "Colette, Henry de Jouvenel et le seigneur chat," in *Album Masques: Colette* (Paris: Masques, 1984), 107.
13. Colette, *Oeuvres,* vol. 2 (Paris: Gallimard, 1986), 587.
14. *LV* 121–122.
15. Colette, "Lac de Côme," in *Les Heures longues.*
16. Colette, *Trois . . . Six . . . Neuf. . . .*
17. *Le Matin,* January 6, 1917; see also ibid., January 8, 1917.
18. Colette, "L'Hiver à Rome," in *Paysages et portraits,* 121–126.
19. *LV* 122–123.
20. Ibid., 124–125.
21. Alain and Odette Virmaux, *Colette au cinéma* (Paris: Flammarion, 1975), 23–27, 279–285, 316.
22. Colette, "Bel-Gazou et la vie chère," in *Les Heures longues.*
23. Colette de Jouvenel, "Lettre à Bernard Gavoty," in *Colette de Jouvenel* (Saint-Sauveur: Société des Amis de Colette, 1982), 24–25.
24. Renaud de Jouvenel, "Lettres de Colette à Renaud de Jouvenel," *La Revue de Paris,* December 1966, 4–5.

CHAPTER 18: Mitsou

1. *LV* 126–127.
2. Henry Lémery, *D'une République l'autre* (Paris: Table Ronde, 1964), 104–105.
3. *LSP* 204.
4. Quoted in Claude Chauvière, *Colette* (Paris: Firmin-Didot, 1931), 88–89.
5. Alain and Odette Virmaux, *Colette au cinéma* (Paris: Flammarion, 1975), 303–309.
6. Sido, *Lettres à sa fille* (Paris: Des Femmes, 1984), 15; Colette Papers, Saint-Sauveur-en-Puisaye, courtesy of the Jouvenel succession.
7. *LV* 205–207.
8. Colette, *Le Fanal bleu.*
9. *Le Matin,* December 19, 22, 24, 25, and 29, 1919.
10. Nicolas Ségur, in *Revue Mondiale,* June 15, 1919, quoted in Jean Larnac, *Colette: Sa vie, son oeuvre* (Paris: Simon Kra, 1927), 168.
11. BN 150.
12. *LSP* 36–37.

CHAPTER 19: Chéri

1. *LSP* 214–216.
2. *LHP* 33.
3. *LSP* 38.
4. Francis Carco, *Colette "mon ami"* (Paris: Rive Gauche, 1955), 39–40.
5. Jean-Luc Barré, "Colette, Henry de Jouvenel et le seigneur chat," in *Album Masques: Colette* (Paris: Masques, 1984), 105.

6. Liane de Pougy, *Mes Cahiers bleus* (Paris: Plon, 1977), 101.

7. Ibid., 108–109.

8. Claude Chauvière, *Colette* (Paris: Firmin-Didot, 1931), 63–64, 212–213.

9. Interview with Jean-Louis Aujol.

10. Colette Papers, Saint-Sauveur-en-Puisaye. André Germain, in *Les Clés de Proust* (Paris: Sun, 1953), says that Colette drafted this plea.

11. *LHP* 31.

12. *LMM* 47.

13. Bertrand de Jouvenel, *Un Voyageur dans le siècle* (Paris: Laffont, 1979), 22–25, 36–38, 54–55.

14. Colette, *L'Etoile vesper.*

15. *LSP* 280.

16. *Vingt-cinq ans de littérature française,* vol. 2, ed. Eugène Montfort (Paris: Librairie de France, n.d.).

17. Colette, *La Naissance du jour.*

CHAPTER 20: *Bertrand*

1. Germaine Beaumont and André Parinaud, *Colette* (Paris: Sevil, 1951), 13, 18, 33–35.

2. Bertrand de Jouvenel, "La Vérité sur 'Chéri,'" in Colette, *Oeuvres,* vol. 2 (Paris: Gallimard, 1986), lvi, and *Un Voyageur dans le siècle* (Paris: Laffont, 1979), 55.

3. *LMM* 53. Misdated; actually written in summer 1920.

4. B. de Jouvenel, *Un Voyageur,* 56, and "La Vérité," lvii.

5. *LMM* 47–48.

6. Courtesy of Anne de Jouvenel, with the authorization of the Colette Estate.

7. Courtesy of Anne de Jouvenel, with the authorization of the Colette Estate.

8. *LMM* 48.

9. *LSP* 219.

10. BN 201.

11. Interview with Jean-Louis Aujol.

12. *Journal de l'Abbé Mugnier (1879–*

1939) (Paris: Mercure de France, 1985), 371.

13. *LMM* 48–49.

14. Interview with Gilles Le Guenec.

15. Frédéric Lefèvre, "Une heure avec Henry de Jouvenel," *Les Nouvelles Littéraires,* March 24, 1928.

16. *LMM* 50.

17. *LV* 138–139.

18. Ibid.

19. François Martinez, "Entretien avec Colette de Jouvenel," *Bonne Soirée Télé,* April 14, 1973.

20. Interview with Esa di Simone, Rome.

21. B. de Jouvenel, "La Vérité," lvii.

22. B. de Jouvenel, *Un Voyageur,* 57, 73.

23. *LMM* 54–55.

24. *LSP* 42.

CHAPTER 21: *My Mother's House*

1. Maurice Martin du Gard, "Colette au 'Matin,'" *La Parisienne,* November 1954, 1216–1222.

2. Bertrand de Jouvenel, "La Vérité sur 'Chéri,'" in Colette, *Oeuvres,* vol. 2 (Paris: Gallimard, 1986), lvii.

3. Colette, "Dimanche."

4. *LMM* 57–58.

5. Bertrand de Jouvenel, *Un Voyageur dans le siècle* (Paris: Laffont, 1979), 57.

6. *LMM* 57.

7. Jean Larnac, *Colette: Sa vie, son oeuvre* (Paris: Simon Kra, 1927), 171.

8. Alain and Odette Virmaux, *Colette au cinéma* (Paris: Flammarion, 1975), 309.

9. B. de Jouvenel, *Un Voyageur,* 57.

10. *LHP* 39.

11. Quoted in Sido, *Lettres à sa fille* (Paris: Des Femmes, 1984), 17.

12. *LV* 146–148.

13. B. de Jouvenel, *Un Voyageur,* 57.

14. In Colette, *Mes Cahiers.*

15. Renaud de Jouvenel, "Lettres de Colette à Renaud de Jouvenel," *La Revue de Paris,* December 1966, 10–11.

16. *LMM* 58–59.
17. *Journal de l'Abbé Mugnier (1879–1939)* (Paris: Mercure de France, 1985), 393–395.

CHAPTER 22. *The Ripening Seed*
1. *LMM* 61.
2. *LHP* 41.
3. *LMM* 61–62; *LHP* 41, 56.
4. Bertrand de Jouvenel, *Un Voyageur dans le siècle* (Paris: Laffont, 1979), 36.
5. Frédéric Lefèvre, *Une heure avec . . . , 4ᵉ série* (Paris: Gallimard, 1927), 138–139.
6. *PC* 85.
7. Renaud de Jouvenel, "Lettres de Colette à Renaud de Jouvenel," *La Revue de Paris*, December 1966, 9–10.
8. *LV* 153–156.
9. R. de Jouvenel, "Lettres de Colette," 10.
10. Bertrand de Jouvenel, "La Vérité sur 'Chéri,'" in Colette, *Oeuvres*, vol. 2 (Paris: Gallimard, 1986), lvii–lviii.
11. Jacques Frugier, "La 'Collection Colette,'" *Cahiers Colette* 5 (1983): 71–84.
12. Albert Flament, "Tableaux de Paris," *La Revue de Paris*, March 1, 1923, 202–206.
13. Quoted in François Caradec, *Feu Willy* (Paris: Carrère, 1984), 284.
14. Sido, *Lettres à sa fille* (Paris: Des Femmes, 1984), 18.
15. In *Comoedia,* quoted in Claude Chauvière, *Colette* (Paris: Firmin-Didot, 1931), 106.
16. *LHP* 48, 50.
17. *LMM* 64.
18. Ibid., 73–74.
19. Ghislain de Diesbach, *La Princesse Bibesco (1886–1973)* (Paris: Perrin, 1986), especially 323–327.
20. R. de Jouvenel, "Lettres de Colette," 12.
21. André Billy, *L'Oeuvre,* August 21, 1923.

22. Benjamin Crémieux, "Les Lettres françaises," *Les Nouvelles Littéraires,* August 25, 1923, 2.
23. *LHP* 51.
24. Diesbach, *Bibesco,* 327.
25. *LMM* 69, 71.

CHAPTER 23: *Ruptures*
1. *LV* 165–166.
2. *LMM* 75.
3. *LV* 167.
4. *LMM* 76.
5. Ibid., 77.
6. Courtesy of the Société des Manuscrits et Autographes Français, with the authorization of the Colette Estate.
7. Colette,*Trois . . . Six . . . Neuf. . . .*
8. *LMM* 77.
9. Bertrand de Jouvenel, *Un Voyageur dans le siècle* (Paris: Laffont, 1979), 57.
10. Interview with Jean-Louis Aujol.
11. *LSP* 126.
12. *LHP* 62–63.
13. André Germain, *Les Clés de Proust* (Paris: Sun, 1953), 237.
14. *LHP* 64.
15. Courtesy of the Société des Manuscrits et Autographes Française, with the authorization of the Colette Estate.
16. *LMM* 78–79.
17. *LV* 173–174.
18. Courtesy of Anne de Jouvenel, with the authorization of the Colette Estate.
19. *LHP* 65–66.
20. Courtesy of the Société des Manuscrits et Autographes Français, with the authorization of the Colette Estate.
21. Courtesy of the Richard Anacréon Collection, Granville, with the authorization of the Colette Estate.
22. *LV* 174.
23. *LSP* 226.
24. B. de Jouvenel, *Un Voyageur,* 57.

25. *LV* 175.
26. B. de Jouvenel, *Un Voyageur,* 57–58.
27. *Journal de l'Abbé Mugnier (1879–1939)* (Paris: Mercure de France, 1985), 438–439.
28. *LMM* 81–83.
29. Ibid., 85–86; *LV* 179.

CHAPTER 24: *The Last of Chéri*

1. *LMM* 84–87.
2. *LHP* 67–68.
3. *LMM* 88.
4. Colette, *Oeuvres,* vol. 2 (Paris: Gallimard, 1986), xlviii.
5. Bertrand de Jouvenel, "La Vérité sur 'Chéri,' " in Colette, *Oeuvres* 2, lviii.
6. *LV* 180–181.
7. *LMM* 99; BN 159.
8. The twelve colums are reprinted in *Le Voyage égoïste.*
9. *LV* 181–184.
10. *La Revue de Paris,* April 15, 1925, 897–899.
11. Ghislain de Diesbach, *La Princesse Bibesco (1886–1973)* (Paris: Perrin, 1986), 339–341, 347; interview with Jean-Louis Aujol.
12. *PC* 11–13.
13. B. de Jouvenel, "La Vérité," lviii.
14. *LPC* 47.
15. *LHP* 72.
16. Quoted in Francis Carco, *Colette "mon ami"* (Paris: Rive Gauche, 1955), unpaginated.
17. *PC* 14.
18. Maurice Goudeket, *La Douceur de vieillir* (Paris: Flammarion, 1965), 12–29, 58. Curriculum Vitae courtesy Richard Anacréon Collection, Granville.
19. *PC* 11.
20. Ibid., 16–18, 31.
21. *LMM* 101–112.
22. *PC* 32, 43.
23. *LV* 185–186.
24. *LHP* 74.
25. Ibid., 75.

26. Goudeket, *La Douceur,* 88–89; *LMM* 112–113.
27. Colette, "La Treille muscate," in *Prisons et paradis.*
28. Goudeket, *La Douceur,* 101.
29. *LMM* 116.

CHAPTER 25: *La Treille Muscate*

1. Courtesy of the Société des Manuscrits et Autographes Français, with the authorization of the Colette Estate.
2. *PC* 185–186.
3. Colette de Jouvenel, in *Colette de Jouvenel* (Saint-Sauveur: Société des Amis de Colette, 1982), 27.
4. *LMM* 116–117.
5. *PC* 28, 61–62, 67–68; Maurice Goudeket, *Ce que je ne crois pas* (Paris: Flammarion, 1977), 101.
6. *LV* 188.
7. *LMM* 124.
8. *LHP* 76–77.
9. Ibid., 79–80.
10. Interview in *Les Nouvelles Littéraires,* March 27, 1926, reprinted in Frédéric Lefèvre, *Une heure avec . . . ,* 4ᵉ série (Paris: Gallimard, 1927), 136–137.
11. Colette Papers, Saint-Sauveur-en-Puisaye.
12. *LHP* 80.
13. Albert Flament, "Tableaux de Paris," *La Revue de Paris,* March 1, 1926, 180–181.
14. Renaud de Jouvenel, "Lettres de Colette à Renaud de Jouvenel," *La Revue de Paris,* December 1966, 13.
15. Colette, "Notes marocaines," in *Prisons et paradis.*
16. *LHP* 81.
17. André Rouveyre, *Mercure de France,* June 1, 1926, 428–431.
18. *LMM* 130–131; *LHP* 83–84.
19. *LMM* 131–132.
20. *LV* 192–193.
21. Courtesy of the Société des Manuscrits et Autographes Français, with

the authorization of the Colette Estate.

22. *LMM* 142.

23. Quoted in Claude Chauvière, *Colette* (Paris: Firmin-Didot, 1931), 249–250.

CHAPTER 26: *Break of Day*

1. *LHP* 86–87.

2. Natalie Clifford Barney, *Aventures de l'esprit* (Paris: Emile Paul, 1929), 201.

3. Colette, *Trois . . . Six . . . Neuf. . . .*

4. Jean Larnac, *Colette: Sa vie, son oeuvre* (Paris: Simon Kra, 1927), 190–194, 205.

5. François Mauriac, "Le Roman d'Aujourd'hui," *La Revue Hebdomadaire,* February 19, 1927, 265–266.

6. *Journal de l'Abbé Mugnier (1879–1939)* (Paris: Mercure de France, 1985), 480–481.

7. Quoted in François Martinez, "Entretien avec Colette de Jouvenel," *Bonne Soirée Télé,* April 14, 1973.

8. BN 127.

9. Deed, March 4, 1927, receipt of June 18, 1927, courtesy of Denise Cabanis; *LMM* 145.

10. *PC* 51–53.

11. *LV* 196–197.

12. *LMM* 147–151; *LV* 200–201.

13. *LMM* 153.

14. *LV* 202.

15. *LMM* 156–158.

16. *LV* 204.

17. Jeannie Malige, preface to Sido, *Lettres à sa fille* (Paris: Des Femmes, 1984), ix–x. See also pp. 126 and 128 for examples of Colette's rewriting of Sido's letters.

18. Quoted in Maurice Goudeket, *La Douceur de vieillir* (Paris: Flammarion, 1965), 116–117.

19. Renaud de Jouvenel, "Lettres de Colette à Renaud de Jouvenel," *La Revue de Paris,* December 1966, 14.

20. *LMM* 161–162.

21. *LSP* 194.

CHAPTER 27: *The Other One*

1. Colette, *L'Etoile vesper.*

2. Courtesy of the Société des Manuscrits et Autographes Français, with the authorization of the Colette Estate.

3. *LMM* 175.

4. *LV* 205–206; *LHP* 85.

5. *LMM* 177–178.

6. *LMM* 187.

7. Ibid., 183; *LSP* 187.

8. *Journal de l'Abbé Mugnier (1879–1939)* (Paris: Mercure de France, 1985), 502.

9. Ibid., 503–504.

10. *LMM* 189.

11. *LSP* 91, 93.

12. *LHP* 106.

13. *LSP* 187.

14. *PC* 75.

15. André Billy, *La Femme de France,* May 5, 1929, quoted in *LSP* 196.

16. *PC* 123.

17. *LV* 208.

18. *LHP* 108.

19. *LMM* 192.

20. *LHP* 111.

21. Colette, *Prisons et paradis.*

22. *LHP* 101–103.

23. André Billy, *Intimités littéraires.* (Paris: Flammarion, 1932), 149–151.

24. Dunoyer de Segonzac, *Le Figaro Littéraire,* January 24, 1953.

25. Natalie Clifford Barney, *Souvenirs indiscrets* (Paris: Flammarion, 1960), 202.

CHAPTER 28: *Claridge's*

1. Quoted in Maurice Goudeket, *La Douceur de vieillir* (Paris: Flammarion, 1965), 111.

2. Notes for *Mémoires d'une européenne* by Louise Weiss, Bibliothèque Na-

tionale, MS NAF 17794 f.12; interview with Richard Anacréon.

3. *PC* 56–57, 93, 107, 129, 145–149, 238.
4. *LMM* 203.
5. *LHP* 112; *LV* 212.
6. Janet Flanner, *Paris Was Yesterday (1925–1939)* (New York: Viking, 1972).
7. *LMM* 208–211.
8. Rachilde, *Portraits d'Hommes* (Paris: Mercure de France, 1930), 46, 58–59.
9. X. M. Boulestin, *A Londres naguère* (Paris: Fayard, 1946), 36. On Willy's debts, see Archives Nationales, SGDL Papers, 454 AP 172.
10. Sylvain Bonmariage, *Le Sang des pharisiens* (Paris: Edition Littéraire Internationale, 1935), 157–160.
11. Colette, *Trois . . . Six . . . Neuf. . . .*
12. *LV* 218.

CHAPTER 29: *These Pleasures*

1. Claude Chauvière, *Colette* (Paris: Firmin-Didot, 1931), 75–81.
2. *PC* 68.
3. Chauvière, *Colette,* 2–8, 201.
4. *LHP* 128.
5. Ibid., 129.
6. Chauvière, *Colette,* 280–281.
7. *LMT* 36.
8. *LMM* 213.
9. PC 74; *LHP* 128.
10. BN 163–164.
11. *LMM* 220–221.
12. BN 141; *LMM* 222.
13. *LSP* 172.
14. *LHP* 143–144.
15. *LV* 220.
16. *PC* 79–82.
17. Quoted in George Wickes, *The Amazon of Letters: The Life and Loves of Natalie Barney* (New York: Putnam, 1976), 252.
18. *LMM* 225.
19. *LV* 226.

20. BN 162–163; *LHP* 147; *LSP* 234.
21. BN 170.
22. Colette Papers, Saint-Sauveur-en-Puisaye.
23. *LHP* 153.
24. *PC* 83.

CHAPTER 30: *The Cat*

1. *LMM* 228; *LMT* 53–54.
2. *LMM* 230; *LV* 230.
3. Maurice Goudeket, *La Douceur de vieillir* (Paris: Flammarion, 1965), 144–146.
4. *LMT* 57, 60; *LHP* 154–155.
5. *LHP* 159.
6. Courtesy of Evan A. Lottman.
7. *LHP* 160, 165.
8. Marie-Thérèse Colléaux-Chaurang, "Etude critique de la correspondance de Colette avec les petites fermières" (Doctoral diss., Université de Nantes, 1986), 9–11, 326, 364.
9. *LHP* 161.
10. *PC* 84.
11. *LHP* 163–164.
12. *LMT* 72–79.
13. *LV* 233–234.
14. *LSP* 277–278; *LMM* 233.
15. *LSP* 332.
16. Ibid., 295, 304.
17. *LMM* 234.
18. *LHP* 167.

CHAPTER 31: *Madame Goudeket*

1. François Porché, *Jour,* August 16, 1934, quoted in BN 101.
2. *LHP* 169; *LMT* 85.
3. *LMT* 86–87.
4. Paul Leroy, *Femmes d'aujourd'hui: Colette–Lucie Delarue-Mardrus* (Rouen: Maugard, 1936), 17–21.
5. Alain and Odette Virmaux, *Colette au cinéma* (Paris: Flammarion, 1975), 219–222.
6. *LV* 238.
7. BN 166.

8. Colette, *La Jumelle noire: Deuxième année.*

9. Colette, *Trois . . . Six . . . Neuf. . . .*

10. PC 96–97.

11. LHP 174.

12. PC 98.

13. Maurice Goudeket, *La Douceur de vieillir* (Paris: Flammarion, 1965), 120–121.

14. PC 99.

15. Bibliothèque Nationale, MS MIC 3322 f.275.

16. LMT 105.

17. Colette, "New York et la 'Normandie,'" *Mes Cahiers.*

18. PC 102.

19. LMT 106–107.

20. PC 104–105.

21. LV 242.

22. LHP 175.

23. Colette de Jouvenel, "Lettre à Bernard Gavoty," in *Colette de Jouvenel* (Saint-Sauveur: Société des Amis de Colette, 1982), 27–28.

CHAPTER 32: *My Apprenticeships*

1. Michel del Castillo, "De Jouvenel à Colette," *Cahiers Colette* 10 (1988): 7.

2. LHP 175; LMT 154.

3. Colette Papers, Saint-Sauveur-en-Puisaye.

4. Anatole de Monzie, "Adieu à mon ami," reprinted in *La Revue des Vivants,* November–December 1935, 1635–1636.

5. Colette Papers, Saint-Sauveur-en-Puisaye; interview with Albert Parveaux, Hotel Castel-Novel.

6. André Gide, *Journal (1889–1939)* (Paris: Gallimard, 1948), 1245.

7. LHP 181.

8. Ibid., 182.

9. Quoted in PC 136–137.

10. Maurice Martin du Gard, *Les Mémo-*

rables, vol. 3 *(1930–1945)* (Paris: Grasset, 1978), 203.

11. Colette, *Discours de réception,* 10, 14.

12. Quoted in Martin du Gard, *Mémorables* 3, 206.

13. Colette, *Splendeurs des papillons* (Paris: Plon, 1936).

14. *Premier Cahier de Colette* (Paris: Les Amis de Colette, 1935), reprinted in *Mes Cahiers.*

15. LPC 33.

16. Claude Pichois, in *LPC* 21–26.

17. Ibid., 152.

18. PC 179.

19. Quoted in *LSP* 308.

20. LPC 41.

CHAPTER 33: *Palais-Royal*

1. BN 97.

2. Diary of Renée Hamon, Bibliothèque Nationale, MS NAF 18711.

3. Sido, *Lettres à sa fille* (Paris: Des Femmes, 1984), 28.

4. LMT 123.

5. LV 251–253.

6. Jean-Pierre Aumont, *Souvenirs provisoires* (Paris: Julliard, 1957), 82–83.

7. Sido, *Lettres,* 21–22; LMT 123.

8. LPC 35; PC 143–144.

9. LPC 38–39.

10. LPC 39.

11. PC 260–265.

12. Germaine Beaumont and André Parinaud, *Colette* (Paris: Seuil, 1951), 39.

13. LPC 46–48.

14. Quoted in Denise Tual, *Au Coeur du temps* (Paris: Carrère, 1987), 163–164.

15. LPC 40, 43.

16. LSP 384.

17. Talk with Denise Tual.

18. Colette de Jouvenel, "Notes et réflexions," in *Colette de Jouvenel* (Saint Sauveur: Société de Amis des Colette, 1982), 5–7.

19. *LV* 254.
20. *PC* 47, 168–170.
21. *LPC* 56.
22. *LMT* 134–135.

CHAPTER 34: *Every War in Paris*

1. *LPC* 57–60.
2. *LHP* 196.
3. *LPC* 61–65, 67–69.
4. *LV* 263–264; *LSP* 131; *LMT* 144.
5. *PC* 171.
6. *LPC* 71–72.
7. *LV* 264.
8. *LPC* 76–77.
9. *LMT* 159.
10. *LV* 265.
11. *LPC* 77.
12. *LMT* 161.
13. Ibid., 161–162.
14. *LPC* 78.
15. Marie-Thérèse Colléaux-Chaurang, "Etude critique de la correspondance de Colette avec les petites fermières" (Doctoral diss., Université de Nantes, 1986), 357.
16. Denise Tual, *Au Coeur du temps* (Paris: Carrère, 1987), 215–216.
17. *LMT* 163–164.
18. *PC* 175–176.
19. *LV* 267–270; *LPC* 78–79.
20. Colette, *Paysages et portraits* (Paris: Flammarion, 1958), 237; *PC* 177.
21. *PC* 179.
22. Ibid., 139.
23. *LPC* 71.
24. *LMT* 165–166.
25. *CSP* 133.
26. Bibliothèque Nationale, MS NAF 18711.
27. Ibid.
28. *LMT* 166–167, 169–173.
29. *LPC* 84.
30. Colette, *Paysages et portraits*, 254–260.
31. *LPC* 86.
32. *LV* 274–275.
33. *LPC* 86–87.
34. *LMT* 176–177.

CHAPTER 35: *Occupied Paris*

1. *PC* 182–183.
2. Colette, "Fin Juin 1940," in *Journal à rebours*.
3. From Madame André Cantegreil and Jean Lalé.
4. Interview with Simone Wertheim.
5. *LPC* 87.
6. *PC* 187–188.
7. *BN* 180.
8. *LPC* 88.
9. *PC* 188.
10. Interview with Simone Wertheim.
11. *LSP* 402; *LMT* 178–182.
12. *PC* 190–191.
13. *LSP* 403–404.
14. *PC* 192.
15. *LSP* 135.
16. *LMT* 185–187.
17. Pascal Fouché, *L'Edition française sous l'occupation,* vol. 1 (Paris: Bibliothèque de littérature française contemporaine, Université de Paris VII, 1987), 142–147.
18. Renaud de Jouvenel, "Lettres de Colette à Renaud de Jouvenal," *La Revue de Paris,* December 1966, 18.
19. Marie-Thérèse Colléaux-Chaurung, "Etude critique de la correspondance de Colette avec les petites fermières" (Doctoral diss., Université de Nantes, 1986), 372–373.
20. *LPC* 93–98.
21. Bibliothèque Nationale MS.
22. *LMT* 189–191.
23. Jean Cocteau, *La Difficulté d'être* (Monaco: Editions du Rocher, 1953), 137–139.
24. *LPC* 99–100.
25. *LMT* 192–196.
26. *LPC* 101–102; *LMT* 196.
27. LPC 103.
28. *LMT* 198–199.

CHAPTER 36: Julie

1. Quoted in Jean-Luc Mercié, *Anacréon le Jeune* (Ottawa: Editions de l'Université d'Ottawa, 1971), 81.
2. *LHP* 202.
3. Bibliothèque Nationale MS NAF 18711.
4. Colette, *Journal intermittent.*
5. Denise Tual, *Au Coeur du temps* (Paris: Carrère, 1987), 253–254.
6. *LMT* 203.
7. Pascal Fouché, *L'Edition française sous l'occupation,* vol. 1 (Paris: Bibliothèque de littérature française contemporaine, Université de Paris VII, 1987), 132–135, 140.
8. Colette, *Le Pur et l'impur* (Paris: Aux Armes de France, 1941), 5. See Fouché, *L'Edition française* 2, 255.
9. *LHP* 203.
10. *LPC* 106.
11. Mercié, *Anacréon,* 80.
12. *LMT* 219–220.
13. *LMM* 239.
14. *LMT* 205, 214–215, 217, 220, 222. See *PC* 194–195.
15. BN 194.
16. BN 184; Richard Anacréon, Granville.

CHAPTER 37: Maurice and Misz

1. *PC* 197–199.
2. *LHP* 204.
3. *PC* 202.
4. *LPC* 111.
5. Colette, *L'Etoile vesper.*
6. *PC* 203–205.
7. Robert Brasillach, *Oeuvres complètes,* vol. 10 (Paris: Club de l'Honnête Homme, 1964), 606.
8. Denise Tual, *Au Coeur du temps* (Paris: Carrère, 1987), 252–253.
9. Sacha Guitry, *Quatre ans d'occupations* (Paris: L'Elan, 1947), 457–458, 479–480.
10. Maud de Belleroche, *Paris Match,*

August 11, 1978, quoted in Marie-Thérèse Colléaux-Chaurung, "Etude critique de la correspondance de Colette avec les petites fermières" (Doctoral diss., Université de Nantes, 1986), 163.
11. Arthur Gold and Robert Fizdale, *Misia: The Life of Misia Sert* (New York: Knopf, 1980), 281–282. Goudeket is the source of this account: letter from Robert Fizdale to the author.
12. Bertrand de Jouvenel, *Un Voyageur dans le siècle* (Paris: Laffont, 1979), 200–203, 397, 402, 426.
13. Colette Papers, Saint-Sauveur-en-Puisaye.
14. Jacques Isorni, *Mémoires,* vol. 1 *(1911–1945)* (Paris: Laffont, 1984), 286.
15. Courtesy of Sanda Goudeket.
16. Marie-Thérèse Colléaux, "Six lettres de Colette aux Petites Fermières," *Cahiers Colette* 10 (1988): 26; *PC* 206–207.
17. Colette, *L'Etoile vesper.*
18. *LMM* 241; *LPC* 113.
19. Guitry, *Quatre ans,* 318–319, 324, 334, 342.
20. *LMM* 242; *LMT* 229; *LPC* 113–116.
21. Colette, *L'Etoile vesper.*
22. *PC* 208–209; Germaine Beaumont and André Parinaud, *Colette* (Paris: Seuil, 1951), 41.
23. *LPC* 119.

CHAPTER 38: Waiting for the Communiqu

1. Marie-Thérèse Colléaux, "Six lettres de Colette aux Petites Fermières," *Cahiers Colette* 10 (1988): 28.
2. *PC* 209.
3. *PC* 63–65. See BN 188–189.
4. *LPC* 120–121.
5. Reprinted in Colette, *En pays connu.*

6. *Les Lettres Françaises* (clandestine), December 1942, 4.
7. *LPC* 121.
8. *PC* 210–211.
9. *LSP* 180–181.
10. *LPC* 125.
11. *PC* 212.
12. *LPC* 125.
13. Renaud de Jouvenel, "Lettres de Colette à Renaud de Jouvenel," *La Revue de Paris,* December 1966, 18–19.
14. *LMM* 243, 252–253.
15. *LPC* 127–128, 130, 143–146; *LMM* 250, 258.
16. Colléaux, "Six lettres de Colette," 29–30.
17. *LMM* 259.
18. Ibid., 269–271.
19. Quoted in *PC* 201.
20. *LMM* 276, 278.

CHAPTER 39: Liberation

1. Jean-Luc Mercié, *Anacréon le Jeune* (Ottawa: Editions de l'Université d'Ottawa, 1971), 69.
2. *LMM* 278–282, 284–285, 287, 289–290.
3. *PC* 213.
4. *LMM* 290–293.
5. Colette, *L'Etoile vesper.*
6. *LMM* 295; *LSP* 246; *PC* 213–216.
7. *LMM* 294–296.
8. Ibid., 297–298; *LMT* 240, 297.
9. Jacques Isorni, *Le Procès de Brasillach* (Paris: Flammarion, 1946), 162.
10. Jacques Isorni, *Mémoires,* vol. 1 *(1911–1945)* (Paris: Laffont, 1984), 285–286, 308–309; Robert Brasillach, *Oeuvres complètes,* vol. 10 (Paris: Club de l'Honnête Homme, 1964), 606.
11. *LSP* 138.
12. Ibid., 137–138.
13. Marie-Thérèse Colléaux, "Six lettres de Colette aux Petites Fermieres," *Cahiers Colette* 10 (1988): 31–32.
14. Ibid., 32; *LMM* 300; Colette, *L'Etoile vesper.*

15. *LHP* 216–217.
16. Colette, *L'Etoile vesper.*
17. Lee Miller, "Colette," *Vogue* (New York), March 1, 1945.
18. *Fraternité,* May 4, August 24, September 7, 1945.
19. François Martinez, "Entretien avec Colette de Jouvenel," *Bonne Soirée Télé,* April 14, 1973.
20. Monica Stirling, "Two Young Talents," *Vogue* (New York), November 1, 1945.
21. Colette, *L'Etoile vesper.*
22. Courtesy of Anne de Jouvenel.

CHAPTER 40: Cures

1. *LMM* 304.
2. Jean Galtier-Boissière, *Mon Journal depuis la libération* (Paris: Jeune Parque, 1945), 239; Georges Ravon, *L'Académie Goncourt en dix couverts* (Paris: Aubanel, 1946), 51–52.
3. Ravon, *L'Académie Goncourt,* 54.
4. Colette, *Le Fanal bleu.*
5. *PC* 224.
6. *LMM* 303, 306–307.
7. *LMT* 254.
8. *LMM* 308.
9. *PC* 225.
10. Ibid., 225–226.
11. *LMT* 265–266, 269.
12. Ibid., 272, 275, 277.
13. *LMM* 315–318.
14. *LMT* 281–282, 286–287.
15. *LMM* 319.
16. *LMT* 288–290.
17. *LMM* 321.
18. Truman Capote, *The Dogs Bark* (New York: Random House, 1973), 12–15.
19. Shari Benstock, *Women of the Left Bank* (Austin: University of Texas Press, 1986), 413–415.
20. Bibliothèque Littéraire Jacques Doucet, NCB C 550.
21. Colette Papers, Saint-Sauveur-en-Puisaye.

22. From the late Dr. Pierre Muesser, who escorted this author through the house.

CHAPTER 41: *Colette at Seventy-five*

1. *LMM* 331; Alain and Odette Virmaux, *Colette au cinéma.* (Paris: Flammarion, 1975), 319.
2. *LMM* 332–334.
3. *LSP* 229.
4. *PC* 229.
5. BN 229.
6. *PC* 248–249.
7. *LSP* 285.
8. Ibid., 252.
9. *LMM* 339.
10. *PC* 242–244, 246.
11. See "Mélanges," in *La Chambre éclairée* (Fayard edition).
12. Virmaux, *Colette au cinéma.*
13. *LMT* 300–313.
14. Interview with Jean-Louis Aujol.
15. *LMT* 315–317.
16. BN 197–198.
17. *LMT* 317–318.
18. BN 158.
19. Quoted in *LSP* 441–442.
20. BN 206.
21. *Les Lettres Françaises,* October 20, 1949.

CHAPTER 42: *Monte Carlo*

1. *LSP* 165.
2. *New York Times Magazine,* January 22, 1950, reprinted in Joseph A. Barry, *Left Bank, Right Bank* (New York: Norton, 1951), 110–117.
3. Quoted in *Autour de Natalie Clifford Barney* (Paris: Bibliothèque Littéraire Jacques Doucet, 1976), 23–24.
4. *PC* 260–262, 269–270, 276.
5. Courtesy of Anne de Jouvenel.
6. *PC* 252–253.
7. *LMT* 322–328, 330, 335.
8. BN 162.
9. *LSP* 166, 259, 286.

10. Quoted in Sido, *Lettres à sa fille* (Paris: Des Femmes, 1984), 23.
11. Bertrand de Jouvenel, *Time & Tide* (London), August 14, 1954, 1075.
12. *LMT* 339–345.
13. *PC* 257.
14. BN 190.
15. *LMT* 344.
16. Bibliothèque Nationale, MS NAF 18704 f. 114–188, with the authorization of the Colette Estate.
17. *LMT* 346–348.
18. Ibid., 351–360.
19. Jean Cocteau, *Le Passé défini,* vol. 1 (Paris: Gallimard, 1983), 166–167.
20. Jean Cocteau, *Colette: Discours de réception à l'Académie Royale de Langue et de Littérature Françaises, 1 Octobre 1955* (Paris: Grasset, 1955), 29.
21. *PC* 274.

CHAPTER 43: *Last Writings*

1. Jean Cocteau, *Le Passé défini,* vol. 1 (Paris: Gallimard, 1983), 279.
2. *LSP* 262.
3. *LMT* 362.
4. *PC* 259.
5. Cocteau, *Le Passé défini* 1, 401.
6. *LSP* 369.
7. Colette, *Paysages et portraits* (Paris: Flammarion, 1958), 267–268.
8. *LSP* 396–397.
9. Dominique Aury, "Colette ou la gynécée," *La Nouvelle Revue française,* March 1, 1953, 505–511.
10. Marcelle Biolley-Godino, *L'Homme-objet chez Colette* (Paris: Klincksieck, 1972), 10–12, 49.
11. *LMT* 370–375.
12. Jean Cocteau, *Le Passé défini,* vol. 2 (Paris: Gallimard, 1985), 41–42, 45.
13. *LMT* 371.
14. Bibliothèque Nationale, MS NAF 18704 f. 210–211, 220, 222–224, 226, with the authorization of the Colette Estate.

15. André-Louis Dubois, *A travers trois
    républiques* (Paris: Plon, 1972), 114.
16. Bibliothèque Nationale, MS NAF
    18704 f. 227, with the authorization
    of the Colette Estate.
17. Courtesy of Anne de Jouvenel.
18. BN 209.
19. Cocteau, *Le Passé défini* 2, 348.

CHAPTER 44: Reckonings

 1. PC 275.
 2. Richard Anacréon Collection, Gran-
    ville.
 3. PC 278–279.
 4. *LMT* 379–380.
 5. PC 279–280.
 6. Pierre Mazars, "Les derniers mo-
    ments de Colette," *Le Figaro
    Littéraire*, August 7, 1954.
 7. PC 281–283.
 8. *New York Times*, August 4, 1954.
 9. PC 238–239; Maurice Goudeket, *La
    Douceur de vieillir* (Paris: Flamma-
    rion, 1965), 165–167, 171, 175, and
    Ce que je ne crois pas (Paris: Flam-
    marion, 1977), 156–157.
10. Graham Greene, "A Propos des Ob-
    sèques de Colette," *Le Figaro
    Littéraire*, August 14, 1954; reprinted
    in Graham Greene, *Yours Etc.: Letters
    to the Press* (New York: Reinhardt/
    Viking, 1990), 40–41.
11. *Le Figaro Littéraire*, August 21, 1954.
12. Ibid.
13. Bertrand de Jouvenel, "Colette,"
    Time & Tide, August 14, 1954, 1075.
14. Jean Cocteau, *Lettres à Milorad*
    (Paris: Editions Saint-Germain-des-
    Prés, 1975), 20.
15. Courtesy of Anne de Jouvenel.
16. From Anne de Jouvenel and Esa di
    Simone.
17. Jean Cocteau, *Colette: Discours de ré-
    ception à l'Académie Royale de Langue
    et de Littérature Françaises, 1 Octobre
    1955* (Paris: Grasset, 1955), 29.
18. Michel del Castillo, "De Jouvenel à
    Colette," *Cahiers Colette* 10
    (1988): 7–10.
19. Virginia Lee Warren, "The Daugh-
    ter of Colette Emerges from
    Obscurity," *New York Times*,
    April 28, 1970.
20. Castillo, "De Jouvenel à Colette," 7.
21. *Le Figaro Littéraire*, Febru-
    ary 3, 1973.
22. Colette de Jouvenel, "Lettre à De-
    lanoë," July 8, 1978, in *Colette de
    Jouvenel* (Saint-Sauveur: Société des
    Amis de Colette, 1982), 30–31.
23. *Le Figaro*, February 4–5, 1978.
24. Colette de Jouvenel, "Lettre à De-
    lanoë," April 4, 1978, in *Colette de
    Jouvenel*, 29; *Le Figaro*, March 21,
    1966.
25. Colette de Jouvenel, "Colette," in
    Colette de Jouvenel, 21–23.

Colette's Works

The list that follows is designed to help readers place Colette's writings in her life. Posthumous publications and shorter texts that were written to accompany art reproductions or were later reprinted in collections of her stories or articles are omitted. Dates refer to the original French publication.

1900
Claudine à l'école (*Claudine at School*)

1901
Claudine à Paris (*Claudine in Paris*)

1902
Claudine en ménage (*Claudine Married*)

1903
Claudine s'en va (*Claudine and Annie*)

1904
Minne (later republished, with *Les Egarements de Minne,* as *L'Ingénue libertine*)
Dialogues de bêtes

1905
Les Egarements de Minne
Sept Dialogues de bêtes

1907
La Retraite sentimentale (*Retreat from Love*)

1908
Les Vrilles de la vigne

1909
L'Ingénue libertine (*The Innocent Libertine;* also *Gentle Libertine*)

1911
La Vagabonde (*The Vagabond*)

1913
L'Envers du music-hall (*Music-Hall Sidelights*)
L'Entrave (*The Shackle;* also *Recaptured*)
Prrou, Poucette et quelques autres

1916
La Paix chez les bêtes (*Creatures Great and Small*)

1917
Les Heures longues
Les Enfants dans les ruines

1918
Dans la foule

1919
Mitsou (*Mitsou*)

1920
Chéri (*Chéri*)
La Chambre éclairée

1922
La Maison de Claudine (*My Mother's House*)
Le Voyage égoïste (*Journey for Myself*)

1923
Le Blé en herbe (*The Ripening Seed*)

1924
La Femme cachée
Aventures quotidiennes

1925
L'Enfant et les sortilèges

1926
La Fin de Chéri (*The Last of Chéri*)

1928
La Naissance du jour (*Break of Day;* also *A Lesson in Love*)

1929
La Seconde (*The Other One*)
Sido (*Sido*)

1930
Histoires pour Bel-Gazou
Douze dialogues de bêtes

1932
Paradis terrestres
La Treille muscate
Prisons et paradis
Ces Plaisirs . . . (to become *Le Pur et l'Impur* [*The Pure and the Impure*] in
    1941)

1933
La Chatte (*The Cat*)

1934
Duo (*Duo*)
La Jumelle noire (first of four annual collections of theater reviews)

1935
Cahier de Colette (first of four, to become *Mes Cahiers* in 1941)

1936
Mes Apprentissages (*My Apprenticeships*)
Chats

1937
Bella-Vista (*Tender Shoot*)

1939
Le Toutounier

1940
Chambre d'hôtel (*Chance Acquaintances*)

1941
Journal à rebours (*Looking Backwards: Recollections*)
Julie de Carneilhan (*Julie de Carneilhan*)

1942
De ma fenêtre

1943
Le Képi

Flore et Pomone (Flora and Pomona)

1944
Gigi (Gigi)

Trois . . . Six . . . Neuf . . . (Places)

1945
Belles Saisons

1946
L'Etoile vesper (The Evening Star)

1948
Pour un herbier (For an Herbarium)

1949
Trait pour trait

Journal intermittent

Le Fanal bleu (The Blue Lantern)

En pays connu

Index